MASTER OF NONE

MASTER OF NONE

The Story of Me Life

Ben Wicks

Canadian Cataloguing in Publication Data
Wicks, Ben, 1926-
    Master of none: the story of me life

ISBN 0-7710-8994-5

1. Wicks, Ben, 1926-   . 2. Cartoonists – Canada – Biography.
3. Authors, Canadian (English) – 20th century – Biography.*
I. Title.

NC1449.W53A2 1995   741.5'092   C94-931546-X

The publishers acknowledge the support of the Canada Council
and the Ontario Arts Council for their publishing program.

Typesetting by M&S, Toronto

Printed and bound in Canada on acid-free paper

McClelland and Stewart Inc.
The Canadian Publishers
481 University Avenue
Toronto, Ontario
M5G 2E9

1 2 3 4 5   99 98 97 96 95

To Doreen

Acknowledgements

THERE ARE MANY PEOPLE who have written their autobiographies only to hear the critics declare that they were much too young and should have waited a few years before telling the stories of their lives. Unfortunately, this will not, I'm sure, be the criticism of those who read this book. I have lived on this planet long enough to be able to look back on a full life that has been, for the most part, a happy one.

For the past two years I have been able to relive this life by penning my way into the past. It has been a journey worth reliving as, once again, I have visited in my memory with the extraordinary people who have played such an important part in my life.

Several people have been kind and generous enough to help jog my memory. Without them the task of filling these pages would have been that much harder. My longtime friend and agent, Matie Molinaro, was once again there to steer me through the jungle known as publishing. My editors, Sandra Tooze and Dinah Forbes, and my copy editor, Heather Sangster, all nudged me into remembering parts of my life that were initially unwilling to surface in my memory. I want to thank them and to thank those others who have shared a moment or two in my life and who, in most cases, are responsible for my wanting to live forever.

Fortunately I have been blessed with a backup arrangement in case I don't live forever. I have my children, Vincent, Susan and Kimberley, to carry part of me through their lives. And, as if this were not enough of a guarantee, I also have six wonderful grandchildren, Brittany, Caleigh, Rhia, Toran, Rupert and Monty. Last and most important, I have my wife, Doreen, my constant companion for thirty-nine years, a woman who remains the most caring and most remarkable person I have ever met. And I've met many, as you are about to find out.

Introduction

DAD WAS DEAD. The kindest, gentlest man I had ever known had finally gone. Seated in the only car that followed the hearse, I watched as dribbles of rain squirmed their way down the window beside my elbow. This winter morning in 1975 was a perfect day for a funeral, if there is such a day. Heavy, dark clouds rumbled over Hertfordshire, just outside of London, and formed a ceiling that threatened to crush the scene below.

The number of mourners at the funeral disappointed me, yet the turnout would have been a comfort to my father. He was never happy in crowds and had even begged off attending my wedding because he felt uneasy mingling with strangers.

None of my parents' friends from Southwark, London, was able to come to the funeral. No old neighbours from their tenement, no one who had ever hurled insults at a rent collector threatening eviction, none of the men who had removed their hats as the daily funeral procession passed by was there to escort Dad on his last journey. I wished that they were. If only the Bastins and the Vidlers, the Barkers and the Stones, were all gathered for a final farewell to my dad, remembering the many times they had spent together in the pub before their Sunday afternoon snoozes or crowded around the pub's battered piano at the Saturday night singsong.

The one consolation I had was that he had lived to see me, his only son, who had left school at fourteen, make a success of my life. I had always sent him my cartoons and stories the moment they appeared in the newspapers and magazines. In return, he had never missed a week of writing to me, thanking me for the clippings and telling me unrealistically good news of home. Between the time of his death and the funeral, my sisters found a scrapbook in which he had collected everything written by or about me. He had carefully clipped and pasted each item on a page together with the date and then had put the book away with instructions that it was never to leave the house. When I saw it, I wanted to go back in time to hug him and tell him how deeply it had moved me.

Inside the car my sisters were whispering, and now my mother began to sob quietly. I turned away and drew a circle on the foggy window. Through this peephole I watched the misty countryside race by, and silently retraced a life that had begun in the shadow of London Bridge.

I

I WAS BORN A TWIN. This news was kept secret from me for forty years, until a family gathering at the home of my sister Doll provided the tip-off. After whispering that I should ask Dad about my twin brother, Doll watched my amazement as I questioned him.

"It's true," he said sheepishly, as he lifted his second beer.

"But why didn't you tell me?" I asked.

"I was too embarrassed."

"Embarrassed because I was a twin?" I was astounded.

"No, embarrassed to tell you what 'appened to 'im. You see, you was born in Guy's Hospital and I 'ad gone in to see you and yer mother. Well, there was two cribs, one on either side of 'er. You was in one, and the other one was empty. So I said to the doctor, 'Where's the bloke that should be in this one?'

"'I'm afraid I 'as bad news fer you, Mr. Wicks,' 'e says. "Your son died during the night, and I'm sorry to say that the responsibility for 'is burial is yours.'"

Dad lowered his drink to the table and turned to face me." 'Well,' I says to the doctor, 'I ain't got no money fer burials. I been out of work fer three years.'

3

" 'I'm sorry, Mr. Wicks,' he says, and wiv that leaves the room.

"On the way 'ome I met me brover Steve, the cabdriver, and told 'im the news.

" 'There's only one bloke can 'elp you,' 'e says. 'Alf Smith, the undertaker.' " I nodded my head. Anyone who had spent any time at all in South London knew Alf Smith, the greatest undertaker of them all.

Dad took another sip of beer. "Anyway, I 'eaded for the Clyde pub and sure enough there was Alf at 'is favourite spot beside the counter. I told 'im the news, how I had been outta work fer three years and 'ad now lost a son.

"He placed an 'and on me shoulder. 'You're in luck,' he says. 'Last night we 'ad a fire in the basket factory and I've got one laid out in the front room. A young woman, she is, 'ardly a mark on 'er. No flames got to 'er, just a bitta smoke. Now then, provided you don't want to know who she is and where she's going, I'll pick the boy up from the 'ospital, put 'im between 'er legs, close the lid and 'e'll get a Christian burial.' "

Dad turned to face me. "And that was 'ow yer twin brother went."

He picked up his glass and began to drink once more. It had been extremely difficult for him to tell me this story. For forty years he had held it inside, afraid in some misguided way that I would feel ashamed if I knew. Yet my reaction was one of immense love for this couple who had struggled most of their lives for the sake of their family.

Two more different personalities would be difficult to imagine. My dad, Alf, a short, dark, slightly built man, was very shy, and my mum, Nell, was robust and ready to dance at the drop of a hat. Unwanted by her mother, she had been handed over to a drunken aunt and her husband to raise when she was only a baby. Although she was bright, her "parents" were too poor to keep her in school, and she had been forced to go out to work at an early age.

She had met my father shortly before the First World War and immediately fell for the shy student. Although he was from a large, poor family – nine boys and one girl – he had excelled at a clerical job to such a degree that the owner of the company was paying for his tuition at a London college. As soon as he finished his studies, Alf and Nell were married. Their first daughter, Doll, was born just as the world went crazy with war.

It was 1914, and all eyes were turned to those strong young men willing to die for their country. Delighted with my father's work, his company tried its best to hold him back from the army, but despite their pleas, Dad soon found himself in uniform. By 1915 he was scrambling through the mucky trenches that crisscrossed Flanders fields. It was four years before my father saw England again; four years of filth, starvation and brutality. The muddied players engaged in a grizzly dance of death, as an audience of generals looked on through long-range binoculars.

The first gas released by the German army oozed across the battlefield and drifted into the trenches occupied by my dad and his mates. The trenches that had once protected the soldiers instantly became their graveyards. Like many of the survivors, Dad quickly urinated into a handkerchief and shoved it against his face. This action saved his life; nevertheless, my father would suffer the effects of the gas attack for the next forty years. He would pace the living-room floor, holding his stomach and biting back his groans for fear of waking his sleeping children. But Nell was always there, holding his arm and gently rubbing his back.

After he returned from France, Dad applied to the company he had worked for before he joined the army. His position had been filled, however, and the bosses who had earlier been so anxious to keep him now found that they could just as easily replace him.

Years later I discovered a tiny tin box. Inside were two letters, both from Dad's company. One described him as an invaluable member of the firm, someone who was indispensable in his position. Pinned to this letter was another explaining why this same position had been filled by another man. Like thousands of others, my dad was now unemployed, and the government just shrugged. Finding these letters shattered my views of patriotism. A government that had taken him from his job and sent him to the trenches of France had turned its back on him when he needed it most. To this day I remain suspicious of how government treats its ordinary citizens.

In the middle of these bad times fell a small bundle of good. A second daughter, Nan, was born and, although it added to my mother and father's financial difficulties, they were delighted. No longer able to afford the luxury of living in North London, the Wicks family moved into a flat in St. Georges' Building, one of the many tenements in Southwark, a borough clustered around the southside of London Bridge.

For hundreds of years Southwark had been the refuge of those unfortunates who searched for the cheapest possible shelter. It was also a haven for those bent on crime. London Bridge had provided them with an access and escape route. They would nip across the river and raid the homes of the wealthy, then vanish across the hump of the bridge into the narrow streets and alleys that snaked between the southside warehouses.

Southwark was a natural choice for prisons, and a number had been built in the 1800s. It was known then as the "Borough of Clink," and the name had stuck. To this day "clink" is slang for "prison."

It was hardly an area to attract outsiders, yet famous names had passed through, none more famous than Charles Dickens, who as a child lived in Southwark with his mother. Anxious to be near her husband, who was serving time in the most famous jail of them all, the Marshalsea debtor's prison, Mrs. Dickens took lodgings nearby. The borough was a mine of experiences for Charles, which he later used in many of his stories. In *The Pickwick Papers*, the character Bob Sawyer, "a carver and cutter of live people's bodies," was a medical student at Guy's Hospital in Southwark. The borough, in turn, mined its connection with Dickens. The playground outside our tenement building was named after his novel *Little Dorrit*. On Lant Street, where Dickens and his mother once lived, the council built the Charles Dickens School. As it was just a short walk from where we lived, my sisters and I all went to school there.

At the time Mum and Dad moved to Southwark, little had changed from the days when Dickens had walked its streets. It was still inhabited by colourful characters who were stuck in Southwark by menial jobs but knew how to support each other. All were aware that should the need arise most likely there was a generous neighbour close at hand. And if not, the pubs were plentiful and provided the means by which daily problems could be swilled away. Common burdens provided the glue that bound them all. This was the world I entered on October 1, 1926; a world full of history, hardship and love.

I was named Alfred after my father, and as a child answered to Alfie. With my parents and two sisters waiting to fulfil my every need, I was more fortunate than many newborns, rich or poor. Near our tenement a nursery had been added to a low building, one of many soot-covered structures within spitting distance of London Bridge. As soon as I was old enough, my mother would wheel me there in my pram each morning and leave me for a few hours while she worked as a cleaner. Before returning to our building, I would insist on saying hello to the white horse stabled across the street. Even though I was only two years old at the time, to this day I can close my eyes and see Mum pushing me over to see this horse.

To my sisters I was a new toy, one they could take on regular visits to the nearby bridge. My elder sister, Doll, dark and attractive, was like a second mother always by our side. Each year, before the annual Guy Fawkes Day celebration on November 5, Doll would persuade me that it would be fun if I allowed her and Nan to do with me as they wished. One year they dressed me up like a scarecrow. I sat in my pram with Dad's old clothes falling off me, straw sticking out from the end of my sleeves and a large board that read "Give a Penny for the Guy" hanging around my neck. I hated it, even though I did eat a disgusting amount of sweets.

Much more to my liking were the outings to London Bridge. Doll would lead the way, holding Nan's hand and steering my pram close to the balustrades so I could see the many ships being loaded and unloaded.

St. Georges' Building, which was owned by a wealthy, absentee landlord, housed kind and decent people, typical of those who struggle to survive in most poor areas of the world. Built in the 1880s, the tenement consisted of five floors of ten flats, each floor sharing a single balcony that ran the length of the building. Three of its sides looked onto small squares, each housing a large rubbish bin. It was a well-planned arrangement, since each of the fifty families had an equal opportunity to smell the rotting rubbish and watch the rats scurrying back and forth as they carried tidbits to their nests. Our tiny flat was on the top floor at the rear, which had the advantage of being close to the wash house. We shared a lavatory with three families.

The dingy staircase we had to climb so many times each day was lit by gas, as was the rest of the building. Anyone returning after dark had to grope with one hand for the chain fixed to the gas mantle and hold a lit match with the other. It was an exercise in patience. And this wasn't the only thing we had to be patient about. Behind the wallpaper in our flat, attracted by the paste, bedbugs nested and bred by the thousands, sleeping during the day and feeding at night. Even though my mother and sisters constantly scrubbed our beds and mattresses with carbolic soap, we would be covered in bites by morning.

Yet my childhood was happy. Despite the hardships, there was little thought of escape. Most people in Southwark believed they had been dealt a particular hand in life and there was little point in complaining.

Dad finally found a job as a printer at the *Daily Mirror*, while Mum worked as an office cleaner at *The Times*, then later at a bank, and life took a turn for the better. They decided that, with our newfound wealth, we should move to the front of the building where we could have a view. Even better, we moved up from sharing a toilet to having one of our very own.

One of my earliest memories is of Christmas 1932, when I received the finest present a child could ever wish for. Now that Dad had a job, we had a choice of presents, within reason. I chose a toy that would later become famous through Dylan Thomas's tale, *A Child's Christmas in Wales*. As did the boy in the story, I found a small bus-conductor's set under the tree. The peaked hat, made of cardboard, was a perfect fit. But even better was the tin ticket-punch with a cord I hung around my neck. Each time I punched a hole in a ticket a bell rang. I quickly punched holes in all the tickets supplied, then turned to punch a hole in any piece of paper within reach. The ding it made was music to my ears, although Dad had another opinion. This was, after all, an historic moment. King George v was about to give the first Royal Christmas message.

"Alfie, stop ringing that bleedin' bell," said Dad. I dropped the toy to the floor and joined him beside our wireless radio set. We did not bother to stand, but were just as attentive as if we had.

"Through the marvels of modern science," said the King, "I am enabled to speak to all my peoples throughout the Empire."

I was surprised. I had seen the King christen some ships on the movie newsreels, but I hadn't realized that he could actually speak like an ordinary man.

Suddenly the King coughed, and with that single action, he

came alive to his people, so much so that *Spectator* magazine remarked, "A King who coughs is a fellow human being."

"You see," said Dad, "didn't I tell you 'e was like one of us?" Dad was quite right, and to prove the point, the King did indeed act like one of us when he upped and died a few years later.

Naturally there were major differences between us. If the King or anyone else of the upper class wanted to bet on a horse, it was well within the law. Not so for the poor. Off-track betting shops were forbidden, and since it was impossible for most people to enjoy the top-hat world of Ascot, any wagering they indulged in was strictly illegal.

This made for memorable Saturdays – betting day. As regular as clockwork, Dad would sit at the table in the morning and scribble on a scrap of paper. Lying beside him was the newspaper, listing the horses running that day. He would tick and then write down the name of each horse he felt had a chance to win. A dozen names soon covered the small piece of paper along with coded betting instructions for the bookmaker. Any winnings from the first horse would go to his favourite in the second race, and so on.

Dad would then walk out onto the balcony and shout down to the bookie five floors below. Mr. Parker would step from a ground-floor doorway and wave an arm. It was the signal that all was clear; it was safe for Dad to wrap his money in his betting slip and drop it over the railing.

Mr. Parker rented that flat from Mrs. Gaffney just on Saturday afternoons. She was quite content to stay there and read while he did his illegal business. Occasionally there would be the sound of running feet, whenever Mr. Tingle, the gallant lookout for our bookie, shouted a warning when the police were heading our way. Badly injured in France, Mr. Tingle could only hop and skip in a desperate attempt to reach the safety of Mrs. Gaffney's flat before the police arrived. All too often the door would be slammed shut by a copper who got there first, and, once again, the arm of the law would grab our sad, limping lookout and lead him away for a couple of nights in the clink. Throughout my childhood, Saturday afternoons were filled with the sounds of banging doors and warning shouts of "Heads up!"

Saturday night was pub night. The entire Wicks family would walk to our local, the Clyde, and my sisters and I would wait, with our feet in the door, while Mum and Dad enjoyed their one evening out a week.

Once we got home, I would lie in bed listening to the drunken voice of Mrs. Murphy, as she slowly zigzagged her way home from the pub. The song never changed, and to this day I remember the words of "There's an Old Mill by the Stream, Nelly Dean."

Although the new flat was an improvement, the walls were still paper-thin. Throughout the building, each and every family shared their lives with their neighbours, knowing instantly who had lost a job, who was sick and who was, once again, on the receiving end of a vicious tongue.

Our new neighbours on one side were the Wallaces, a family of twelve living in two rooms. A blanket hanging on a rope across one room created the illusion of an extra room. The Bastin family occupied the flat on the other side. One of their sons, Johnnie, a great fan of Bing Crosby, not only constantly played the records of the great crooner, but also frequently sang his own rendition of "In the Blue of the Night."

Sunday afternoons would bring out Johnnie Bastin's competition. No sooner had the pubs closed for the afternoon than the street singers would appear. Their dreadful voices would echo through the building, prompting most of the residents to throw them coins in the hopes that, once paid, they would quickly move to another location. Knowing this, even a street singer with a voice like Pavarotti would try his best to screech and wail his way through the most popular melodies of the day.

Weekends were hard for my mother. Forced to share in the cleaning of the building's halls, toilets and stairways, she would try to avoid the constant arguments that floated up and down the stairwells as each neighbour claimed that the other had neglected to do her share.

"Wot d'ya mean, it's my turn to clean the stairs? I cleaned 'em last week!"

"Of course I cleaned the copper when I finished me wash. Don't I always?"

Yet the close quarters bred a certain trust among us. Through a hole in each door a string hung down, attached to the lock on the inside. One tug was all that was needed to enter a flat. Yet I don't remember a single burglary. Of course, we all knew that, once inside, there would be little of value to steal anyway.

With Mum and Dad both working for newspapers, our flat was constantly full of reading material. Although these were not books I was reading, I was still learning the printed word. Little was said in the evenings, as Mum and Dad caught up on the day's news. My interest in reading was just as intense, although I stuck to fiction. The newspaper comics gave me my daily "literacy shot." What was Rubber Man doing today? What was Tarzan up to? Looking back, I can now see the value of growing up in a household of reading.

Comics helped me pass the many days I was forced to stay home from school. Whatever illness was going the rounds I would get. My mother's reasoning, I learned later, was that my dead twin's share of sickness had passed to me. One of the numerous illnesses that kept me home was impetigo, a dreadful skin disease that covered my face in sores. On the day the sores erupted, Mum had left early for her cleaning job, so Doll rushed me to Guy's Hospital. The disease was so contagious that she was infected from just carrying me there. Luckily neither of us was permanently scarred by it.

Although many families in more prosperous districts of London had pet dogs or cats, there were none in St. Georges' Building. Not that there was any lack of love for animals, but the space we lived in made our choice of pet dependent on size. Our first pet was Joey, a budgie. Dad took me to Petticoat Lane Market, in the centre of London, to choose just the right bird. Because it was suspected that sparrows caught at one end of the market were sprayed with gold paint and sold at the other end as canaries, we set our hearts on a budgie. Joey was blue and had not been painted. For months he sang and swung on his perch inside a small wooden cage nailed to the outside of our window.

The roof of St. Georges' was a favourite haunt of most of the children, and it was there that I was given my first lessons in sex by Bill, the mentally handicapped son of a neighbour. Bill knew how to masturbate, and soon gathered a fascinated group of boys around him, each attempting to fill a spoon with the sticky outcome of listening to his amorous stories. Unfortunately, word got out and the poor soul was led off by the police, never to be seen again. Without Bill's stories to encourage us, boredom quickly set in and we were soon back to a more acceptable form of play.

A narrow sidestreet led to the constantly crowded surgery of Dr. Stone, a wonderful Scot who was loved throughout the district. Speculations of how he came to be living in the area ranged from dedication to the poor to a liking for booze. Whatever the reason, without him life there would certainly have been a lot shorter than it was.

Next door to Dr. Stone was the Barkers' two-storey lodging house that sheltered the street people. Mostly tramps, they would trudge up the half-dozen steps that led into the dark building and find a dry place to sleep for the night. The first floor was relatively expensive, sixpence for one of six beds, complete with blankets. There was a rule that you could not come back if you wet the bed, one that played well for the strange man who cleaned the lodging house. Each night he would urinate in a bottle and pour a little on the sheet of one of the sleepers. Waking the hobo, he would point to the damp patch. "Look wot you've done. No more beds fer you when I tell the Barkers . . . unless you'd like to give me a couple o' pennies fer a pint."

Down a set of stairs and below ground was the same size space, yet thirty tramps could shelter there for two pence each. Three ropes were stretched across the room three or four feet from the floor. The men slept standing up with their arms looped over one of the ropes. My friends and I would shout through a grate in the pavement into this room, trying our best to scare these unfortunate creatures into falling off the rope.

A regular visitor was the Welsh poet and tramp W. H. Davies, who wrote a poem known by every British schoolchild: "What is this life if full of care, we have no time to stand and stare . . ." Certainly there was a great deal to stare at in our area.

Milk Bottle Annie was a familiar figure. She derived her name from her habit of placing an empty milk bottle on her window ledge when she was busy with a customer. In spite of her profession, she lived quite happily with Freddy. They were a generous couple, who, I was told by a local publican, would offer a bed to anyone who needed it, whether or not he was a customer of Annie's.

Later, in the midst of the war, Freddy spent three nights sleeping beside Annie, unaware that she was dead. When the police asked him to explain his strange behaviour, Freddy said, "I always took Annie a cup a tea in the morning and one in the afternoon. It was when I saw six cups of tea still sat there untouched that I thought, blimey, somethin's 'appened to Annie!"

Life for the poor in Southwark was not solely confined to the streets of the borough. The Trinity movie house provided a means of escape. It was cheap and one of Mum's favourite places to take us children. Dad would wait for us at the local pub and listen patiently as Mum described the show we'd seen. Although she enjoyed most of the features, the one thing she hated was the high singing voice of Jeanette MacDonald. I shall never forget my mum dragging me to my feet in the middle of one of her movies and declaring in a loud voice that this was the biggest load of old rubbish she had ever heard. Music-hall singers and singalongs in the pubs were more to her liking.

The same movie house showed films on Saturday mornings especially for kids. The two-penny rush was just that, a mad crocodile line of pushing and shoving children. Since the downstairs seats were the first to be filled, all of us were trying to get to the back of the line in order to grab seats in the balcony. From this vantage point we could pelt the kids downstairs with orange peels and garbage before and during the movie. From the start to the finish of each show there would be constant interruptions from children gatecrashing through the side doors and being chased out by attendants. Meanwhile, the lights, which were within easy reach, were repeatedly turned on whenever the various cowboys were told to "Stick 'em up!"

For those interested in more brutal sports, Blackfriars Ring was close by. Since the end of the 1800s, fighters both big and small had boxed here. I watched many of them through a crack in the back door, only to run off with my mates at the first bellow of rage from an irate and burly doorman.

There was one activity that gave most Cockney families a short break from their soot-covered world: hop picking. Hop picking meant we could breath fresh air and be paid while doing it. The hop is the vital ingredient needed to make the magic potion – beer – and in England it grows best not that far from London.

Each summer families headed to Kent for six weeks of hop

picking, and we were no exception. Piled into the back of lorries, most of us sang in high spirits as we nosed our way deeper into the glorious clean air of the English countryside. Dad never went with us, but no doubt he appreciated the time we were away, which he could spend reading the newspaper without constant interruptions from me and my sisters.

Once we arrived at Tunbridge Wells, we gathered straw to sleep on from the main shed in the farmer's field and took it to the small hut that would be our home for the coming weeks. As the sun rose so did most of the pickers. By six o'clock in the morning, most of us were already in the fields standing beneath the long lines of hop vines that grew high overhead along wire frames.

Mum's fingers would fly across the vines, plucking the hops and dropping them into a canvas bin. Although she enjoyed picking, my sisters and I hated it. In the early morning the hops would sometimes be covered in frost, and soon our fingers would be numb from stripping them off the vines.

"Come on, come on!" Mum would shout. "Call that pickin'? 'Ow do you expect us to earn any money wiv you lot standin' around pickin' yer noses?" Once again we would make motions resembling hop picking, all the time watching my mother who, I am convinced, would have won a gold medal if it had been an Olympic event.

At the end of each day, we would stagger across the fields to the hut. Mum, no doubt, would be counting the number of bins we had filled and calculating the amount of money we had earned. As night fell, open fires would throw a glow on the faces of friends and neighbours gathered round, and we would soon be lifting our voices in familiar songs. When the final days of our six weeks approached, most of us quickly put the hardships of picking out of our minds and wished that this "holiday" would go on forever.

At age fifteen both Doll and Nan left school and began working in nearby factories. They would leave each morning before I left for school, giving me the opportunity to be naughty to them. As they emerged from the building, I would run to the end of the balcony and shower them with pieces of coal. They would take shelter under an overhang, and the whole building would hear them shouting that, unless Mum stopped "her rotten kid," they would be late for work.

I was spoiled, being the only boy and the youngest, but my sisters still managed to have fun at my expense. At almost every Sunday meal, we would have canned pineapple as a treat for dessert. Either Nan or Doll would draw my attention to something outside the window, and while my head was turned, they would take from my plate the few pieces of pineapple I had been saving for the last.

At age nine I left Charles Dickens School to continue my education at Orange Street School, just a five minute walk farther on. To my friends and I there was little difference between the two schools. The new one still had teachers and boring lessons. I did not enjoy school, but one event did brighten an otherwise tedious day.

Above the sounds of children playing at recess came one high-pitched scream: "Come and see! Freddy Price 'as just 'ad 'is finger chopped off by the iron door and it's laying on the floor!" And it was − a tiny bloodied finger left behind by a teacher who had been more concerned for Freddy than any part of him left in the grit of the playground.

Few children in the area could escape the constant ravages of various diseases. One time I was sick at home with a bad cough that worried Dr. Stone so much he decided the best place for me was in a hospital bed. My mother pleaded with him to keep me at home. He finally relented, and for two weeks she stayed with me day and night beside a roaring fire in the hope that this would cure me. It did not. The cough developed into pneumonia and Mum was forced to send me to hospital. I have never forgotten the sensation of being lifted onto a stretcher and carried to a waiting ambulance with my mother holding my hand.

After a short stay in the hospital, the doctors found that the illness had left a cloud on my lung and decided that I should finish my recovery in a convalescent home. I was forced to leave my friends at Orange Street School for Stowey House, an open-air school that took one hour to get to on the tram. In the grounds of the house there were several wooden platforms sheltered by sloping roofs. This is where we were given our lessons, regardless of the weather. Fierce winter winds would blast right through these shelters, where we sat bundled in heavy scarfs. To this day I am puzzled to know why the teachers were condemned to such conditions.

I was cold and bored at school, no matter whether it was Stowey House or Orange Street. Home was where I loved to be. At least I was warm, and I could play with my beloved Plasticine. Dad would lay a long piece of board on the floor, and day after day I created small figures until, months later, I had completed a full Coronation parade. It marked the beginning of the artistic leaning that has played such an important part in my life.

Occasionally Mum and Dad would find that they'd saved up enough money for an outing to the sea. Off we'd go to Southend, a favourite seaside resort for most Cockney families. It was located within easy reach of London, and the hour's train ride would quickly transfer us from a black, sooty slum to the fresh breezes of a seaside town inhabited by sellers of cockles and whelks. Once off the train, we would head for the beach. The tide would be out. The tide was always out. Rolling up our trousers and hitching up our dresses, we would begin the mile-long trudge to the water's edge. Once there, Dad would remove his tie and collar stud and, after a quick glance around to make sure he was not being watched, he would cock his thumbs under his braces and declare with immense pride, "This is the life!"

And so it was for me and my sisters. Full of the knowledge that we were truly loved, we made our way through those early years never far from these two remarkable people, Nell and Alf Wicks.

2

AS THE SUMMER OF 1937 began to unfold, the papers were filled with the news of events in Europe. A little man with a Charlie Chaplin moustache could be seen in newsreels at every movie house. Adolph Hitler seemed determined to intimidate everyone within marching distance of Germany.

Although it had been nineteen years since the end of the First World War, little had changed for the poor of Britain. Our lives continued in the same squalid manner, and those who had given the most for their country continued to receive the least in return. The coal miners marched on London and returned to their Welsh valleys with little to show for their efforts. Unemployment was rampant, and to add to the misery, there was the unwelcome appearance of Sir Oswald Mosley, a fascist whose band of misguided followers began to seek out the disenchanted poor in the streets of London.

I was ten years old when I witnessed my first Mosley demonstration. A group of men in black shirts with their banners flying had turned the corner into our area when the mounted police suddenly charged down the street. My father pushed me into a doorway, and we watched as truncheons, sticks and bottles filled the air.

Life was changing for the Wicks family. At the age of twenty-three Doll fell in love, a surprise to us all. Although she was attractive and dressed well, she had not previously seemed to be interested in the latest fashion or in men. There was a stability to her character that lead us all to think of her as a homebody, the home being mostly ours. She loved this role, but still enjoyed the one night a week she went dancing. It was there, at the local dance hall, that she met Howard Talbot from the nearby borough of Lambeth. Within the year, Howard and Doll were heading for St. George's Church to get married.

The wedding was of such importance to the family that even Dad felt obliged to attend. I was made to wear a cap. In short trousers and with my cap at a jaunty angle, I stood at the front of the wedding party on the church steps for an all too rare family portrait. My sisters and I were no strangers to the church since we had been constantly shunted through its door each Sunday. Like most Cockney families Mum and Dad had little interest in religion – the trenches of the First World War had cleansed Dad of any belief in God. But despite these feelings he did find the church a convenient babysitter when the need for quiet was essential after his regular Sunday lunchtime visit to the local pub. Doll and Howard took a small apartment nearby and began to set up their home. Unfortunately they had little time to enjoy it.

It was March 13, 1938, and thousands of stiffly outstretched arms appeared as if by magic to welcome Hitler onto the streets of Vienna. Britain began a desperate search for volunteers. A million men and women was the government's target. Less than half that number stepped forward. Howard was a member of the territorial army and was soon seen in his uniform marching off to the local drill hall for weekly training.

Disappointed with the result of its appeal, the government turned to a woman it thought might have better luck in persuading the required bodies. Lady Reading stepped smartly into the limelight and formed the Women's Voluntary Service, calling upon women "in every sphere of life . . . to prepare patiently and thoroughly . . . a protection . . . for our loved ones and our homes." There were no takers in Southwark that I remember. Everyone in the neighbourhood was too busy staying alive in a time of peace to think about volunteering for war. Considering the condition of the flats in St. Georges' Building, few of us could be convinced that they were worth saving.

Molly Reid, the local money-lender, was certainly not about to join any group; she was too busy at the head of a queue of people waiting to pay her the interest on loans she had made them. Molly could be seen most evenings sitting at the end of the bar in the Clyde, wearing a big apron with deep pockets. Her business continued to thrive despite the approaching war.

Many other aspects of life in Southwark continued much as before. Alf Smith, the local undertaker, presided over the seemingly daily burials, dressed in black and wearing his top hat. Everyone in the neighbourhood would lower his head as Alf passed. This was not so much out of respect, but because of the rumour that if Alf caught your eye and lifted his top hat, you would be next on his list.

Mr. Lee, a neighbour who worked in the docks, was caught with a quarter-pound of tea that he had pushed in his pocket when unloading a ship. The local judge, Sybil Campbell, gave him six months, despite his pleas that it was a first offence and he had four children at home depending on him for food. Such was the treatment of the poor. Whatever the crime, the local magistrate would hand out a heavy penalty, believing that the greatest deterrent was to make an example.

As the tension of living under the threat of war spread to St. Georges' Building, families began to foresee the possibility that their loved ones would be called away to fight for their country. Those of Dad's age remembered the First World War. The thought that such a terrible event might happen again filled them with dread, especially if they had children of military age. Those with younger children were also worried by predictions that the war would be played out in the skies above Britain.

Arguments were common, and although most consisted of shouting, occasionally a confrontation that involved more than just a raised voice or two would break out. Sally Pepperell moved into the building only to find that a longtime inhabitant, Mrs. Collins, was in a fighting mood. Their shouting and screaming filled the narrow stairwell as Mrs. Collins pulled Sally's hair. Sally left the building soon after, and weeks later news filtered back that two of her three children had died of diphtheria within days of each other.

While the government continued to appeal for volunteers, Hitler turned his eyes towards Czechoslovakia. Few people felt he would stop there. Many in Southwark believed that, although our borough was not much to look at, there was a real danger that soon we'd all be goose-stepping our way to work. More and more men in uniforms appeared on the streets as volunteers stepped forward.

The news that Hitler had invaded Czechoslovakia spurred a new flurry of activity in Southwark, as did the arrival of some of the thirty-eight thousand gas masks distributed throughout Britain. It was, to my mind, the first free package of anything that had arrived in the borough. The rubber mask with its strange eyepiece was uncomfortable to wear and gave off a strong odour. Most children resented wearing the masks until word spread that, by forcing air through the side of the mask, a loud farting noise could be produced. The masks now became quite popular, much to the disgust of the teachers during school practice drills. Wearing a mask was particularly difficult for my mother, since like most women she wore her hair in a bun.

Frustrated, she eventually threw the mask into a corner where it stayed for the duration of the war.

The government cranked up its appeal for volunteers, and posters began to appear everywhere. People who had been largely ignored suddenly felt wanted. The most successful appeal in Southwark was for volunteer firemen, since a large fire station was within easy reach of St. Georges' Building and most of the local volunteers felt duty bound to sign up. The imprisoned Mr. Lee was also willing and able, and vowed that the moment he was released he'd have his name on the dotted line faster than you could shout "Fire!"

The need for women telephone operators and ambulance drivers was a top priority, although the poorer areas of Britain seemed hardly to be a likely area to search. Most women there had never even sat in a car, let alone driven one, but still they joined up.

Across the country jobs were suddenly opening up as Britain prepared for battle. Aircraft and tanks were now filling assembly lines that had recently lain idle, and those who had volunteered for the reserve army were reporting for duty. Doll and her husband were awakened at 2 A.M. to find a policeman on the doorstep. Howard was needed. He dressed and left immediately to join his unit.

The children in my schoolyard were quite aware of the dangers ahead. As with so many childhood concerns, this worry was acted out in games of "good guy versus bad guy." Few of us wanted to play the part of Hitler since all the games ended with his violent death. Many children imagined the coming war would consist of thousands of planes weaving across the sky, twisting and turning, with machine guns spitting out fire along their sights.

Over the last few years I had developed a love of flying. My Plasticine modelling had changed focus from people to planes. The long piece of board once home to my Coronation models was now an airport. I spent hour after hour on the floor of our flat, zooming and twisting around the room with small models held high, battling for control of the living room. I discovered that by sticking birdseed under the models' wheels, each plane could slide along the floor to a smooth stop, safe after battle. Art class at school was no different. I covered every piece of paper with planes bearing the familiar insignias of Britain and Germany.

My tenth birthday had been magical. My sisters had saved diligently for my present: a ten-minute plane ride. I climbed into an aircraft at Croydon Airport to take my first flight. Although I remember little of it, the thrill of being airborne has never left me. When I rejoined my sisters on the tarmac, my flushed face told them their money had been well spent. What other present would remain with a person more than fifty years after the event?

More than ever my days were filled with dreams of being a pilot, taking off to do battle with any German who dare show his face overhead. Despite this brave play-acting, children, like adults, were under no illusion of what this would mean. Film from the wars in China and Spain had shown the horrified and desperate faces of civilians and how terribly they were suffering, mostly as a result of bombing. Each scene conjured up images of what might occur in Britain should war come here. However brave we appeared to be, all were agreed that peace was a better alternative.

Life in Southwark changed little despite the threat of war. Most of the adults had enough to worry about. Those without jobs continued to hope that they would find one and those with jobs continued to wish for something less boring. Dad appeared to be happy in his job, and at 5 P.M. he could be seen making his way along the alley as he headed home. Once inside the house, the bundle of newspapers he brought from work was soon opened and a discussion about the events of the day would begin. Most of the news concerned our seventy-year-old prime minister, Neville Chamberlain, who was visiting Hitler. He returned waving the now-infamous piece of paper.

For a short while we felt that war had been averted, yet plans to defend ourselves against a possible attack continued. Leaflets began falling on doorsteps everywhere. For Mum, who took great pride in whitening the step outside our flat twice a day, this was an added irritation. I cannot remember ever entering our home without having to take a large step over this white hurdle. Now strangers were dropping papers on it by the dozens, spoiling its purity. The leaflets had titles like "YOUR GAS-MASK" and "MASKING YOUR WINDOWS," but Mum threw most of them in the wastepaper basket before anyone had a chance to read them.

A major concern to parents was the news that almost three and a half million children between the ages of five and fourteen would be moved to places of safety outside the potential danger areas if war seemed imminent. Many parents did not react well to the idea of handing over their children to strangers for the war's duration. So the government started a major poster campaign, telling parents that keeping their children at home was not only unwise but would play into the hands of an enemy intent on destroying as many of Britain's future citizens as it could.

The Wicks family did not discuss my leaving, since Nan had met a fellow and most of our conversation was about their wedding plans. I liked John Hill. He lived just around the corner and loved football (soccer). In order to curry favour with my sister, he impressed her by showing an interest in her young brother. Most weekends the two of us would go to the local football stadium to see our favourite team, Millwall. As the team played in a rough part of town, I needed someone of John's build to protect me in the event of trouble. Few fights occurred among the crowd while in the stadium, but once outside many fans took out their frustrations at losing on whomever was the closest.

Nan and John's wedding plans came as no surprise. Unlike Doll, Nan had thoroughly enjoyed her social life outside the home. She was attractive, extremely outgoing, generous and had many men to choose from. Her choice of partners turned out to be as good as Doll's had been.

The weather during the summer of 1939 was glorious. Nan's wedding forced us to cancel our annual hop picking "holiday," but most of our neighbours who did go returned with a healthy tan and the sad suspicion that the blue skies over Kent's hop fields would soon echo with the sounds of gunfire. What they didn't realize was that they would never work in the hop fields again. After the war, machinery would replace these hardy and diligent field labourers.

Towards the end of the summer London schoolteachers were called back to work to hear that they were expected to lead thousands of children to the safety of the British countryside. Many of them were already prepared for the task, since they had been part of a rehearsal that involved five thousand children from twenty London schools. All of them had reached the nearest railway station without mishap.

Stowey House had been involved in the rehearsal. The school lay on the edge of a common, and the job of leading a group of children across its expanse and back again was no problem. Orderly lines of children marched from the school gates and strolled to a nearby pond, then turned around and strolled back, leaving both the teachers and children confident that any escape from London was a piece of cake.

So we settled back in our open-air classrooms and waited for the government's instructions. Meanwhile the first trickle of civilians, most of them clerks and typists, boarded trains and were on their way to safety in the countryside. The office workers were not alone. Many other civilians decided that a city about to be bombed was hardly conducive to one's health. Almost two million people evacuated to safer locations. Most of them left by car. For this reason, few were from Southwark.

Such a warm and beautiful summer made it difficult to believe that war was on its way. A new craze hit the alley beside St. Georges' – building scooters from two pieces of wood formed into an L-shape and adding wheels with ball bearings. The loud squeals and rattles of the scooters as we chased around the block forced many to yell out in protest from the balconies above.

As the last days of summer began to fade, parents were told over the radio that they should be prepared to say goodbye to their children. Little did I realize what was in store for me as I lay down to sleep on the evening of August 31, 1939. German troops on the Polish border were also settling in for the night. By daylight each one of us would be involved in an historic event: I would be part of the largest evacuation of children that the world had ever seen; the Germans would be invading Poland, signalling the start of war.

September 1, a Friday, began as any other school day. The best that could be said for it was that the end of another week was close. I arrived at school and was told to make my way to the assembly hall. There we were told to go home, collect our belongings and come back to the school in two hours.

When I arrived home, Dad had left for work. So it was up to Mum, who had returned from her early-morning office cleaning, to say the farewells and reassure me that it was just a matter of weeks before I'd be back. She had not packed a bag. We didn't have a bag. She threw my socks, underpants and a shirt into an empty pillowcase and, after one last hug, off I went. I was twelve years old, and despite what Mum had said, it would be two years before I saw Southwark again.

We assembled in the schoolyard at Stowey House. Each of the name labels we wore was checked, and the lids of our little gas-mask boxes were opened to see that the masks were inside.

Satisfied that everything was as it should be, we set off to join thousands of children in snaking lines that wove their way to the nearest railway station. For many of the older children, it was a happy excursion, a first trip on a train and a journey into a countryside few had seen before. But most important of all, it was a Friday and a school day had been cancelled. For those who were as young as five, it was a time of great stress. Many of these youngsters held tightly to their mothers before being sent off.

As our train shunted out of the station, I tried my best to squeeze my head around the arms and bodies of those already leaning out of the windows to wave a final goodbye. Mum had obeyed the school's request not to come to the station, but many parents didn't and could be seen with tears flowing down their faces until smoke from the departing trains finally hid them from view.

For the next few hours most of the carriages were quiet. Through the windows the countryside provided all manner of wondrous new things for us to stare at. There were horses without carts to pull, cows standing in fields and, adding to the pleasure, the friendly waves and smiles of the country folk. The train came to a stop at Eastbourne, a seaside town on the south coast.

Once on the platform, we were led to buses by the dozens of volunteers. We assembled in a small schoolyard in town and waited to be chosen. What had started out as an adventure soon became a tragic meat market, as fingers pointed at various children: "I'll take him;" "Give me her;" "I'll take the boy, but I don't want his sister."

A young woman pointed to me and I followed her to a motor car. It was my first car ride, and I felt fortunate to have been chosen by someone this wealthy. The family, although not rich, was comfortably off, and lived over the grocery store they owned. I settled down to enjoy my time living with the couple, their son and the woman's father. Their son was the same age as I was, so the arrangement appeared perfect. It would not be for long, I thought, and I'd soon be home again. How wrong I was.

Along with my new family, I sat beside the radio and listened to the prime minister that first Sunday morning as he declared that Britain was at war with Germany. What had begun as a short trip to the countryside had now taken on a vastly more sinister aspect.

My life with the Eastbourne grocer lasted only a few weeks. Their son had an electric train set. Both he and I were playing with it when we began to argue and fight. We were separated by a shocked mother, who immediately called an emergency meeting of the family. With only the grandfather showing support for my side, they decided that the arrangement was not as they had hoped and one of the children must be asked to leave the house. It did not go to a vote.

The billeting officer arrived and I followed him in a search of a new home. This was not easy, since I was now an evacuee who had been found unsuitable. Halfway up a hill, we turned into the front walk of one of the many attached homes whose bed and breakfast sign had been removed and stored safely for the war's duration.

A roly-poly woman with a ruddy face and kind smile met us at the door, placed an arm around my shoulder and led me inside. She was taking care of two other evacuees, both boys, and once again my initial feeling was of tremendous luck at finding such a home. She was without children of her own and was obviously happy to have three young boys living with her.

It was suppertime before we met the man of the house. As I sat in the kitchen eating my first meal, the door burst open to reveal a fat, drunken slob. He staggered to the table and promptly threw his and everyone else's meals across the room. He then made his way to the settee in the parlour and went to sleep. A different man awoke, one full of fun and games. His earlier behaviour was soon forgotten.

Unfortunately bedtime arrived and with it an even more revolting human being emerged, one who revelled in giving each of us hugs and lingering kisses. For most of the year we stayed with the couple, we welcomed our time at school and, back at the house, dreaded the arrival of the old man.

By the time the first Christmas of the war arrived many of the evacuees had returned to their homes. Little had happened since the declaration of war and few families felt the need to be separated from their children any longer. Unfortunately, because they lived in the obvious target area of the East End of London, my parents decided that I was in the best place. They had no reason to be concerned for my welfare since, like most of the children who had left their homes, I wrote letters to them full of glowing reports of my new life.

In April 1940 the war began in earnest. German armies rolled into Denmark and Norway and were soon advancing across France. A new British leader appeared, a cigar-champing figure who quickly declared that we were about to start the greatest fight of our lives and continued, "I have nothing to offer but blood, toil, tears and sweat."

Mum and Dad were relieved that they had decided to keep me where I was. But as the German armies advanced across France, it was quite apparent that those living in a ten-mile zone along the coast from Norfolk to Sussex would, in the event that France fell, be closer to the enemy than anyone else. Since this included the area occupied by many of the evacuees, including me, plans were made to move us out of danger. Where would we go? What would the next billet be like? Would it be better than the one we were in? I was convinced it had to be better than where I was. I would miss the wonderful woman of the house, but I hoped her husband would quickly be taken prisoner by the Germans should they land in his street.

Following the example of our army in France, the evacuees on England's southern coast began a retreat. Our stay in Eastbourne was over, and once again we boarded trains and were shunted off to safety.

The children from my school all headed west into Wales. The people of Llanelly waited to receive us, then packed us into buses and sent us deeper into this incredibly beautiful and gentle land. After what seemed like hours of driving through green hills (in later years I would find it was just twelve miles), we came to a village hugging the base of a giant slag heap. The whitened windowsills and doorsteps of the Cross Hands cottages gleamed, evidence of the constant battle to keep back the coal dust that drifted down from the slag heap. Once again I found myself paraded before a group of strangers, and once again I set off to a new home.

Mr. and Mrs. Jones had been married for a number of years, and the announcement that evacuees from London were about to arrive in the village presented them with the chance to conduct an experiment. They had been debating whether they should have children, and this test run would give them the answer.

My bedroom was one of two on the first floor of their modest bungalow. A small front room and even smaller kitchen and bathroom comprised the rest of the house, and I quickly realized that this cramped home was hardly equipped to handle an extra body. Yet the Joneses, like thousands of others, had hurried to schoolyards to find a stranger to share the little that they had. They were compassionate people who did their best to make me happy. Like most men in the village, Mr. Jones worked in the local coal mine. He was proud of being a miner, and on the first Sunday I was with him, he showed me where he worked. The trip shaped the respect for miners I've held to this day.

The tiny cage dropped like a stone down the throat of the mine and came to a sudden stop in a dark, damp tunnel. Far off, I heard the sound of dripping water. The lamps on our helmets pointed the way down a steep slope leading to the main tunnel. A mile-long walk through puddles finally brought us to a ladder leaning against a wall. I followed Mr. Jones up the ladder, crawled through a hole and into a passage leading to an area four feet square and three feet high. This hellhole was Mr. Jones's working area, eight hours a day, six days a week.

He lay on his side and handed me a shovel. "Alfie, take a piece of souvenir coal," he grinned. I gently tapped the side of the tunnel and placed a bit of coal in my pocket. "I said a *piece* of coal," laughed Mr. Jones, then he took a pick and drove it into a seam of coal. I don't remember what fell out of the wall, but I do know that, despite our lamps, the rising dust completely hid him from view. Coughing and choking I eased my way backward to the ladder and crawled down to the main tunnel. I could still hear Mr. Jones laughing but he quickly broke off to cough – a nasty hacking cough, which in a few years would kill him. He would be just another son of Wales who gave his life so the rest of us could live in comfort.

Work at the mine was done in eight-hour shifts. The afternoon shift would end as I arrived home from school at four o'clock. Mr. Jones would crawl out of his hole and make his way with dozens of others to the foot of the shaft. Above ground once more, they would shield their eyes from the light and set off for their homes, the thick black dust clinging to their clothes. There were no showers at the pit heads, so each miner was forced to carry the filth home. There in the bath, Mr. Jones would scrape and scrub away at the dust that had worked its way into his skin.

His hobby was jigsaw puzzles, and night after night he would sit for hours placing hundreds of pieces together to form the country scenes he no doubt dreamed about when he was underground. I once made the mistake of trying to help him. He immediately slapped my hand and told me that it was bad manners to interfere with someone else's hobby.

The news from home was both good and not so good. Doll had given birth to a baby boy, but within weeks Howard had been sent with his regiment to North Africa. Nan's husband was now in the army, but fortunately stationed close to London, so he was able to keep in weekly contact.

I loved my time with the Joneses, but there was one big problem: the toilet. The small wooden hut at the bottom of the garden was surrounded by demons and devils just waiting to pounce on me after dark. Most times I was able to limit my visits to daylight hours, but one night it was impossible.

I was in the bath when my guts gave me the message that it was time to go. It was dark outside and, rather than face the demons of the night, I removed the bath plug, hoping that the swirling water would carry away the evidence. The scheme was a miserable failure and, once again, I was following a billeting officer as we headed for my fourth home.

By now Cross Hands had taken all the evacuees it needed. Few homes were ready to open their doors to take another, certainly not a naughty one like me. I was not going to find a line-up of people ready to show they were capable of succeeding where others had not. Yet I learned at an early age that, although there are some lousy people in this world, most are good. Mr. and Mrs. Roberts, who had a daughter my age, were good. He was the village smithy and everything a smithy should be − a short, strong, gentle man with arms capable of holding still the largest horse as he hammered home a shoe.

Why would he have decided to take in a strange boy who had been rejected by another village household? I soon found the answer. I was thirteen years old and, although not a strong lad, I was able to help in the smithy for the most minimum of pay − nothing. My job was to pump the bellows, which I did every day before and after school.

Every night after I was in bed I could hear an odd and persistent clicking sound coming from downstairs. One evening I decided to peek at what was going on. I could see Mr. Roberts hunched over the kitchen table, still wearing his cap. In front of him were little piles of coins ready for their daily counting.

Like the other cottages in Cross Hands the Roberts' home, next door to the working-man's club, had a gleaming white doorstep and window ledges as a result of Mrs. Roberts's handiwork. Inside, it had low wooden beams, which gave it a warm and cosy atmosphere. Neither Mr. or Mrs. Roberts could speak English, yet with the help of their daughter, Rachel, I had no difficulty in communicating. In fact I soon learned enough words of the rhythmic Welsh language to feel part of the family.

I spent much of my free time in their small farm at the back of the cottage, which should have given me a love of farming. It didn't. This was due to the morning that Mr. Roberts shook me awake; the sun was about to come up and he had a job for me. I was needed to help him and four neighbours slaughter a pig. Since killing anything other than humans was against the law during war, 4:30 A.M. was the ideal time for the job.

As we snuck out the back of the cottage, the pig seemed to have gotten wind of the fact that this was its last day on earth. It began to squeal, and the closer we got, the louder it squealed. After much shoving and pushing, we managed to get it into the shed. With Mr. Roberts stumbling around the five of us and shouting orders, we reached down to lift the pig onto a small table and turned it on its side. Mr. Roberts placed a bucket in the general area he expected blood and, grabbing a long, thin skewer, thrust it into the neck of the unfortunate pig. With an action that would have made Errol Flynn proud, he withdrew the skewer in a sweeping motion and watched with pride as a long stream of blood arched into the bucket. We lay across the body of the dying pig until the last squeal had faded and then slowly returned to the house for a well-deserved breakfast. I've never fancied farming since.

Just fifty yards from the house was the entrance to the school.

A long dirt driveway led to an open field, in the middle of which was a low, red-brick building. Along one side was a series of windows that allowed each classroom to wallow in light. The size of the school had been ideal for the children of a Cross Hands at peace, but this was war. And war was able to affect the lives of those in the most sheltered corners.

The arrival of the evacuees made this perfect little school vastly inadequate. The obvious solution suited us pupils: the evacuees and local children alternated going to school, with one group going in the mornings and the other in the afternoons. Most of the brief time I was in class I spent staring at the healthy bosom of Mrs. Jones, the teacher and the wife of the headmaster (not the couple I first stayed with). Our afternoons were spent in the true manner of country folk. In a nearby field used to grow vegetables, I learned to double trench – a method of digging that involves turning the soil into a previously dug ditch. The healthy exercise did wonders for me and no doubt helped me grow from a sickly London schoolboy to a strong, healthy lad.

The war seemed a million miles away, but the wireless radio and newspapers gave us what continued to be bad news. Particularly hard was news from London. The city was being bombed regularly and, since most of the evacuees in Cross Hands were from the capital, letters from home were anxiously awaited.

Although the war was at its height in the early autumn of 1941, my time with the Roberts family was coming to an end. I was fourteen, an age when all evacuated children were asked to return to their parents. It was not a happy parting for me. The cheery cottage of the village smithy had been my second home. I knew that Mr. Roberts would miss my help in the forge, but as he pressed a miniature horseshoe into my hand for good luck, I could not help feeling that he would miss me more as a son.

3

I RETURNED TO LONDON in the autumn of 1941. While I was away, Southwark had been heavily bombed, yet, although many buildings were now in ruins, the heart of the district remained. Each night the German bombers would fly overhead, and moments later we would hear the sound of bursting anti-aircraft shells. Shrapnel would fall like rain, and the next day my mates and I would be able to add to our collections of shell pieces.

There was not much to do after dark. With a complete blackout in place throughout Britain, the streets offered little by way of entertainment. The bombing that had started in 1940 forced most families in the area to take shelter during raids in the Borough tube station. At 4 P.M. each day the queue would start. Families carrying blankets hoped that by being early they could lay their bedding on the platform farthest from the toilet buckets. I joined my mother in the station for two nights, but the smell was so bad that I decided to stay with Dad back in the flat.

Dad had reasoned that by staying at home he would be on hand to tackle the small incendiary bombs that fell by the dozens. The bombs would land, sizzling and ready to spread fire within seconds. The many government leaflets and posters instructed us to cover the menace immediately with a bucket of sand.

None hit our roof. If they had, Dad would have been quite unprepared. At night he happily tucked himself into bed, and within minutes he would be fast asleep. Nothing could wake him, not even the sound of the large anti-aircraft gun that rode the railway tracks behind our building. Each time I heard its wheels approaching, I prayed it would not stop behind St. Georges' Building to blast away at the German aircraft over-head. The few times it did, it made the windows and doors shake, threatening the whole building with demolition from friendly fire.

I was not as calm as Dad. The quiet of the countryside had not prepared me for the constant wailing of warning sirens fol-lowed by the roar of planes and the screams of the falling bombs. Most nights I would pull the bedclothes over my head and tell God that whatever he wished me to do with the rest of my life, I was his. Just let the whistling bombs miss St. Georges' Building and hit the many sinners I was sure lived close by.

Having now graduated from Stowey House at its wartime location in Cross Hands, Wales, I set off to find work. Dad was currently employed by the *Daily Mirror*, a newspaper with one of the largest circulations in the world. He did his best to encour-age me to follow him into the newspaper business, so I went for an interview with a union official at the paper, who suggested I take a job as an assistant to a press photographer. I turned him down. I was also prepared to turn down Dad's second suggestion, that of becoming a shipping clerk, but to keep him happy I agreed. The pay was awful, yet because Dad had started as a clerk, he felt this job was just the thing for me. It was one of the few jobs I have ever hated. Most days the manager was as miserable as Scrooge was on his worst days. When my constant whistling threatened to send him around the bend, he told me that it was time for me to move on. I did so, happily.

Doll suggested that I work with her at Charles Letts, the famous maker of diaries and wallets. It was a simple job. As an assistant to the wallet maker, I had to run a hot iron around the edge of each newly glued wallet to strengthen the binding. My companion and expert teacher was a wonderful old craftsman with a permanent cigarette dangling from his lips. He sat hunched over the bench all day, coughing and gasping for air. At one end of the workshop a group of six sewing machines hummed away as the dainty fingers of the operators turned and manipulated the wallets under the needles. To break the monotony, the twenty workers held contests. Typical of them was the one to find the most attractive girl in the group. The winner was always the girl who organized and encouraged the event – the most attractive one of the group. Although she regularly won this contest, she fell far short of my ideal of beauty. The girl I dreamed of worked in the office, not with us in the factory.

Rennie Price had an incredible figure and the most beautiful chestnut-coloured hair I have ever seen. We were both fifteen. Once a day she walked past me while carrying out some errand. The world stopped while I watched Rennie walk the length of the floor. I just had to see more of her, but I didn't know how I could. One day, it came to me. In a corner of her office there was a large roll of brown parcel paper. That's it, I thought and off I went. It worked like a charm. My gentle knock on her door was answered by a sweet "Come in," and there she was, sitting at her desk with a smile that would melt the snow of Mount Kilimanjaro.

"Er, can I have some brown paper, please?"

"Certainly." Rennie came around her desk and, tearing a sheet from the roll, handed it to me. She was so close that our hands touched, or if they didn't, they should have. By the end of two months we had enough brown paper at our house to wrap King Kong.

Finally I got up enough courage to ask Rennie for a date. She refused, but in a way that encouraged me to try again. The following weekend I travelled a few miles to attend a special dance. While I was waltzing around the floor with a stranger we discovered that we were from the same area. She shared a funny story her friend had told her. It seemed the friend worked in an office, and every day this really ugly guy, his face covered in pimples, came in and asked for brown paper. We both laughed, and I hurried off the dance floor before the lights could go up and she could see that her partner's face was covered in acne. I never went to ask for brown paper again.

The news about Doll's husband, Howard, who was fighting in North Africa, was not good. The desert war, like the war on most fronts, was not going well. His letters were censored, but the newspapers were full of the achievements of a new German general, Rommel, who had stopped an advance by British forces in its tracks. Then the desert town of Tobruk fell, and thousands of British prisoners were taken. More than ever we were concerned for Howard's safety.

One lunchtime Doll and I, as always, walked home from Letts together. Doll was anxious to see her son, who was being cared for by our mother. As soon as we got home, we could tell something was wrong. My mother's face was wet with tears as she handed Doll a telegram. Howard was missing and believed killed. I had half-expected to hear news like this, but it still came as an awful shock. More surprising was Doll's reaction. She wouldn't believe the news, and insisted that he was still alive. We hoped she was right, but we didn't share her conviction. Then, a month later Doll received another telegram, this time from the Red Cross, telling her that Howard had been spotted in an Italian prisoner-of-war camp. There was rejoicing in the Wickses' house.

Up to this time Hitler's bombs had been conventional ones, but there were rumours of a new secret weapon he had prepared especially for London. One Wednesday night I was once again wakened by the anti-aircraft gun travelling the railway lines behind our building. I got out of bed and stood on the balcony. It was a bright, moonlit night, and from my vantage point I could see the Thames stretching away from London Bridge to the out-skirts of London. Searchlights were sweeping the sky. Suddenly the lights formed an X. Trapped in the centre of their beams was an aircraft that appeared to be, from the flame that roared behind it, on fire. London's anti-aircraft defences came alive. Dozens of exploding shells surrounded the target as it made its way up the Thames towards me. Suddenly the flame behind the aircraft went out. There was silence for a moment, then a rush of air followed by a huge explosion as the local post office blew up. The first of the flying bombs, the V-1, had arrived.

Although I shook my father awake and tried to tell him the news, all I got in return was "Yes, yes, Alfie. Now go back to sleep." It was no doubt trivial compared with what he had wit-nessed in France in 1916.

In the months that followed, the south of England was bombed by thousands of these pilotless planes – doodle bugs, we called them – as they spluttered their way to their targets. The V-1 was a brutal weapon that had no way of distinguishing between military and civilian targets and invariably fell on the latter when its fuel ran out.

Although our Spitfires managed to eliminate hundreds of V-1s, many more broke through the coastal defences and made it to London. They were a common sight during the day. It was when the engine stopped that the panic began. As long as the plane glided away from the onlookers, things were fine for them. If not, it was time to run for shelter.

Other than watching for doodle bugs there was little to do. Then, as if in answer to our need for a place to go in the evenings, Cambridge University took over an old house in Southwark and transformed it into a club for us. It was a place with free tea, table tennis and an anxious supervisor ready to organize anyone who came to the front door. It quickly became a regular hangout for the youth in the area. Most of us were happy to brave the German onslaught on our way to and from the club if it meant we could link up with new friends.

With the encouragement of the supervisor, we formed a cricket team. Although I preferred football, I still joined. Our team, Cambridge House, failed to win a single game in its first year. It was an ignominy that the club supervisor turned into a dubious honour by telling us we were the strongest in the league because we were supporting everyone else.

The turning point for our team came with the help of a V-1. A match between Cambridge House and another team was interrupted by the sound of an air-raid warning. Both teams stopped to watch a small plane approaching. Sure enough, it was a doodle bug. We all held our breath as it got closer. Suddenly the engine stopped and the bomb made a slow turn and headed towards us. We all ran in different directions. The V-1 finally crashed and exploded in the field beside us. The game was cancelled and declared a draw. Although our team had not won, more importantly, we had not lost.

The best part of being a member of Cambridge House was the new friendships. Four lads in particular seemed to have the same interests as I did, and soon we were going everywhere together: George Bailey, a redhead with a permanent smile; Phil Parnell, a bright, good-looking lad with a sharp mind for finance; Sammy Verrico, a slim Italian; and Arthur Biggs, dark, lean and generous to a fault.

We spent most of our Sundays playing card games at Phil's home. During one game the air-raid siren started to wail. George, with ears as sharp as a deer, held up his hand for silence. Over the siren we could hear the sound of an approaching doodle bug. Then its engine cut out. We dove under the table and held our heads as a loud swishing noise warned us that the explosion would be close by. When the roar stopped, we ran through the streets, heading for the pillar of smoke.

I can still remember Arthur's face as we turned the corner and saw that it was his house that had been hit. We scrambled over bricks and into the ruins in time to see his mum and dad staggering out of what had once been their home. Its front had been demolished.

"Where's Gran?" shouted Arthur.

His dad turned to follow Arthur, who was already at the foot of the stairs. Suddenly an upstairs door opened and an old lady appeared, covered in soot and dirt.

"What the bloody 'ell was that?" she shouted, to gales of laughter from the first-aid workers and wardens.

My lack of progress with the love of my life left me with no desire to stay in the employ of Charles Letts. I was sure there was better money to be made elsewhere. I decided to try my hand at making clogs. As it was piecework, I was paid by the number of finished clogs I turned out each day. I would be earning more money than I had made at Charles Letts. A narrow strip of tin secured the wooden clog to its upper, and within days my hands were a mass of cuts and bruises. I had second thoughts about the job and quit.

I began making women's purses for Mr. Francis, a wonderful Jewish man. During the war, it was the law that, on the sounding of an air-raid siren, all companies had to allow their employees to take shelter. Being young and stupid and in love with flying, instead of taking cover I used to head for the roof to watch the aircraft fighting. Aware that I was nowhere to be seen during the raids, Mr. Francis asked me where I had been going. When he heard that I had been on the roof, he immediately told me that, since I felt little need to take cover during the raids, I might as well continue to work. I did, and with every air raid regretted my previous disobedience.

Like most people, I was anxious to earn extra money wherever I could. Phil suggested that I help his dad in the East Street Market in Walworth on weekends. I leapt at the chance and headed for the market the next Saturday morning. Mr. Parnell was short and wore horn-rimmed glasses, the kind usually depicted in cartoons of American tourists. He had recently opened a bookie business on the side and needed someone to help on his fruit stall. After introducing me to his assistant, he left to answer what he hoped would be dozens of phone calls from gamblers.

"Ever worked in the market before, son?" asked his assistant as he began to set the apples on the cart. "Remember, it's always the best ones in the front, the lousy ones at the back."

"Yes, sir."

"Now, the first thing we're gonna show you is 'ow ta ring the change." This was the slang term for shortchanging a customer.

"Now, why do you fink all the fruit is priced at awkward numbers? Like the apples are tuppence ha'penny a pound and here," he reached over for a pear, "these are three pence ha'penny a pound. Why do you reckon that is?"

I struggled to come up with an answer.

"I'll tell you why. So that the bleedin' customer don't know wot the 'ell is going on when you count out the change, that's why. Right, let's start the first lesson."

He took one of my hands in his. "Now, I say to you, 'That will be sixpence ha'penny, guvnor.' You gives me a shilling. I says, ''Ave you got the ha'penny?' Then halfway frew, I says, 'Give me the penny and I'll give you . . .'" I was completely lost, but whatever he did I was a penny short when he finished giving me change.

He continued, "One fing you must remember: Shortchanging must never be done to a woman. A man is too stupid to count his change before 'e returns it to 'is pocket." He clenched a fist and opened it. "The woman will always count her change before puttin' it in 'er purse." It was my first lesson in human behaviour from a man without schooling. Like most of those who worked in the market, what he did have was a lot of street smarts and that most valuable of all attributes, common sense.

The market was full of characters who worked hard for the little they got in return. Although fruit selling may seem a simple exercise, requiring only a loud voice and the ability to make change quickly, in order to compete against others in the market one needed ingenuity. There were lessons that I learned as a barrow boy that I have never forgotten. One has proved invaluable. "Never try to sell someone oranges if all they wants is apples," said my market teacher. He was right. Give the customer what he wants and you'll never go wrong.

During the war what the British wanted was something that would take the taste of Spam and fake foods from their mouths. It was no longer possible to obtain many of the foods that had been plentiful during peacetime. One luxury in particular, sweets, was rarely seen. Mr. Parnell hit on a way to overcome this problem: he bought a large number of coconuts. Each morning we sat in a shed near the market and, after breaking open the coconuts, cut the white insides into squares. We then placed the squares in tiny bags, with a sprinkling of sugar in each. All that remained was to think of a name. Mr. Parnell opened a dictionary and came up with the longest name he could find. We quickly ran out, as customers lined up to buy this newest of confections with the unpronounceable name from an exotic source that Mr. Parnell refused to divulge.

One day a moving truck backed up to the edge of the market crowd, and the rear doors were flung open. The driver stood in the back, auctioning off cheap sheets and china. A crowd quickly gathered. Suddenly a small, rough-looking man appeared below the tailgate of the truck and began tugging at his sleeve. The auctioneer stopped and bent down, as the man whispered in his ear.

"Ladies and gentleman," the auctioneer called to the crowd.

"Ernie 'ere," he pointed down at the man, "'as just found a wallet. Those of you who has lost one can form a line at the front of the lorry."

Everyone laughed and he continued the auction. Why the interruption? They had planted three pickpockets in the crowd. Each of them was watching to see who was checking their wallets and, even more important, which pockets the wallets were returned to.

I worked in the market on weekends for six wonderful months, always at Mr. Parnell's cart and always surrounded by rogues. Listening to the various market con men I learned an important lesson. If you want people to listen, entertain them. If you want people to buy what you have to sell, describe what it will do for them in the simplest of terms. Eventually, although I enjoyed my days in the market, I realized I couldn't make it my life. There were other ways I wanted to spend my time.

I had loved drawing since I was a child, and when I heard there were evening classes in still-life drawing at the Dulwich School of Art, I rushed to sign up. At the end of two weeks, my teacher advised me that I was wasting my time, that I would never make a living in art and should look to other areas of interest. I was not happy to be discouraged so emphatically but quickly turned my attention to another love. From the moment I took my first flight around Croydon Airport on my tenth birthday, I had longed to be a pilot, and nothing was going to stop me now.

I joined the Air Training Corp, an organization like the Boy Scouts, and attended classes on aircraft recognition and navigation three evenings a week at a nearby school. I loved it, and while my friends were following the exploits of football players, I was learning the name of every war ace, including some of the German flyers.

At age seventeen, I volunteered for the air force and sat for an initial exam for pilot training. I waited eagerly for the results.

When they arrived I was told that, although I had passed, pilots were no longer needed, but since I had volunteered for service, I would receive a call from the army. I felt duped, and to this day, I distrust anything military.

I passed the army medical and was sent to Scotland for six weeks of training. After completing the course – I have never heard of anyone who failed it – I was posted to Canterbury to join the BUFFS, an infantry regiment that, like most regiments, celebrated the battles in which they had lost the most men. From early morning to late afternoon, my days were filled with constant drilling and shouting. There were thirty men to a platoon, and each of us ate and slept never more than a few yards apart. If any of us reached out while sleeping we would hit the person in the next bed. There were no sheets, just two blankets and a pillow to each soldier. Although this bothered many of those who had enjoyed a comfortable upbringing, those of us who had picked hops in Kent found the sleeping conditions more than adequate.

A few weeks after I joined the BUFFS I was excited to read on a bulletin board that volunteers were needed to become glider pilots. A tremendous number of glider pilots had been killed at Normandy and Arnhem and needed to be replaced. This was the chance I had been hoping for. I quickly applied and was called for an interview.

The officer leaned across his desk and asked the all-important question, "Are you willing to die for your country?"

I was astonished and shot back what I thought was a sensible answer: "Certainly not."

He recommended me for officer training.

Others must have disagreed with his assessment; at the time I arrived at the airborne training centre, I was still a private. The initial training for all glider pilots took place on Salisbury Plain, a mile from Stonehenge. The closest inhabitants were German prisoners of war, who stood looking glumly towards our Nissan huts from four hundred yards away. It was an ideal location for training as it was impossible to escape. All day we ran, jumped, swung from trees, climbed and learned to kill through unarmed combat.

After six weeks of this tough treatment we left for our elementary flying school at Hatfield, a town just north of London and the home of de Havilland Aircraft. Here we would first learn to fly power-driven aircraft before being sent on to glider school. We were billeted in a large Elizabethan manor that would have made the perfect setting for a Gothic horror novel. Dark and gloomy, it encouraged the dozen of us residents to make our true home at the local pub.

Our time at the airfield was split into half-days of flying and of classroom instruction. We flew Tiger Moths, small biplanes with open cockpits. The instructor sat in the front seat and directly behind him sat the pupil. The need for glider pilots was so desperate that little or no time was spent in the training process – nine hours of flying instruction, then it was off solo. After my nine hours I was still so unsure of what I was doing I was convinced the instructor would fail me.

He said nothing as we made our way to the aircraft and climbed in. I called to a ground-crew member that we were ready for him to spin the single propeller, and then began to roll the Tiger Moth towards the runway. The instructor's voice came through the earphones. "Take the aircraft over to the hangar and stop." I did as I was told. He climbed out, saying, "Its all yours. Good luck." He waved an arm and strolled away.

I vividly remember the thrill of that flight. As the biplane began to climb, I felt overwhelmingly excited and relieved to be free of the instructor's badgering. I flew around the airport as instructed then gently lowered the Tiger Moth to the ground. It was the best landing I would ever make.

I passed the test but, unfortunately, the glider school was full. Those on the waiting list were requested to remain at their airbases until space became available. Since I had passed the elementary training, I was automatically made sergeant, probably the youngest sergeant in the British army.

The Germans, meanwhile, had been developing a deadly weapon. The V-2 rocket was a forerunner of the Russian and American space vehicles. Fired from Northern France, the rocket would arch its way towards London. Travelling faster than the speed of sound, its arrival was silent and unheralded. Hundreds died in London as Hitler, in a last gasp at victory, aimed rocket after rocket at a defenceless capital.

The rocket that hit the factory next door to St. Georges' Building landed at 5 P.M., an hour when most workers were about to leave. Many died but, fortunately for me, Mum and Dad were not among them. Minutes before the rocket hit, Dad had sensed imminent danger and had thrown Mum and himself under the table. The windows crashed around them, spraying them with broken glass. Mum was cut on her head, but it was not a serious injury. Later, when I asked Dad to explain how he could have felt the peril, he just said that he had the same feeling of apprehension that he had often had while serving in the trenches of the First World War.

It was weeks before I heard about the incident. True to form Dad kept it from me. His weekly letters continued to be filled with good news and happy thoughts. Some months after the event I arrived home on leave to find a hole where most of the factory had been and learned of Mum and Dad's remarkable escape.

The delay in my move to gliders meant that I had many relaxed, carefree days. On the last of them, I took off in my tiny biplane the morning after a particularly eventful evening at the local pub. I decided that the best cure for a wicked head would be a series of loops and turns ending with a wild swaying approach before touching down. It was great fun, but, alas, the chief flying officer witnessed my antics.

He called me to his office, and to my horror told me that, although what I was doing was no doubt enjoyable, troops riding in the back of a glider I was piloting would hardly share my enthusiasm. I was out. I pleaded with him, but nothing I said changed his mind. It was a bitter moment and, as I opened my locker and removed my helmet, goggles and parachute, the tears rolled down my face. For eight years I had lived for the day I would fly. Now it was over, and I was being sent back to a regiment I hardly knew.

The commanding officer of the BUFFS looked at the report from the Glider Pilot Regiment. The airborne was sending him a sergeant he would have difficulty in placing. He had no intention of embarrassing me or the regiment by putting me within shouting distance of the parade square, which was a foreign place to me. His solution was simple. A lifeguard was needed at the outdoor swimming pool, and I would be it. So I spent the summer of 1945 reading in a deck chair with a lifebelt by my side. Happily, few people ever used the pool and those who did were able to swim, something I couldn't do.

When the war ended, there were parties on Britain's streets, and I missed them all. Unable to get leave, I spent a happy VE-Day on the base in Canterbury. Our celebration was like most of the others throughout the country: boisterous. I did my part by downing as many pints as I could at the local pub. Although I had seen no action, I was more than happy to accept the free beer constantly passed to "one of our brave lads."

The war continued in the Far East, but for us in Europe the fighting was finally at an end. Most of those who had been called into the services were just waiting for the day they could say a final farewell to their uniforms. I was as anxious as the rest to get back to civilian life, but I still had some years to go in army service. Eventually I was sent on a course to learn small arms and weapons instruction. I was surprised to find that I enjoyed teaching and to discover that my experience selling fruit in the market had prepared me to face students and explain the workings of most weapons in a simple manner. It's called communication, and I realized that I was good at it. My ability to build models was also useful, and I was soon putting together small demonstration models that showed the angles and trajectories of various weapons.

To entertain myself and keep track of the days remaining, I made a huge calendar and hung it on the wall. I attached a small bowler hat to the calendar and each day I would move it one square closer to the last day. When the hat finally fit squarely on the head of the figure at the end, my army days were over.

The suit handed to me when I was demobbed was a loud check and, although the fit was pretty good, the sight of it was enough for me to head for the nearest civilian tailor. I wasn't about to go home wearing *that*.

Back in Southwark at St. Georges' Building, I quickly became aware that I was not the same lad who had left. Mum and Dad were thrilled to see me back, and I was glad to be home, but I felt uneasy. I had expanded my horizons far beyond the borough.

The new experience I valued most was a love of music. One of my army friends was a classical music lover who had constantly played records, and I had always been ready to listen. Now, the moment I had sufficient money, I bought an old windup record player. From it some of the greatest singers in the world invaded our small flat. Never once did Mum or Dad complain. Their only comments were "That's nice" or "I like that" about almost everything I played.

Mr. Francis was good enough to give me back my job in his leather-goods shop, but after life in the service, I found the job tedious. A future of gluing leather pieces together for eight hours a day, hoping they resembled a woman's purse, was not the kind I was looking for.

My old friends had returned to Southwark, and all of them

were as bored as I was. Most of our time was spent at the Biggses' new home. Like me, Mr. Biggs loved classical music. The news that the great Italian tenor Beniamino Gigli was about to make his first appearance in London since the war resulted in a race for tickets. The concert at the Albert Hall sold out in hours, so an extra fifty tickets were made available, on the stage. Mr. Biggs succeeded in buying two of these, and since I was the only other person he knew who was interested in classical music, he offered me his spare ticket.

On the evening of the event, Mr. Biggs and I took our seats. I thought the hall was magnificent. As it began to fill with people, I was as excited as any artist about to entertain six thousand people.

As Gigli's large figure appeared onstage followed by his pianist, the audience erupted in applause. War had restricted many international entertainers from coming to Britain, and Gigli was one of them. For four hours this great Italian tenor lifted us away from our problems. I was close to the piano and, unfortunately, could only see his back. His voice would fill the hall and float back to those of us sitting on the stage.

Suddenly he turned, waved a signal to his pianist and, with his back to the packed hall, Gigli sang "Mattinata" to us. It remains my favourite song to this day. It has been sung beautifully by Pavarotti and Carreras, but there is only one voice that rings in my ears – Gigli. He received encore after encore that night, and each time the great man strolled out to sing some more. When it seemed daylight would soon be upon us, I witnessed an extraordinary sight offstage. At Gigli's suggestion, his pianist lay down on the floor and Gigli dragged him back to the piano by his arms. It brought the house down. This evening made me a convert to the world of great singers forever.

A few nights later, as the gang and I sat in the local pub discussing both Gigli and a new kid named Frank Sinatra, we decided to start a band. Who would play what? Phil Parnell was no problem. He could play the piano – sort of. Sammy Verrico was also off to a flying start. His father had a drum set he would bang on every year at his Christmas party. Although Sammy had never drummed, he was willing to follow in his father's footsteps and try banging along with whatever it was we might be playing. George Bailey, who had been a wonderful glider pilot, couldn't carry a tune. We told him to buy a banjo.

I was sent to the nearest pawnshop to see what instruments they had for me to play. The window outside advertised a flute. I remember the wording to this day: "Flute for sale. Easily concealed." Did this mean that it was possible to sneak into a party, surprise guests by whipping out a flute from an inside pocket and deliver an unwanted concert? I never did find out since the rest of the gang felt that this was not the kind of instrument that would lead us to the world stage. I ended up with an old clarinet.

For months our group of dedicated "musicians" met on Mondays and attempted to play traditional jazz, but finally the others gave up. Me? I felt anything was better than sticking pieces of leather together. I hunted out a teacher, Freddy Datchler, who suggested that learning the saxophone was the fastest route to becoming a professional musician. He was certainly in a position to know, since he worked for one of the leading bands of the day. I agreed to take weekly lessons at his house and to buy an alto saxophone.

"How long will it take me to become a professional?" I asked him.

"That depends on how much you're willing to practise," he answered.

Determined to leave the world of woman's purses behind as fast as possible, I practised like a fiend. It was not easy. Our thin walls forced others to suffer the wailing of a saxophone in pain. Mum and Dad tried their best to shield me from any embarrassment.

Dad opened the doors to our wardrobe, set a music stand between the coats and hung a torch from the rail. Taking my place between the doors, I would sit half in and half out of the wardrobe. Dad would then enclose me with blankets across the doors and down my back to muffle any escaping sounds. With my saxophone pressed against the coats, there I sat night after night practising scales. This is just one more example of the incredibly supportive parents I was fortunate to have.

I stuck with my lessons and was delighted with my progress. Even our neighbour Mrs. Lee failed to dismay me when she remarked one day, "Alfie, I think that trumpet of yours is beginning to sound lovely." She may have had the wrong instrument, but her goodness of heart did give me encouragement, so much so that I felt confident enough to give up my job and devote myself full time to music. I had worked hard, and for as long as I can remember I have always been confident that, given time, I can accomplish anything.

An advertisement in a musical newspaper I regularly read mentioned that a new band was forming and those wishing to join should apply at the stated address. It had been almost six months since my first lesson, and this was my first audition.

Roy Kenton, the drummer and would-be leader of the proposed band, was short and dark, with a lively personality. He held my audition at his home in nearby Kennington, where he lived with his family, all as bubbly and enthusiastic as he was. After I played a few tunes on the saxophone in front of the whole family, everyone applauded. Although the way I played hardly warranted their zeal, their response convinced me that the life of a professional musician was just around the corner. Roy's dad was the most excited of all, and danced around the room slapping a pair of spoons on his leg to the rhythm of the music.

Roy accepted me as a member of the Roy Kenton Band and began to develop a plan of action. He had heard that the owners of a dance hall in Cornwall, in southwest England, needed a band for the summer season, and he was determined we would get the job.

There was much to be done before the all-important audition. First, we needed a band. After a series of auditions six other members joined. Doug Proudly, whose round, jolly face sat on an expansive body, was a fine pianist and a natural choice. Pete Probert arrived with a string bass and stood beside it grinning and throwing his fingers around the strings. A young, good-looking lad, his ready smile would later snare a whole gaggle of women. Frank Rashbrook was thin and had nerves that seemed stretched to the limit. But when the trumpet hit his lips, there was no question that Frank could place his signature on the dotted line. Three other sax players were signed up, and we were almost ready to hit the road. We needed to rehearse and to create a logo for the band. The letters *RK* would be prominent on the front of every music stand, followed by the first name of each band member. This presented a problem. Although I was proud of my name, it was not to Roy's liking.

"There's no way I'm going to have the name 'Alf' on the music stand of my lead sax player," declared Roy. "In future you'll be called Benny." And I was. A new chapter of my life was beginning. I was about to enter the world of music, and Alfie would be left behind. Ben had arrived, and he has remained to this day.

4

ALTHOUGH IT WAS DIFFICULT for Dad to understand how anyone could give up a secure job to be a musician, both he and Mum were happy that I was setting out to earn a living doing something I loved. I was twenty-two years old, and they felt that I knew my own mind. Whatever lay ahead, St. Georges' Building would remain my home, they assured me, and they would always welcome me back.

The band was naturally excited about our audition for the job in Cornwall. The photos of the Blue Lagoon Ballroom that Roy passed around showed that the dance hall was on the top of a cliff overlooking the ocean. The idea of passing the summer months playing in a seaside town prompted one smart-alec to suggest that if we didn't get the job, we should offer to pay them to play there.

Mr. and Mrs. Coster, the owners of the Blue Lagoon, came up from Cornwall and rented the upstairs room of a local pub for our audition. Roy had rehearsed us well, and we could play most of the popular favourites of the day. The Costers were pleased with what they heard. We signed the contract and headed to Cornwall for the summer.

It is easy to feel that when God created Earth the place he chose as a garden was Cornwall. "And here," He said, "I'll place Newquay." The harbour and village of Newquay lie at the foot of steep cliffs on the southwest coast. A perfect beach stretches below the towering rocks, which reach their highest point near the edge of town. Sitting on top was the Blue Lagoon, our place of work for the next three months. It was the only dance hall in town and a gold mine for the Costers.

The first task upon our arrival was to find accommodation. This was fairly easy since it was early in the season, and those who were renting rooms knew that we would be there for the whole summer. I took an attic room above the local butcher's shop with Pete, the bass fiddle player. Although it had only one small window, which looked out on a sloping roof, our land-lords were friendly.

The more comfortable first floor above the shop was reserved for the regulars: actors who arrived each year as part of a reper-tory company. Repertory is the backbone of the British acting profession, and few actors have not begun their careers touring with the reps. Each morning we would sit at breakfast, hardly daring to breath as these incredible people memorized a different role for each night. How they did it I have no idea, but they loved the theatre as much as we loved music.

The Roy Kenton Band began playing each evening at 7:30 P.M. and finished at 11:30 P.M. (This left us all day to spend on the beach, doing our best to strike up conversations with the most attractive girls who strolled by.) We enjoyed playing the big-band music to happy groups of holiday-makers circling the large, crowded dance floor. A wall of windows ran along one side of the room, and as the sun sank into the sea each evening it threw an orange glow across the ballroom floor.

Saturday was a special day. We would visit the local train station in the afternoon to say goodbye to the girls we had met the week before, then wait for the next train to arrive carrying the newcomers. We hoped that by that evening each of us would be escorting a new girlfriend home. Although most girls were smart enough to allow only kissing at the front door, the stories we told the rest of the band were filled with inventive amorous details. As these girls circled the dance floor for the remainder of the week, the band members without girlfriends would watch and pant.

Since the holiday-makers could be staying a great distance from town, we took care to find where a particular girl was lodging before we offered our services as an escort. Even so, many romantic evenings ended in a long and fruitless mystery tour.

I had experienced my share of disappointing evenings, but this didn't stop me one day from falling into the trap of fanta-sizing an ending to a romantic evening that turned out to be anything but. The girl was gorgeous, but after a quick kiss she vanished inside her boarding house and I turned to face a three-mile walk back across the cliffs to town. It was a beautiful moonlit night, but it was already 2 A.M., and I was tired and anxious to get home. Suddenly I heard a hoot and there on a fence post sat an owl. I stopped and watched as it blinked at me. I decided to get closer and was within a few feet when it sud-denly flew off, only to settle again on another post up ahead. Once again I got close, and once again it took off for another post. This continued all the way into town, and as I walked along the empty High Street, the owl followed. Eventually I left it sitting on a shop awning and climbed the stairs to the attic.

Pete was reading in bed. "You're not going to believe this," I said, "but a bloody owl just followed me home." He was about to ask what I had been drinking when there was a flurry of wings outside the window, and the owl perched on the window ledge. Both of us were speechless. It was difficult to know whose eyes were open the widest, the owl's or ours. After a few minutes it flew off. I have heard that old sailors come back as seagulls, but I have yet to find out who returns as an owl.

The summer ended all too quickly, but we left happy in the knowledge that not only had we enjoyed ourselves but so had the owners of the Blue Lagoon. We agreed to return the following summer and signed contracts to that effect. In the meantime, those of us without jobs for the winter had to beat the bushes for work.

Archer Street, in the West End of London, was the meeting place for musicians. Each Monday hundreds of musicians would crush together in the various clubs and coffee houses on the street, hoping to meet friends or find work. I shouldered my way through one crowd and headed for a few faces I knew. A friend told me that an agent was booking musicians to play at the American camps in Germany and France and if I was interested I should give him a phone call. I should have been tipped off when this agent offered me a six-month contract to play the American camps in Germany without hearing me play.

Two weeks passed without a word from the agent. One Saturday afternoon I was at a major football game watching two of London's most famous teams play for a crowd of fifty thousand. Halfway through the game there was an announcement: "If there's a Ben Wicks in the crowd, it is important that he report to the front office immediately."

I was stunned. I was sure that such an announcement would only be made in an emergency. Had something happened to Mum and Dad? I hurried to the nearest police officer, who directed me to the front office. There I was told the message was serious; a member of my family was in trouble. I rang the number they gave me, fully expecting to reach a hospital. It was the agent. "Sorry for the scare, kid. Figured it was the only way to get you the news. You have to be in Germany by Monday night." He told me the tickets were waiting for me and that I'd best forget the football game and go straight home.

A few hours later, Dad said goodbye to me at the railway station. He was convinced that joining a strange group of show people on the continent was the height of madness, but still he gave me his typical stiff hug and wished me well.

It was late Monday afternoon when I arrived at a tiny hotel in Frankfurt. I had been travelling for two days, but as it was my first time out of England, I was anxious to see something of the town. The nearby tavern was crowded with people both in and out of uniform and, as I leaned on the bar, I was surprised to hear some of the civilians near me speaking English. They were, I learned, also musicians who had signed on to play the American camps. We began to compare notes. I explained that in the morning I was to meet the cast of the show I would be touring with, and after rehearsal we would be heading for Vienna. Another saxophone player mentioned that he had never been to Vienna and that the show he would be travelling with was on its way to Berlin, a city he had seen before. Would I like to trade? Since both shows were expecting strangers, no one would be any the wiser. I agreed that it sounded like a good idea, and anyway I was just as anxious to see Berlin as he was to see Vienna. We shook hands and that was that.

It was ten o'clock the next morning before I found out the real reason for the switch. I went to the hotel listed in my travel instructions and entered its small ballroom. The Gypsy Markoff Show consisted of nine American showgirls in their early twenties and a piano player, who later confessed his preference for men. At first glance I was sure I had won the lottery. The girls were incredibly beautiful and the piano player, Wayne, was just friendly enough. We tried out a few numbers that seemed to go very well. Wayne was a good pianist and we had no problems following the music the girls supplied.

She was an hour late. The sound of high-heel shoes clicking in the outside passage gave warning that she had arrived. Gypsy Markoff was extremely short – well under five feet – and as she drew closer, it was apparent that she had seen better days. Both

Wayne and I introduced ourselves. She lifted her hand to the side of her face and tossed aside her long black hair. "And where are the useless good-for-nothings who showed up yesterday?"

I was ready to answer "On their way to Vienna," when she threw a pile of music at poor Wayne and removed her accordion from its case. I tried to help Wayne unfold what turned out to be an arrangement for the twenty-eight-piece Brooklyn Navy Yard Band. As we spread it out on the piano, Gypsy began to play an incredibly involved arpeggio that ran the length of her keyboard. She paused, and I had hardly lifted the sax to my lips before she was away again like a racehorse. As I remember it, Wayne won, or at least he finished first. Gypsy came in second, and I made up the rear.

She lowered her accordion to the floor and opened her mouth to speak. What came out was a scream. She hitched up her skirt like a showgirl, lifted her legs and brought them down in a show of rage in the centre of the room. Wayne and I looked for cover. There was none. When the tirade was finally over, all I could think about was the sneaky sax player who had cajoled me into switching jobs and was now off to Vienna.

There was no out for any of us. Gypsy was stuck with us, as we were with her. We approached our first concert, in Wiesbaden, with trepidation. Although most of the showgirls had played Broadway, they still were nervous of what might happen. Gypsy's reputation had followed her from Italy. There, the girls told us, Gypsy had decided that a general was making too much noise during her performance and had given him a shrieking lungful of abuse from the stage. To no one's surprise, the company had received orders to move out of the country at sunrise.

There were many military brass present at the Wiesbaden concert. We hoped there was not a noisy general among them. The performance went without a hitch and, although Wayne and I continued to have difficulty keeping up with Gypsy's brilliant accordion playing, she seemed pleased and enjoyed the attention she received at the officers' mess after the concert.

The greatest advantage of travelling with nine beautiful young women, apart from the obvious, was the treatment we received from the audience. Every show was a hit, with men standing and shouting regardless of whether the girls sang, danced or stood on their heads. Royce Wallace, a beautiful blues singer, was followed by an equally attractive magician. A former beauty queen of China circled the stage and adopted various poses. Although this act might appear to lack substance, few performers could have attracted more response from an audience of GIs than Lee Wong. Sherry danced and showed her shapely legs to a grateful audience as a blonde whose name I've forgotten sang a medley of songs from *South Pacific*. At each stop Gypsy would do her stuff under a spotlight and, after the show, sweep into the officers' mess on the arm of a colonel. We tagged along behind and, although Wayne and I obviously lacked the attractiveness of the girls, we were at least allowed to enjoy the plush surroundings.

We travelled to most of the American camps by bus. Late at night, after the last show of the day, we would climb aboard, stop at a hotel on the way and continue the following morning to the next camp on our itinerary. Once we caught a plane because of the long distance we would have to travel to get to Berlin. With army assistance we hopped on a DC-3 military aircraft and flew down the narrow air-corridor that split the Russian sector surrounding the city.

The theatre in Berlin astonished me. It was a large opera house with ornate gold fixtures and beautifully carved figures. Wayne and I entered the orchestra pit and looked aghast at the space that would normally be occupied by dozens of musicians. Slowly the opera house began to fill, until two thousand rowdy American servicemen were seated and shouting for the show to start.

Our magician completed her act to thunderous applause. Few cared where the rabbit had vanished, provided that her figure was still visible in her shiny, tight-fitting dress. Then Royce glided onto the stage in a sultry manner while thousands of eyes followed her every move. During these two acts a fat, very drunk sergeant was leaning across where we were playing and shouting obscene remarks at the girls. They returned the abuse with their usual ad-libbed banter.

The lights were dimmed for the entrance of the star and, as everyone peered into the darkness, the sounds of an accordion arpeggio filled the air. A spotlight pierced the blackness and circled Gypsy as her fingers danced back and forth over the keys. She was a dazzling musician, and her opening to the "Hungarian Rhapsody" usually held most people, but not the drunken sergeant.

"What the fuck is this crap? Bring back the girls!" he shouted.

Gypsy stopped and took a few paces to the edge of the stage. She puffed herself up to her full four feet six inches and stared down at him. With a loud scream she declared, "The show is over, and you can thank your drunken sergeant for the early finish." With that she walked off the stage. The house was in an uproar. Beer cans flew through the air and hit the curtain like balls thrown at a carnival coconut show. We were not invited back to the officers' mess, but made our way as quickly as we could to the railway station.

The train travelled through the Russian sector with the blinds down; we had strict instructions not to look out the windows. Most of the troupe were exhausted and had no intention of doing anything other than sleeping. I, however, was too excited to sleep and waited anxiously to arrive at the checkpoint between the Russian and American zones.

The train slowed and threw clouds of hissing steam towards the platform before coming to a stop. It was past midnight and, peeping around the blind, I watched in fascination as six Russian soldiers exchanged papers with six American soldiers. No words were spoken and, with the steam swirling around their legs, the station took on the appearance of a Hollywood movie set. Then the train began to move again and the sound of blinds snapping up signalled that we were back in the American zone.

After a month-long tour of France, the Gypsy Markoff Show went to England. Our first engagement was in Oxford. The bus pulled to a stop outside our hotel, and Gypsy swept into the lobby. As per her instructions she was first in line, and as we sat or stood around, we watched her perform her usual duchess act. Unfortunately for Gypsy, this was England not Germany. These people had not been defeated and were not prepared to bow and scrape to her. The elevator was out of order and, as the porter followed her up the stairs, Gypsy looked distinctly unhappy. While we stood waiting to register, she suddenly reappeared. She was dissatisfied with her room and demanded what any person of her importance was accustomed to – a suite.

"We have no suites available, Madam," said the desk clerk.

"I demand to see the manager," said Gypsy.

The demand was made in such a loud voice that the manager appeared from a small office behind the desk and asked, "Is there a problem?"

"There certainly is. I'm not happy with the crappy room I've been given," said Gypsy, "and furthermore I'm not happy with your staff."

He glanced at her from under half-closed eyelids. "I'm sure there's something we can do to make you happy. Please accept my apologies." He then turned to a phone and made a call. Satisfied, he turned to Gypsy, scribbled on a piece of paper and handed it to her.

"There you are, Madam. It's a hotel down the street that, I've been informed, have vacancies. Good day." With that he turned and made his way back into his office.

There was little Gypsy could do. She had been thrown out of a hotel for the first time in her life and did not enjoy the humiliation.

The tour finally came to an end. We had been travelling together for almost nine months and were now like brothers and sisters. There were plenty of tears when we parted. We vowed that we would meet again, but it would be twenty-five years before I ran into anyone, when I discovered one of the girls performing on Broadway in *Funny Girl*.

As any professional musician knows, jobs are not easy to come by, but I was one of the lucky ones. After just a few weeks' break, I headed for my second summer season in Newquay with the Roy Kenton Band. It was the perfect job and, after the extensive bus travel, I looked forward to having a whole summer to relax and breathe the sea air on one of the finest beaches in the world. The whole season went as smoothly as the first, and again we spent our days dallying with girls on the beach and our nights playing at the Blue Lagoon.

Roy had grandiose ideas for all of us when the summer season ended. In order to attract would-be bookers, he publicized the band as recently completing a world tour. Since I was the only member who had ever ventured beyond England's shores, this was hardly an accurate claim. But it worked. An agent booked us into Barrow-in-Furness, a northern town where at early light workers trod the cobbled streets on their way to the factories. From the beginning it was apparent that we would get little sleep.

The theatre had seen better days. It was called Her Majesty's Theatre and, although I doubt Queen Victoria would have claimed any connection, it did have an old-world charm. Unfortunately when the Roy Kenton Band played, it also had a number of empty seats. In fact, with the exception of the first two rows and a nutcase who sat in a box every night wearing tails and a top hat, the rest of the theatre was empty.

The Roy Kenton Band topped the billing, and among the other acts was Mona and her Magic Rings. Mona was a friendly woman with a set of rings that she would slowly squeeze through to the tune of "Deep Purple." Dressed in a bikini, she would bang the rings on the floor and declare, "These rings are solid steel and will not bend." As they hit the floor our drummer would lightly tap a cymbal to make the appropriate sound, since the thud of her rubber rings would not have impressed any audience.

For the three young showgirls this engagement was their first appearance on any stage. They had paid their own fare and, although they could not dance, they were anxious to please.

Roy decided that we had to watch the magician closely. Since he was the one who booked the acts, he was the one with the money. At the end of the first week, it was apparent to everyone that there would not be enough money from the box office to go around. Each of the band members took turns standing backstage outside his dressing room to ensure he would still be around at the end of the two-week booking.

On the second Friday night, one night short of the engagement's end, I stood smoking near the magician's dressing room. When his door opened quietly, I eased back and watched as a suitcase appeared, then the magician. He may have been a good magician but he was lousy at disappearing. We reminded him that the show was not over but was, in fact, just about to begin. After the final curtain, we crowded into his dressing room to decide who was getting paid. At the end of a shouting match it was agreed that the showgirls should take whatever money there was to get them back home to Scotland. Poor Madame Mona could do nothing but nod her head. She cried as she packed her magic rings and prepared to leave.

Once again the Roy Kenton Band was without work, and we went our separate ways. Back in London I headed for a small café on Archer Street and joined a group of friends. During the usual banter and stories of past gigs, one musician mentioned that he had been playing saxophone on the giant ocean liner the *Queen Elizabeth*. He had made six trips to New York, but was already bored with the job and would be leaving after the next trip. I was instantly interested in stepping into his shoes. This was the most modern liner in the world, plying back and forth across the Atlantic between Southampton and New York, a city I had never seen.

I began with my standard question: "How good a musician do you have to be to get the job?"

"Are you joking? I'm talking about playing in the band of the *Queen Elizabeth*."

"So you must be good, right?"

"Wrong. Let me explain. The guy who does the auditions is named Barber. He is tone deaf and knows nothing about music."

I was about to interrupt when he held up his hand. The others lowered their cups and leaned into the table.

"Barber's mother was a musician and when she retired she started up her own agency. It did very well, and one of the clients she nailed ran the *QE*. Anyway, she retired and left the business to her son."

"The one who's tone deaf?"

"Right. So forget worrying about the audition. Do you read music?"

"Sure."

"Can you play without it?"

"Most songs."

"Well, don't worry about it. Barber knows only two tunes. One is 'The Lady Is a Tramp' in the key of C, and the other is 'Night and Day' in E flat."

I left the group and headed for the nearest phone.

"Okay, show up here in a week and bring your sax and clarinet with you," said Barber and gave me an address close to

Trafalgar Square. One week later I climbed three rickety floors above a tobacconist's shop in Charing Cross Road and faced a door labelled "Barber Agency." I knocked on the glass and walked in.

The desk that trapped Barber against the wall was almost as big as the room. On one side of the office was a set of shelves holding hundreds of pieces of music.

"Wicks?"

I nodded.

"Right, let's get started." He reached up, handed me some music and pushed his horn-rimmed glasses farther up the bridge of his nose. I took out my saxophone and placed it on the stand.

"This is a trumpet piece, Mr. Barber."

"Just play it, Wicks."

"Shall I pick it up at the melody?"

"No, start at the top."

I looked at the arrangement that had been written for a full orchestra.

"Er, that's a harmony part, Mr. Barber."

He looked up. "So play me some harmony."

I began to play. The notes wailed around the room. Barber stood and came around the desk. Taking a piece of cloth from the drawer, he stuffed it into the end of my sax.

"We don't need any of those sounds on board our ship, Mr. Wicks. We're looking for sophistication."

I started to blow once more. It was not easy, but a weird sound did manage to sneak out.

"That's more like it. Now, how are you at playing without music? We have lots of passengers who want to hear their favourite tunes."

"I'll play anything you'd like to mention."

"How about 'The Lady Is a Tramp' in C?"

It had happened. I didn't think it possible. The guy knew

only two tunes. I began to blow. It was wonderful. It should have been. I'd practised nothing else for the past week.

"That's okay. Now how are you on clarinet?"

"Fine," I answered.

"Then try this." He handed me a fresh sheet of music. It was "Swedish Rhapsody," a familiar piece often played as background to travel films. My first thought was that a flock of pigeons had run back and forth across the manuscript. As I squeaked my way through the first page, Barber got up and squeezed his frame around his desk. Standing just inches away from my squawking instrument, he suddenly spoke.

"When the hell did you last clean that thing?" he asked. "You'll be playing in first class, and what's some foreign king going to think when he dances past an instrument like that?" He paused. "Now what about playing the clarinet without music?"

"Anything you'd like to mention," I answered and placed my fingers confidently on the keys that would begin a version of "Night and Day" in E flat.

"Okay, lets hear . . . er, let's hear . . ."

I waited. My god, the man could not think of "Night and Day." Should I suggest it? Yet to pick that particular tune may appear suspicious.

"Let's hear . . . er . . . er . . . Oh, to hell with it. Let's hear the middle bit of 'Lady Is a Tramp' in C."

Incredible as it may seem, I had met a man who only knew one tune.

I returned home convinced that my squeaky clarinet had lost me the audition. It hadn't. It took just one week for Barber to call. There had been a sudden opening on the *Queen Elizabeth*. I headed for Southampton that winter with Barber's last instruction ringing in my ears: "And get that damned clarinet cleaned before you get on board!"

As I walked towards the *Queen Elizabeth*, it was easy to see why Bea Lillie, a British actress who had travelled to New York on the huge liner, had asked the deck steward, "What time does this place get to America?" The "place" was huge, and it took more than a few directions before I located my cabin. After what seemed like miles of corridors, I found myself at the stern of the ship in an attractive cabin with a porthole.

Jeff, the musical director of the three small bands on board, was a small, pleasant man in his fifties who played the violin (Barber's instrument of choice, since he felt it gave the right tone for those wealthy enough to travel across the Atlantic on the QE). I was never sure what part of the country Jeff came from, but after touring most of the hotels in Britain he had decided to switch jobs and become a ship-board musician. I was told he had been on board the QE for more than three years. Since he had no relatives on shore, for him the ship was home.

The final goodbye ribbons were thrown and a farewell blast from the ship's horn sounded as I followed Jeff towards the dining room for the afternoon-tea performance. I felt uncomfortable. Here I was a dance-band musician about to play semi-serious stuff. I had no need to worry. Tiny Clark, the friendly drummer, was the first to push forward and hold out a hand in welcome. He was a former wrestler who hit the drums as though he were pounding the floor with an opponent's head. The bass-cum-cello player and the pianist were quiet fellows whose names have faded from my memory.

We took our places on the stage. Jeff decided that "Teddy Bear's Picnic" would be a good opening number since many in the room were children. Jeff lifted the violin to his chin and with a nod of his head began to play. It was not the sweetest music this side of heaven. I tried my best to take my mind off Jeff's wretched efforts and concentrate on the clarinet part. The tune was a familiar one, and the children and their parents appeared to be having a good time. Encouraged, our small group then turned its attention to a Viennese waltz and ploughed on.

Suddenly Jeff tapped his music stand and pointed excitedly with his bow. A recognizable face had stepped into the room. My heart stopped. One of the greatest violinists in the world, Yehudi Menuhin, and his sister were entering for afternoon tea. I sank lower in my chair. Much as I liked Jeff, he was a lousy violinist.

"Quick," said Jeff. "Put up eighty-four."

We did as we were told and rustled through the music until we found number eighty-four. It was "Handel in the Strand," a popular afternoon-tea classic. We began to play. With his violin under his chin, Jeff stepped from the small stage and slowly toured the room. Stopping beside an astonished Menuhin, he continued to play. The great violinist and his sister had their cups part way to their lips. They stayed like this throughout the entire piece, at which time Jeff lowered his violin and with the deepest of bows, returned to the stage. There was some applause, and I am sure Menuhin and his sister would have joined in if they had not been busy wiping the spilled tea from their clothes.

Life at sea was wonderful. Although the standard of music left much to be desired, the passengers seemed prepared to enjoy themselves no matter who was assigned to entertain them. The three bands on the *Queen Elizabeth* took turns playing for the different classes on board. Although first class was fine for the passengers, it was not a favourite of the musicians, since the bow-tie crowd liked to stay up late and most of us preferred to get to bed at a reasonable hour.

After completing the eight-to-midnight shift playing for a dance, it would be time to take a turn playing in the tourist, or third-class, section of the ship. The nightclub there was a popular area, not only for the musicians but also for many of the first-class passengers. The classes on the liner were separated by locked gates in the gangways, but for a small tip a steward would be happy to allow the bow ties into the "peasant" quarters far away from the pomp and nonsense of first class. The room was filled with emigrants, many from Ireland, or first-time travellers. They were constantly in a happy mood and wanted nothing more than to sing and dance.

Playing in third class gave Jeff, our gallant leader, the opportunity to put away his violin and try his hand at the saxophone. I never once heard him play the instrument. Each night would be the same. Fond of a few drinks and having had little to eat all day, he would arrive at the club distinctly the worse for wear. He would unpack his sax, then sit with it in his lap in the dimly lit room and fall asleep. It was a nightly ritual for Tiny and I to carry him, still on the chair, into a dark corner behind the piano and wake him when the session was over, usually around 2 A.M.

As our ship approached New York, Tiny asked if I liked classical music. I replied that, although I was not an expert, I did like the more popular pieces.

"Great, you can come with me and meet my old buddies at Carnegie Hall," he said. "The New York Phil is in town. It should be great." I answered that I was more keen on getting to the most famous jazz club in the world, Birdland.

"So we'll go after the concert." He was difficult to turn down.

After the initial thrill of seeing the Statue of Liberty came the excitement of watching the largest liner in the world manoeuvre, with the help of tugs, into a reserved dock.

The pianist agreed to accompany me ashore, and as we walked along Broadway we decided to stop for our first hamburger. When the waitress placed a glass of water beside me, I asked the pianist why, since I had not asked for water. We continued to discuss this strange ritual on the street. He was sure that it was for drinking. I thought otherwise. We made a bet and went back inside the crowded shop.

"Excuse me, Miss. My friend and I would like you to settle a bet."

"Sure, honey. What would you like to know?" She had a typical Brooklyn accent.

"Would you mind telling him that the glass of water is there to be used as a finger bowl."

She was drying a knife with a towel and slowly lowered it. In a loud voice she faked an English accent: "Of course it is, me lud. We're all out of finger bowls but if you would like me to wipe your little fingers with a nappie, I'd be more than honoured."

Laughter followed my red face outside.

The sizeable crowds outside Carnegie Hall indicated the importance of the Philharmonic Orchestra. I pushed through the ranks of tuxedoes and evening dresses towards the giant in the middle of the foyer. There is one thing about making an arrangement to meet a former wrestler, he's easy to find. Before I reached him, Tiny was shouting across the heads of those crunched together. "Over here, Ben, me boy."

Throwing an arm around my shoulder, he held me in a head-lock as he introduced me to a distinguished looking man wearing a bow tie, and a carnation in his buttonhole. "Ben, meet Rudolf Bing." I stared at the famous general manager of the New York Met as he grinned and took my hand.

Satisfied that the evening had started out well, Tiny grabbed my arm and led me down a long corridor. Program sellers and ushers grinned and greeted him by name as we passed through a door that led us backstage. From the wings we could see the timpanist for the New York Philharmonic tuning his drums. Without pausing an instant, Tiny strolled out onstage towards him. I followed and suddenly found that we were in full view of an audience taking its seats.

"Okay, Issy, stop the nonsense, I want you to meet a friend." The irritation on the face of one of the world's finest timpanists quickly changed to a smile, and he grabbed Tiny's hand. Introductions were made. Tiny took me by the arm, promised his friend that he would try to see him in the intermission, and with that sauntered into the wings. We watched the concert from a box, naturally. I enjoyed it and the companionship of the remarkable Tiny Clark. At the end of the concert it was difficult to refuse Tiny's invitation to join his friends in a post-performance celebration, but I was anxious to get to Birdland.

It was smaller than I had imagined and certainly a far cry from Carnegie Hall. A dwarf took my ticket at the door and pointed to a seat at the back of the room. I could not have been luckier. Lester Young and his trio were warming up the crowd before Count Basie and his band squeezed themselves into position. Within minutes Basie's great sound was filling the room. Hours later, as I walked back to the ship, his music was still running through my head. Back on board, I lay in my cabin, closed my eyes and dreamed of what it would be like living in the most exciting city on earth. New York had lots to offer, I thought, but then so did the *Queen Elizabeth*.

As the giant ship eased its way out of its berth and began the long journey back to Britain, the purser took a quick look at the passenger list to see if any of the new arrivals were entertainers. Quite often there were famous stars aboard who could easily be persuaded to give a free concert for the first-class passengers. Although most readily agreed, this time one did refuse.

Gracie Fields had only been on board a few minutes when the purser made his move. "Sorry, lad," said the superstar. "If the crowd in first wants to hear me sing, they can pay for the honour." With that she turned and disappeared into her cabin. After dinner she appeared once more, not in the first-class dining room, but in the Pig and Whistle, a pub far below the water line, reserved for the crew. On each of the four nights it took to cross the Atlantic, "our" Gracie would sing for the crew. She was one of the greatest stars I ever met – a rare human being.

In Southampton, the great ship had a forty-eight-hour turnaround, just enough time for me to head to London for a quick visit to Mum and Dad. As the *Queen Elizabeth* slid from the docks for my second round-trip, there was bad news. Our regular pianist was sick and a replacement had arrived on board.

Barely speaking to anyone, he played the first of the teatime sessions then vanished into his cabin.

During our first meal together he suddenly dropped his soup spoon and declared in a loud voice, "He's trying to poison me."

"I beg your pardon?" said Tiny.

"Was it you?" said the pianist. "So, you thought you could get away with it, did you? I'm on to you . . . you . . . big fat drummer, you. Paid the chef to get rid of me, did you? Well it didn't work."

With that he stomped out of the room as an astonished group of musicians looked on. Jeff hurried after him and returned a few minutes later to say that the pianist had locked himself in his cabin. The only sounds coming from inside were of him praying.

It was difficult to know what to do. The mid-Atlantic was no place to find a replacement pianist. We decided to allow him to play the evening session and hoped for the best.

We were already in position when he arrived. He was a good pianist, and few noticed or seemed to care that he glared and mumbled at the keys. A woman passenger approached the band and tapped the pianist's shoulder.

"Excuse me. It's our wedding anniversary." She made a gesture towards an older man who was beaming at her. "Could you play 'Blue Moon' for us?"

The pianist continued to stare at the keys.

"Er, excuse me," she tried again. "I was wondering if you wouldn't mind playing 'Blue Moon?'"

No response. The woman tried once more: "I don't mean to be a pest, but I wonder . . ." She got no further.

The pianist whirled around and pushed his face into hers. "Fuck off!" he yelled.

The purser arrived on the scene and tried his best to make amends for the insulting remark. The pianist stomped from the room and was not seen again until we docked back at

Southampton. Some weeks later we heard that he had gone to London and thrown himself under a train on the underground.

It was difficult to know if the next replacement played the piano or not. The moment we left the dock, he began to feel seasick. He went below deck, only coming up just before we docked in New York. After twenty-four hours of fun and games, he came back on board and claimed to feel seasick again. Back in Southampton he gaily marched down the gangplank carrying a briefcase holding, I presumed, untouched music.

Since our orders were to play until the last passenger went to bed, it was important at the start of each trip to have some idea of who was likely to give us the most problems. Before the ship sailed we would check the passenger list searching for the regulars who were known late-night dancers and drinkers. Movie stars seemed to be the worst. The wonderful Bette Davis and her husband, Gary Merrill, would dance the night away apparently believing that beds were not to be occupied before daybreak. Other famous stars were often on board and proved surprisingly approachable and friendly.

For Tiny their approachability was vital. He would grab each star around the shoulders soon after he or she came aboard. The ship's photographer, paid by Tiny, would be ready and, before the startled personality knew what had happened, Tiny had his picture. I remember watching his act with Bing Crosby. Tiny moved to stand beside him, threw his arm around Crosby's shoulder, saying, "Hi there, Bing! Loved you in . . ." Flash, and that was it, Tiny was off.

I was told he had a boarding house in Bournemouth where hanging on every wall were pictures of himself with the most famous people of our time: Lord Beaverbrook, Anthony Eden, Gracie Fields and many more. Under each photograph Tiny had written a glowing message to a "dear and loving friend."

On one trip back from New York, I watched in awe as the great Stan Kenton and his band came on board. They were heading for their first British tour, an event of some importance. Initial difficulties with the British Musicians' Union had been overcome by an agreement that the British band leader, Ted Heath, would tour the States at the same time.

This event was important for me personally as well. The British music press were clamouring for interviews once Kenton arrived in Southampton, but I would have access to the man for four days *before* he arrived. Although I had never written for a newspaper, I approached the *Record Mirror*, a large London music weekly, and offered to write a six-part series. They agreed. I spent four glorious days interviewing Stan Kenton and the members of his band. My series was published, and Dad clipped out the first of my newspaper articles. He was proud of me, although he never showed it.

I was thrilled to see my name in print, but realized that I had been lucky to be in the right place at the right time. Writing other stories and getting them published would be difficult. Since I enjoyed drawing, I thought, why not attempt to get some cartoons published instead? I sent some work to the *Daily Mirror*, Britain's largest daily newspaper, and was pleasantly surprised to have it accepted. The pay was good, but not good enough to consider giving up my work on the ship.

After making six round-trips to New York in the years 1951 to 1954, it was time to leave. I realized I would miss both Jeff and Tiny, but the Atlantic was not the place I wanted to spend any more time. It had been fun, but it was time to get back on shore once more. Roy Kenton was again packing his bags and heading for Newquay, and I intended to join him there.

5

IT WAS GOOD TO BE BACK in Newquay. Since our first season at the Blue Lagoon, Roy Kenton had found better digs for us than our old rooms over the butcher's shop. Tody and his wife, Dora, had opened their house to holiday boarders and were more than pleased to accept early bookings from the members of our band. They treated us like royalty, and I settled in to spend the summer of 1954 enjoying the hospitality of the friendly people of Cornwall. I was not aware that before the summer was over my life would change forever.

It happened one Saturday night when the dance hall was packed. Many young people had arrived on the afternoon train and were settling in for a week or two of holidays with or without parents. Their happiness showed on their pale faces, which within days would change colour to a golden brown or fiery red. I surveyed the scene from the vantage point of the stage and began to make a mental note of whom I would approach during the intermission.

She was fair-haired and gorgeous. I was sure I was not the only one in the band who had noticed her, and I made plans to approach her the moment we took a break. Fast as I was, someone else was there faster. I walked home alone and joined the rest of the band back at the house.

The blue skies that greeted me the next morning heralded another hot day. I went to the beach as I usually did. I was sauntering along, glancing at various attractive girls, when I suddenly saw her. The fair-haired beauty from the previous night was sitting with a friend. I strolled over as casually as I could and wished them both a good morning.

"May I sit down?"

"If you want," they said.

"I'm Ben."

They nodded their heads.

I turned my attention to the one who attracted me. "I saw you last night."

"Did you?"

"You didn't see me?"

"I don't think so."

"I was in the band."

"I never look at the band."

It was a setback. I was sure that all girls looked at the band. I had fired my secret weapon to no avail.

I turned to her friend and held out my hand. "Hi, and who might you be?"

"Her sister Joyce, and this is Doreen."

My opening gambit seemed to be working, so I sat down. Doreen offered me a toffee from the bag beside her. I learned that Joyce had arrived from her home in Bristol and Doreen was in her second year of nurse's training at a London hospital. The two of them were in Newquay for a week.

And that is how I met the woman with whom I would spend the rest of my life. Doreen's recollection of the meeting is a little different to mine. She claims that I ate all their toffees, then borrowed a pound before getting up to leave. One thing we do agree on is that we have been together ever since.

I saw her every day of her holiday, and when it came time for her to leave, I realized that for me this holiday romance was vastly different from my others. Although I hated writing letters and, in the past, had rarely sat with pen in hand, now there were few days that I missed writing to this wonderful nurse. The moment I was back to London, I looked her up. Within six weeks I had taken her hand, as we sat on a small wall beside Nelson's Column in Trafalgar Square, and asked her to marry me.

We were married in Bristol, where Doreen's parents lived, on March 31, 1956. My mother and my sisters travelled from London for the event, but most of the other guests were from Doreen's family. Dad felt too shy and stayed home; but we knew he loved Doreen and was happy for us. Doreen's family had hired a hall, the Hotwells Labour Club, for the reception. We had a wonderful time, and once Mum, who considered a bottle of Guinness a day vital to her well-being, knew that we had ordered sufficient Guinness, she was happy. She looked the picture of good health as she spun around the hall with almost every man present. The only glitch in the day was that the best man, Roy Kenton, and his girlfriend, Jean, missed their train and were not present. Another friend, Dennis Jackson, stood in for him.

We had had no trouble deciding where to take our honeymoon, and so we headed off to Newquay in a rented car, with various bits and pieces of rubbish tied to the back bumper. We were sure that we could make the three-hour drive before dark. We would be staying with Tody and Dora, my summer landlords, who had promised to have everything in place.

At midnight we were just an hour away from Newquay when a large coach came around the corner. So close did we come to a head-on collision that the coach sheared off the door handles on one side of our car. Both vehicles were near to the centre of the road, so we were no doubt equally to blame for the accident. It was the narrowest of escapes. We sat in the police station of a tiny village and suffered the ribbing of the coach driver and his passengers once they realized that we were on our honeymoon. It was 2 A.M. when we finally arrived at Tody and Dora's, shaken but otherwise none the worse for our accident.

Although it was early in the season for Newquay, Doreen and I knew that we had chosen the perfect place to launch our life partnership. The weather was glorious for strolling around the town and along the deserted beach past the place where we had first met, just a few months before.

After the honeymoon, we looked for a place to live in the South London area, where rent was cheap and there was good public transportation. We found a small flat in Clapham, on the top floor of a three-storey house, with renters on each floor. The neighbours below us were emigrants from India and Pakistan. They were very generous, offering to share many of their meals with the young newlyweds upstairs.

Doreen now had her nursing degree, and although she enjoyed work at the hospital, decided take a position in Harley Street assisting a specialist in dentistry. My job on the *Queen Elizabeth* was available, but I realized that if I wanted to be near Doreen, being on an ocean liner travelling back and forth to New York was hardly the place for me. Fortunately Roy Kenton was booked to play at the Wimbledon Palais, a large ballroom in the suburbs, and I joined him there. Since the last train for town left seven minutes after the dance was over, we dashed through "God Save the Queen" at top speed. Most of the anthem was played with one foot off the stage.

The Wimbledon Palais was a far cry from the wonderful dance hall in Newquay: it was much larger and the crowd was not in the holiday spirit. Although most came for the dancing, a few came for a more serious sport. Fights in the bar were frequent, and some would spill out into the dance area. We had a first-class view of the action from the stage until the management reminded us that our job was not to stare, but to play faster and louder in the hopes of diverting attention away from the brawlers.

By chance I met a trumpet player there who had been with me on the *Queen Elizabeth*. He mentioned that he owned a house in Streatham and was sure that his wife would be happy to rent the front room to us. Since the rent he mentioned was lower than what we were paying, we decided to take his offer. It was a mistake. He was easy going, but his wife was not. It soon became apparent that the move was not a good one. We moved again.

Our next apartment in Brixton consisted of two upstairs rooms. Again, although the landlady's husband was extremely nice, she was a battle-axe. As a musician, my hours were not regular, and it was usually well past midnight by the time I got home. Eventually the sound of the toilet flushing in the early hours of the morning became too much for our landlady, and her husband asked us to leave.

Doreen's work in Harley Street paid fairly well, but after the busyness of the hospital she felt lonely in a small office. When a part-time job serving in the bar of the Wimbledon Palais became available, she took it. Not only was the pay pretty good, but we would no longer be passing each other on the doorstep as I left for work and she arrived home.

The days of the big bands were fast becoming a thing of the past, and long-haired skiffle groups were beginning to replace them. From a management point of view, it made good business sense. If dancers were willing to buy tickets to hear a four-piece band, why book bands of eight or more musicians? The Wimbledon Palais cut us back to three nights a week. Although Doreen continued to work as a nurse and as a barmaid, our finances were stretched to the limit. I set off to find day work.

I searched the papers and answered a want ad for an electrician's mate. I was told that before I could start I would have to be accepted by the union. There were about two dozen men in the union hall when the leader arrived to give us a short speech, after which I was asked a few questions and was accepted as a fellow brother into this communist-dominated union. Now I was eligible to apply for the job itself.

Following the short interview with the electricity board, I headed for the Temple Bar. This is the historic area at one end of Fleet Street where many of Britain's barristers and solicitors have their offices. I entered the square and headed for the doorway marked on the small map I had been given. After taking a flight of steps down to the basement level, I found myself in a warren of tunnels, dimly lit by small lamps on each side of the wall. Far away I could hear voices echoing along the tunnel and began walking towards the source of the noise. Three electricians and two mates were sitting around a small table drinking tea. I explained that I was the new electrician's mate, and was invited to join them.

Jim, whom I would be assisting, handed me a mug of tea. "Know anything about electricity, Ben?"

"No."

"Not to worry. I know enough for the two of us." He explained exactly why we were in this rabbit warren. A giant underground ring of cables had been strung around London, and our job was to link up the Temple Bar with this ring. After their tea, the electricians each got out a newspaper and began to read. I was amazed. It was three o'clock in the afternoon before someone suggested that maybe it was time we did something. All I did was hand Jim the tools he pointed to.

To fill in most of the time, the group played chess. It was a game that had always intrigued me. They agreed to teach me and, in exchange, I would give them lessons on the clarinet. And that's what we did for three months. There beneath the city of London sat five "workers," dressed in overalls, learning the subtleties of the clarinet.

After three months I was tired of doing only an hour's work a day and set off to consider new fields. A job on a building site with a group of friendly Irish bricklayers, although it also paid well, was the total opposite of my last job. There was no sitting around allowed, and eight hours of throwing bricks to the fastest bricklayers in the world left me exhausted. I still had to drag myself to Wimbledon to play with the Kenton Band in the evenings. After a month, I had had enough.

A few days later I chanced to chat with a window cleaner in Southwark who convinced me that this was the job I had been looking for. I set out selling my services door to door and soon had a lively list of customers. I bought a ladder and off I went.

My major customer was the biggest pub in the area. It had plenty of windows, but the trouble was that most of them were out of reach. I was forced to step from sill to sill on the upper floors. Reaching over to swing myself onto a ledge five floors up, I suddenly found myself, to my horror, looking through a bathroom window at the publican's daughter. I was so stunned I found it impossible to get back down and was trapped on the sill as she screamed, pulled up her knickers and ran to tell her father that there was a Peeping Tom outside. When the publican stormed outside, I quickly explained from my perch on the ledge what had happened and, after a good laugh, he helped me inside.

One morning as I was cleaning the pub windows, I was asked by another window cleaner if I would care to join him for a cup of tea. It was the start of a lifelong friendship. Every morning Bill Coates and I would stop for a tea break, and he would bring me a book. Although I had been brought up on Dickens, I had not developed a love of reading. That is, not until Bill came along. His wife, Hilda, worked for the book chain W. H. Smith, which gave Bill access to all sorts of new books.

Bill was also a musician and had led a fascinating life. Orphaned at an early age, he and his brother had spent their childhood years in the care of others. When he was still a boy, he joined the army as a musician. He had been captured in France in 1940 while working as a stretcher bearer and spent almost five years as a prisoner of war in Germany. Bill was bright, caring and extremely friendly. His experience as an army musician had given him a tremendous grounding in the basics and he was an excellent musician. He now freelanced, as I did, in the evenings with various bands. I was not surprised that he missed being a full-time musician and was waiting for the right opportunity to come along. It presented itself with an offer from overseas. The Canadian army was on the lookout for musicians of Bill's calibre and offered him a sergeant's rank and assisted passage. Despite the short time we had known each other, we were fond of Hilda and Bill, and when they left it was a sad farewell.

The letters the Coateses wrote to us from Canada in the coming months were full of glowing reports of their new home in Calgary. The more Doreen and I discussed their lives, the more empty ours appeared to be. Because of my limited education and my Cockney accent I knew my opportunities in Britain were limited. Michael Caine, the movie star who had grown up in my neck of the woods, had it right. He maintained that a Cockney was the Mickey Mouse of British society, a happy, friendly chap whom everyone liked but no one wished to employ. Doreen and I wanted a family and we felt that the lives we were leading were not ones we wanted for our future children.

Almost all of our conversations ended with us talking about whether we should emigrate. The way Bill and Hilda described Canada in their letters encouraged our feelings of restlessness. Doreen still had a good job as a nurse but I no longer had steady work as a musician. The four-piece bands at the Wimbledon Palais were now bringing in more dancers than our eight-piece band, and we had been given notice. The members of the Roy Kenton Band once again went their separate ways. I looked for freelance jobs, but they were few and far between.

The window-cleaning business was successful, but I was not happy. I missed my tea breaks with Bill. At the same time, the

international news was doing little to liven my spirits. Prime
Minister Anthony Eden had decided that Britain had a right to
invade Egypt, an action that I found appalling, as did my Sunday
newspaper, the *Observer*. Their stand cost them fifty thousand
readers and Doreen and I a number of friends. It seemed that
only a strange Canadian with a lisp, Lester B. Pearson, could
persuade the United Nations to intervene and stop the British
troops as they ran up the beach. It was an embarrassing moment
for a nation that had so often prided itself on defending the
rights of those unable to defend themselves. Disappointed with
my country I was more than ever determined to leave it and find
a home elsewhere.

I was tired of window cleaning and was searching the newspapers for a new opportunity – something that would allow me
to save some money towards emigrating. One almost jumped
off the page: "Coffee Wagon for Sale. Cheap." A fantasy of life
on the open road immediately leapt to mind – thousands of
people scrambling to get to a Wicks's tea wagon.

I contacted Roy Kenton and his wife, Jean, who were as
enthusiastic about the idea as Doreen and I. The four of us
hurried to the address advertised and walked around the vehicle.
It was a small van that had done gallant service during the war,
serving cups of tea to exhausted firemen during the Blitz. In the
back was a small cooking area with a hot plate and a side that
lifted up to reveal a tiny counter. Along with the van came hundreds of thick china cups and a pair of the hottest licences available. They would allow us to serve tea and sausage sandwiches
outside two of Britain's most popular football grounds. I had
been a football fan since falling out of the cradle, and just the
thought of running my own business that close to the game had
me kicking the tires and haggling over the asking price.

We were all anxious to satisfy the grubby hands that reached
out for their food at most football grounds. With eighty thousand people flowing out of a football stadium all wanting tea

and a sausage sandwich, the future began to take on an absolute glow. From what the seller told us, it seemed like it would be only a matter of weeks before the money was rolling into our empty bank accounts, and Doreen and I would have enough airfare to take us around the world and maybe catch Canada on the way back.

The next Saturday we loaded up the van with cups, saucers and food. After first making sure there was air in the tires, we set off for the football grounds, arriving two hours before kick-off. We opened the side of the van and the four of us began to prepare for the rush.

"You want me ta take care of yer parking?" A scruffy individual with one leg and two weeks' growth of beard leaned against the van.

"What parking?"

"The parking of the cars be'ind yer van."

"You mean people will pay to park behind us, and we take the money?"

"S'right. I collects it and gives it to you."

I leaned out of the van and looked around. The street where we had parked was a dead end. What he said made sense. There was room for a dozen cars behind us.

"What do you get out of it?"

"Free grub: a couple of sausage sandwiches and a cuppa."

We agreed to his terms and went back to preparing the stack of sausage sandwiches that would soon be needed.

Things could not have gone better. The first cars arrived and our one-legged friend quickly found spaces behind our wagon for them. No one seemed particularly hungry, but we knew they would be by the end of the game. At the sound of a whistle from inside the grounds, the street quickly emptied. We had ninety minutes to wait for the final whistle and the rush for food. We drank tea and leaned back, anxious to get as much rest as we could before feeding the multitudes. With forty-five

minutes to go we went back to our preparations. Sausage sandwiches flew off the end of the cutting board with the speed of
lightning and were piled neatly at one end of the counter for
easy serving.

There was a roar inside the stadium as the final whistle blew.
This was it. With the till open and the kettle ready, we stood fast.

At the same time as the first people began to leave the exits,
the first clap of thunder hit. Within seconds the rain was falling
in buckets. With coats over their heads, eighty thousand potential customers ran past us with one thing in mind – home.

It was a waste of time shouting. No one was interested.

Our one-legged friend appeared. He was soaking wet.

"Can I 'ave me sausage sandwich and cuppa?" he asked.

"How about a hundred of each?" I answered.

Our first day had been a huge disappointment, but we con-
soled ourselves with the knowledge that there would be others.
It was a week until the next football game. Roy suggested that
rather than wait, we should set up on one of the motorways to
the coast since they were crowded on weekends. We could
ambush enough travellers to make up for what to now had been
a disastrous start.

We set out early the next morning. The Brighton Road had
yet to see the hundreds of cars that would soon be heading for
the coast. Arriving at a likely spot, we lifted the side shutter and
began to prepare our standard fair: sausage sandwiches. Cars
began to stop and before an hour had gone by, money was going
into the till faster than we could count it. Then a police car
pulled alongside. We quickly offered him free tea and eats.

"No, thank you," he answered politely as he took a notepad
from his pocket.

"Is something wrong, officer?" I asked.

"You mean you don't know?"

Each of us looked at the other. "Know what?"

"What you're doing."

"Well, I thought we were selling sausages and tea," I answered.

"I'm talking about where you've parked."

"Yes, I know. Lovely little spot. Doing real good we are and pleased of it."

"And do you know why you're doing so well?" he asked.

"'Fraid not."

"Because, my little feathered friends, you've parked in the driveway of a restaurant." He pointed up the driveway to a small house behind a group of trees. "This morning the owner and staff woke to find that there was no business. And do you know why? Because you was here nicking all his customers."

We shut up shop and moved on. The next few weekends we were out again, trying our luck with the travelling-restaurant business. Whatever the reason, people passed us by. Thoroughly fed up, we pulled down the shutters and decided to sell.

We placed a similar ad to the one that had enticed us and waited for calls. Finally a car dealer called, anxious to see our vehicle and make an offer. As we waited for him to arrive, we noticed that the tires were flat. Fast as we could we pushed the van to the nearest gas station and corrected the problem. Back at the house once more, we watched and kept our fingers crossed as the dealer slowly circled the van. The price was right and yes, he was interested. Each of us said a silent prayer. God answered. The dealer did not kick the tires.

Roy was still able to get the odd booking for his big band, but these jobs were few and far between. Even if I were able to get regular work, I realized, the life of a musician was not one for a married man. I was determined to switch to a completely different way of living. It was time to quit the music business and try my hand at something else.

If I was going to start a new life in Canada, why not as a journalist? I had enjoyed my brief stint writing for the *Record Mirror*, and I could enjoy writing stories as much as playing music. But how to get started? Then I chanced upon a newspaper story that mentioned a name that most people in Britain knew – Roy Farran, an ex-major in the British army and one of the most decorated officers of the Second World War. He had started a new weekly newspaper in Calgary, and I was sure he would be in need of staff.

I wrote to Farran, telling him that I had followed his life with interest and had enjoyed his autobiography, *Winged Dagger*. The good news for him was that I was about to move to Calgary and would be in need of a job. He replied and suggested I call on him when I arrived.

Doreen and I had been working hard and saving what we could to cover our eventual move to Calgary. I sold my last possession of any value, my saxophone. All that remained to do was to visit the emigration office and sign the official documents. It was May 1957 and, along with thousands of others in Britain, we began to pack and prepare for a new life far from the place we had called home.

Mum and Dad were sad when they heard we would be leaving but, as always, they were completely supportive. Saying goodbye to me had become a habit for them. It is only now that I have a family of my own that I can appreciate how upsetting it must have been for them. This was hardly a trip to the countryside. This was the other side of the world – distance that would make it impossible for them to visit us. We promised that we would be back soon for a visit, but no one really believed we would. Today air travel is widespread and relatively cheap, but in 1957, travel to North America was a luxury for most people. For the family I was leaving behind it was an impossible dream. I was going to miss them both, dreadfully.

It was even more difficult for Doreen to say goodbye to her family. She had seven brothers and sisters and a mother she absolutely adored. This remarkable woman had protected her children from an abusive husband, and although her parents still lived together, Doreen had never forgiven her father and poured all of her love onto her mother. Doreen was heartbroken as she hugged her family on the Bristol railway platform and they said their final goodbyes.

We left for the airport to board a large four-engine Super Constellation plane for a twenty-four-hour trip to Edmonton. With only twenty-five dollars in our pockets, a twenty-one-year-old nurse took the arm of her new husband, climbed the stairs into the plane and headed west.

6

THE CHARTER FLIGHT TO EDMONTON was long and exhausting and, to make matters worse, decidedly uncomfortable. Bill Coates was kind enough to meet us in his car, and for hour after hour we watched the flat Alberta landscape slip by as we made our way to Calgary. I felt far from excited by the adventure. Rather, I was beginning to think I had made a mistake.

But my spirits picked up when we got to Calgary. The mountains in the distance formed a perfect backdrop to the city, and it was easy to see why first-time visitors are always so impressed. We had left behind a city of chimneys and entered a world of peaks and valleys. We drove through the downtown section, where the few tall buildings threw their shadows across streets that had retained their western flavour. I started to think maybe I had been wrong to doubt whether we should have come. Maybe we had made the right decision after all.

The city seemed to us Londoners to be small enough to cover on foot. A hot sun had persuaded Calgarians to go outdoors. Wearing brightly coloured dresses, the women were swinging their way along the sidewalks in and out of the busy Eaton and Hudson Bay stores. My Hollywood notion of a typical western town complete with saloons and cowboy hats evaporated. The sight brightened Doreen, who had convinced herself that her new wardrobe would have to consist of jeans, plaid shirts and cowboy boots.

The traffic was as dense as we had left behind in London. Although I was not naïve enough to expect to see a sheriff's posse trot its way along a dusty street, I was surprised at the lack of horses. As we reached the edge of town, a vast expanse of prairie appeared, stretching to the foot of the Rockies. It is a sight that never leaves the minds of Calgarians wherever they travel, and for good reason. Each morning most of them greet each other with a comment about the beauty of this rocky range.

Bill was now a sergeant in an army band, and he and Hilda had moved into married quarters, two-bedroomed houses that were available for families of servicemen. But the biggest news of all was that they had a new member of their family – Alan, an adopted baby boy.

Although Bill and Hilda could not have been more kind, it was too crowded to stay with them. We wanted to find a place of our own, but first we needed jobs. Fortunately for Doreen, nurses were in big demand. Out-of-work musicians were not. Doreen applied at the Holy Cross Hospital and was immediately hired.

I phoned Roy Farran to tell him I was in town. He invited me to his house for an interview. His home was impressive, even intimidating, to someone sharing a house with three other adults and a baby. I knew that his remarkable war record had resulted in a couple of Military Crosses, admittance to France's Legion of Honour and a personal letter of thanks from the president of the United States. Quite frankly, I didn't know what to expect. The person who opened the door was in his forties, of average height, with a bronze face and rugged complexion. Farran grinned and, in a distinctive Irish accent, asked me in.

After a quick tour of the house we sat down to discuss what

it was that I could bring to his newspaper, the *North Hill News*. I exaggerated and said that I had worked for some of Britain's top music newspapers.

"How's your spelling?" he asked.

"Pretty good," I lied.

"We'll soon see," he answered and asked me to spell a relatively easy word. I got it wrong.

"You're hired," he said.

"Doing what?" I asked.

"Proofreader," he answered, "at thirty-five dollars a week."

Now I knew why I'd been hired. If I'd have spelled cat with a *k* I would have still been accepted. The wages were hardly enough to buy groceries, let alone pay rent. Today, whenever I read about new immigrants to Canada, I think back to this time. Like I was, they are all so anxious to get work they are vulnerable to those who will take advantage of them as cheap labour.

Although Farran's offer was not generous, I left his house happy. I had only been in the country two weeks and already I had a job. Fortunately, Doreen had also already landed a job that paid twice as much as mine.

Since Doreen had to start work early every morning, we decided that the best place to look for a home would be close to the hospital. We searched the newspapers and after a brief tour of the other apartments advertised, we found ourselves at the door of the Peterson family.

How lucky we were. This large house was just a block from the Holy Cross Hospital but, more than that, it housed a warm and generous family: Mr. and Mrs. Peterson, a sister and their ninety-five-year-old mother. Mrs. Peterson asked us in and within minutes we were made to feel like one of them. Whatever needs an immigrant has, none is more important than finding a loving family to help fill the hole of the family left behind. The Petersons were this and more.

Mr. Peterson took us to the back of the house and, as we

climbed the wooden stairs, we already knew that whatever the inside was like, we were going to take it. The door at the top of the stairs led to a small kitchen. The sizeable living room had a large window that looked out onto the garden. I opened what looked like a cupboard door and stared for the first time at a piece of Canadiana – a Murphy bed.

Bill and Hilda Coates and their friends scrambled to find furniture for us and helped us move in. Alone at last, we finally had the opportunity to talk. Doreen confessed that she missed her large family, and as we lay in each other's arms that first night, I wondered again, and not for the last time, whether we had done the right thing in moving to a new land.

Within weeks of arriving in Canada, we along with thousands of others went to the most famous cowboy show in the world – the Calgary Stampede. Were we really six thousand miles from London or were we part of some American western movie playing in Leicester Square? Men in white cowboy hats were everywhere. Doreen had suggested that I wear one, but it was too soon. Just weeks earlier I had been in a tide of bowler hats that bobbed and bounced its way over London Bridge. Now I felt as if I was among a whole new breed of human.

Suddenly the past was there before us – horse-drawn wagons, marching bands, cowboys and, most impressive of all, Indians. To my eyes they had leapt in all their finery from the Saturday morning movie screen and miraculously come alive. Amid the crowd's shouts and screams of delight, I heard Doreen gasp, yet to be convinced, and in one excited whisper ask, "Are they real Indians?"

My work at the *North Hill News* was not going well. Given nine jobs to do by a publisher who believed in running a small, tight ship was very stressful. Not only did I have to proofread, I also had to list market reports, television and radio programs, write community news, answer the phone and deliver the paper should the boy fail to show up. Of all these jobs, the worst was answering the phone. Most of the calls were prompted by Farran's editorials, in which he violently attacked the government for allowing the fluoridation of drinking water, a scheme that Farran was convinced was a communist plot to poison the nation.

The first and last interview I conducted was on the phone with the mayor. Halfway through the interview, he confessed to having had a few too many drinks the night before. Having let this slip, he hoped I would not report it. I thought that no one would give a damn whether the mayor had a drink or two at a party, so I assured him the information would not be used. As I was about to replace the phone, I heard a distinct click and realized that Farran had been listening in. He put his face around the door.

"Report it? Of course we're going to damn well report it!" he screamed.

The fact that Farran was listening to my calls added to the strain of working at the paper. I felt that the anguish I was suffering should at the very least be rewarded with something more than thirty-five dollars a week, especially since I was expected to stay until 10 P.M. on Thursdays to put the newspaper to bed. I asked for a five-dollar increase and was promptly given a counter offer: "How about leaving instead?"

An ad for a commercial artist at a small advertising company sent me scurrying for an interview with the English owner, John. I confessed that I had no experience in the field, which didn't stop him from offering me a job, but only at slightly more money than the newspaper had been paying. It seemed that I would have no difficulty getting work in Canada provided I was willing to work for an amount just above starvation wages. I took the job, and each day I sat at a cramped desk attempting to draw to John's instructions.

After six months in Canada, Doreen was still homesick. My own feelings were constantly changing. Weekends with friends were wonderful, but my low-paying work was a problem. I was prepared to stick it out and make a success of our lives in Canada, but Doreen was not happy. Most nights as I listened to her quiet sobs, my thoughts were of how to make enough money for us to go back to England.

John's advertising business wasn't going well, and after a few months he laid me off. Meanwhile Doreen had been offered a job in a dentist's office, and since the money was more than she was making at the hospital, she took it. It meant long hours and hard work, but now that I was out of a job, she couldn't refuse the offer. The small amount of money that we'd saved when we first arrived had dwindled to fifty dollars. Since I did not qualify for government assistance of any kind, my search for work was desperate.

My first visit to the unemployment office was a disappointment.

"What do you do?"

"I'll do anything you've got in the way of a job. I'll even dig ditches." I'd heard this line somewhere and was sure it would impress the clerk.

"Have you ever dug ditches?"

"Er, no, I haven't."

"Look, let's be honest with each other. You're going to take one of the ditch-digging jobs I have here," he waved a piece of paper, "and during your lunch hours you're going to search for something else, right?"

I confessed that it was not my intention to get a degree in sod turning, and that was the end of the interview. Once more I walked the streets looking for work. I approached the loading dock of a large dairy. It was mid-morning, and since most of their milk trucks were now out on delivery, it seemed like a good time to bother the paper-shufflers in the office. I was in luck. They needed a milkman, and although I had no experience, the boss was sure I would quickly get the hang of things. The pay was far better than I had been getting.

On my first day I left the garage at 7 A.M. with an experienced milkman. He was kind, and for the first time since arriving in Canada, I felt I had a job I enjoyed. The trucks, though not large, were difficult to drive. They had a long gearshift handle and an emergency brake that needed a champion tug-of-war team to lock it in place.

After a few weeks I was given my own route and, with a wave from the boss, I set out with a truck full of milk to deliver to the most expensive houses in Calgary. Initially honoured at being given such a prestigious group of customers, I quickly learned why it was not a favourite: Mount Royal was full of hills. The streets were treacherous to drive on when icy. Still, the customers were pleasant and many of them would greet me with a cup of coffee and something to eat. I was afraid that refusing would cause neighbours to ask, "So why does he take coffee with the blonde up the street and turn me down?" so I accepted all offers. Most days I was the last milkman to arrive back at the garage.

Doreen and I were now into our third year of marriage. Both of us adored children, and our greatest wish was that Doreen would one day wake to morning sickness. Morning after morning she woke up feeling fine. Eventually we went to a doctor to see if either of us had a problem. He found nothing wrong with Doreen, and so asked me to provide a sperm sample. He looked at it under his microscope and smiled.

"I want you to take a look at something."

I looked into the microscope.

"What do you see?" he asked.

"I can see a lot of wriggly sperm."

"What are they doing?"

"Swimming?"

"No, they're not." He appeared annoyed. "That's just what they're *not* doing."

"What's wrong with them?" I asked.

"They're lazy, that's what's wrong."

I was astonished. No one worked harder than I did, and to think I had an army of little rotters in my scrotum begging off duty was disappointing.

"Do you know why they're lazy?" I thought of Billy on the roof of St. George's teaching me to masturbate and struggled to think of the answer he would have given.

"I have no idea."

"How many times do you have intercourse?"

"I don't know. About four times a week."

"Four times a week?" He looked surprised. "I see. Maybe it's time to ease off a little."

I brightened. Far from having a few thousand sperm dodging their duty, what I really had was a whole mass of little buggers too exhausted to get up and have a go.

"There's something else you might try."

"What's that?"

"Camping." He continued, "You see, fresh air can make a big difference. Get out to the mountains, and let some mountain air get to them."

It made sense. A deep breath of mountain air sure made me frisky, why not the little sperm?

Determined to have children and willing to try anything to get Doreen pregnant, we set off to buy our first car so we could go camping. The Volkswagen Beetle was certainly cheap enough. The heater didn't work, but the engine did. Next we bought sleeping bags, a tent and a camping stove, and we were ready. I hurried home from the dairy on a Friday to find that Doreen had already packed. Although it was early in the season for camping, I turned the key on our little German friend and pointed its nose towards Banff, in the Rockies. As the miles rolled away, we talked about the crib and diapers we would be needing in nine months' time.

We pitched our tent beside beautiful Two Jack Lake with the opening facing the lake to ensure a perfect view. It was a mistake.

With a clear path across the water, the wind blew straight into our canvas home, and we shivered in each other's arms all night. There were times when I was so cold I was quite prepared to forget the whole exercise and remain childless for the rest of our married life. At first light I turned the tent around. To hell with a view of the lake from the opening. I started a fire to prepare breakfast and watched in amazement as a black bear washed itself in the shallow waters of the lake. The rest of our stay was idyllic, and driving back to Calgary we both agreed that, childless or not, we would come back time and time again.

I enjoyed the job of a milkman but not the hours. I was up at 5:30 A.M. and home by 2 P.M., with nothing to do but wander around our one large room waiting for Doreen to come home. Doreen suggested that I try cartooning again. Although the newspaper that had bought my cartoons in Britain had only accepted half a dozen, it had been fun to draw them. I phoned the two daily papers in Alberta. By some strange quirk of fate, the editorial cartoonist of the *Edmonton Journal* had just quit, and they were on the lookout for a replacement. I was asked to apply in person.

First I needed a day off from the dairy. Doreen called to explain to the boss that I was sick in bed. In the meantime I set off early that same morning for the two-hundred-mile drive to Edmonton. After showing examples of my work, the editors decided that, whatever they were looking for, I was not it. The news that awaited me back in Calgary was even more depressing. My boss, concerned about my health, had visited our apartment. When no one answered the door, he had inquired downstairs.

"Oh, Mr. Wicks," said dear old Mrs. Peterson. "He went to Edmonton to apply for job."

It was the end of my employment as a milkman. Fortunately there was good news to balance the bad. Doreen was pregnant. Although the timing was lousy, we were thrilled.

Once again I searched for work. A new friend who had heard me play the clarinet suggested that I join the band of the Lord Strathcona Horse, a Canadian army unit which had long given up the horse for the much more manageable tank. Fortunately, band members were kept as far as possible from both the iron monsters and the drill square. I signed on for three years. The money was the most I had been paid since my arrival, and Doreen and I were ecstatic. With a baby on the way, we certainly needed the income.

Vincent was born on April 9, 1959. We spent many nights in his first few weeks of life staring at him to convince ourselves that this was indeed our child. Although neither Doreen nor I are religious, from the day of his birth I knew there are such things as miracles. They happen every day, whenever a child is born.

Life in the army was good. My fellow musicians were first class, and the clarinet players were vastly better than I was. I was rightly placed in the position of fourth clarinet in the thirty-five-piece orchestra. Most of the music on the stand was far beyond my ability. Fortunately my fellow musicians were loud enough to drown out the racket I was making.

The band produced the most glorious music; but marching seemed to be beyond their grasp. Any time we had to parade past the saluting base, all of us would have to skip to keep in step with the man ahead. It didn't go unnoticed. A visiting general first congratulated the battalion on a fine turnout, then added, "It's a pity that keeping in step continues to be beyond the capabilities of the band."

We were a happy crew. Hidden away from the rigours of regular army life in our tiny band shed, we practised hard. Our days began at 9 A.M. and finished at noon. The hours were short, but not short enough for most of the musicians. Long before noon, they were shuffling their feet impatiently, anxious to leave the barracks and rush home to their paying music students. It was the easiest job I had had since being an electrician's mate. If it hadn't been for the uniforms we wore, even we would have found it hard to remember that we were in the army.

Although we rehearsed for only three hours a day, it was enough to keep us in form to perform at numerous half-time football events and officers' mess functions. The mess events often went late into the night. Slowly these leaders of men would disintegrate before our eyes, as we played their ridiculous music requests. As regular as high tide, towards the end of the evening one officer or another would stagger towards the band mumbling, "Post Horn Gallop Time." We would place the sheet music for this British call to the hounds on our stands and Staff Sergeant Simpson would grab a nearby rifle. He'd calmly place his trumpet mouthpiece into its barrel and begin to play. It always brought the house down. Fortunately, it also signalled that the end of the evening was near.

Our second child, Susan, was born sixteen months after Vincent, in August 1960. Now that Vincent had a sister and a friend who would rarely be far from his side, we felt we were a complete family. Each day I would charge home to be with them, and I never ceased marvelling at how quickly they grew. From the moment they could walk they played "house." Vincent, dressed in my clothes, and Susan, in her mother's, acted out the father arriving home from work to be greeted by his wife. They were kind to each other and made friends with others easily. Life seemed perfect.

Doreen still missed her family in England but the family she now had was the one she held closest in her heart. I was happy as an army musician, but I wasn't convinced that this life could last. Once again I began to seriously consider cartooning in my spare time. Since all I required was a pen and some paper, I had all the tools I needed. But I wasn't sure how to prepare the work and send it to North American publications. The local library supplied the know-how. In the magazine *Artists and Writers* I read a chapter on how to submit cartoons. Even more useful was a two-page list of magazines interested in buying cartoons, ordered according to the rates they paid. Heading the list was the *Saturday Evening Post*, followed by the *New Yorker* and on down to those magazines who paid the price of postage.

I set about scribbling ideas until I had drawn six cartoons. Away they went to the magazine at the top of the list, the *Saturday Evening Post*. I didn't expect them to be accepted; after all, cartooning was only a pastime. Some people collect baseball cards; I would draw cartoons.

Six weeks passed. I was strolling home from the barracks as usual when I turned the corner and saw Doreen grinning and waving a letter in the air. The editor of the *Saturday Evening Post* had written to say he would be interested in buying my work but since neither he, nor anyone else on the staff, had ever heard of me, would I be kind enough to send three letters of reference? I quickly sat down and began to write. Although I had an extremely high opinion of myself, I tried to tone down the glowing remarks. I sent them off and they did the trick. It was the start of a wonderful three years of drawing for one of the top magazines in the world.

7

MY THREE YEARS OF ARMY SERVICE were coming to a close and I had to make a choice: would I make my career in music or cartooning? Doreen and I decided that cartooning held more promise, but because there was little opportunity in this field in Calgary, we thought we should move to Toronto.

Our Volkswagen was much too old for the trip. Pulling our rented trailer almost did it in, and we were very relieved when we finally staggered into Toronto.

We had been told that accommodation would be cheaper outside of the city, and we initially stayed in a trailer park near Oakville, a beautiful town just west of Toronto on the shore of Lake Ontario. It took three weeks to find a suitable house for rent – a comfortable bungalow located in a field of grazing cows at the end of a long driveway. The children loved it, but with just one car between us, its isolation was a problem. I rented a small office on the main street of Oakville, and each day I would sit there drawing for various magazines and hoping that a staff job would open up and rescue me from the precarious ledge of freelancing.

I contacted the *Toronto Star*, Canada's largest newspaper, in the hopes that they would be impressed that I drew for a top American magazine. A call came back within a few weeks. The critic Nathan Cohen needed someone to illustrate his column. Would I be interested? I certainly was and so began a working friendship with one of Canada's greatest theatre critics.

A large man with horn-rimmed glasses, Nathan's very presence commanded attention. Never without a silver-headed cane, he would squeeze his frame into a theatre seat, completely aware that all eyes were on him. Years later he spotted me in a theatre queue and delivered a wonderful line: "Well, if it isn't Wicks. And what's this I hear about you becoming a colossus?"

Although the *Saturday Evening Post* and the *Toronto Star* were buying my work, the combined moneys were far from assuring us a comfortable living. After a few months, I began to doubt whether the success that I had hoped for in Toronto would ever be forthcoming. Worse, Doreen was not happy being stuck at home without a car. Something had to change. We agreed that I had jumped too quickly into cartooning. The timing was off. The more we looked back on our life in Calgary the rosier it appeared. The regular paycheque of the army band now seemed very attractive, and the more we talked about Calgary, the more we missed the friends we had made there. Finally, I phoned the bandmaster, who told me they would be more than happy to have me return to the Strath band. I was relieved and delighted.

I knew I wasn't going to find it easy to break the news to Nathan Cohen that I was leaving. He had been wonderful to work for and I was going to miss his wit. When I finally told him how unhappy we were as a family and that we had decided to return to Calgary, he was very sympathetic. He wished me good luck, and handed me my final cheque in an envelope. When I got home, I gave it, unopened, to Doreen, who discovered he had paid me far too much. Although we were packed and ready to leave, we both felt that I should go to Toronto and return the cheque. I did this only to have a solemn-looking

Nathan hold up his hand, saying, "That, my dear boy, was a deliberate act on my part. It is my way of showing gratitude for the way you have worked. I trust that the little extra will prove useful."

It was hardly a good time to drive twenty-one hundred miles across Canada. Winter was already breathing down our necks, and we weren't at all confident that our car would make it back. But once again we rented a trailer, and once again we set off on a search for success.

Within a day of leaving the lights of Toronto behind us, winter began to track us. By the time we hit the flat lands of Saskatchewan, a full blizzard was sweeping across our path. Our windshield wipers were barely able to cope with the blinding snow. Radio announcements repeatedly warned motorists to get off the highways, but we had no idea where exactly we were. Worse, black ice was beginning to form on the road, and at the slightest bend in the road we would slip slowly sideways into the oncoming lane.

A sniffle that Vincent had caught before we left had developed into a hacking cough. For hour after hour, Doreen rocked him while also attending to Susan as I drove, white-knuckled, through the blizzard. Large trucks swept by, throwing wet snow and grit against the car. We were desperate to find a room for the night and, with luck, a doctor for Vincent. Eventually a small motel appeared by the roadside and we stayed there until the storm had passed. When the weather cleared, so did Vincent's cough.

A few days later, when we finally drove into Calgary, neither Doreen nor I could hold back the tears of relief.

I signed on for another three years with the army band, and we resumed our previous life in Calgary. Without the stress of money worries, I found drawing much easier, and I was soon exploring other areas of cartooning. An unused patch in this field was about to open up. It began with a comment made by a

Calgary city council member that I thought was stupid enough to warrant a cartoon. I headed out the door for the offices of the morning newspaper, *The Albertan*. The managing editor, Eric Watt, listened as I described the cartoon that I felt would illustrate perfectly the stupidity of the remark. I suggested that he use it on the editorial page. He explained that they employed an editorial-page cartoonist and were not about to replace him with an army musician. I wasn't about to give up, so I suggested he use the cartoon on the front page instead, as newspapers in Britain often did.

"How much do you want?" he asked.

"How about five bucks?"

He agreed, and the next morning my small cartoon ridiculing the councillor appeared on the front page of *The Albertan*. The subject of my drawing was so upset that at the first meeting of the day at City Hall he asked for something to be done about this cartoon that was "maligning the intelligence of the city council." The councillor's reaction delighted my editor.

"Could you do this every day?" Eric asked me.

"I don't see why not," I answered.

Within weeks, other newspapers in western Canada were asking about my cartoons. I was happy to sell them copies of what I was drawing, and so I stumbled into the world of syndication – drawing the same cartoon for several publications.

Despite my success in Calgary, the East was where the large newspapers were. About a year after I had returned to Calgary I took a week's leave from the army and set off for the East to pitch my one-column cartoons. I met with incredible success. The *Ottawa Journal*, the *North Bay Nugget* and the *Montreal Gazette* were intrigued with the idea of a small cartoon brightening their otherwise depressing front pages. But Toronto was my target. Upon my arrival I headed directly for the Toronto *Telegram*. Here, at last, was a newspaper large enough to have its own syndicate. A bright executive, Ray Argyle, headed up the operation, and a few minutes after I introduced myself, he led me towards the cafeteria. The first hint that an offer was about to be made came when he paid for lunch. Then I heard the wonderful words, "How would you like to sign a three-year contract with the Toronto *Telegram* Syndicate?"

There was one fly in the ointment. I still had two years of my three-year army service to complete. Ray brushed the problem to one side, saying that the publisher, John Bassett, would take care of this minor matter. Even better, the paper would arrange for my family to be moved to Toronto. I would work out of their offices and there was a good chance of being published daily on the front page. There, in bold type, he described, would be the name Ben Wicks.

I returned to Calgary to give Doreen the news that we were about to move again. She was delighted. Although she was happy in Calgary, she had never enjoyed the constant waiting for me to return home from one tour or another. As well, Toronto was that much closer to her mother in Bristol. Both of us waited anxiously for the syndicate to complete its plans for our move. In the meantime, the Seattle World Fair was about to open, and the Lord Strathcona Band joined other military bands from across Canada in Vancouver for six weeks of rehearsal before performing in a tattoo at the fair. Since so many of the musicians who would be coming to Vancouver were talented in other areas of entertainment, we decided to organize a concert. I was saddled with the job of booking other acts for the event.

I was told that Fred, a musician in one of the military bands, would be well worth auditioning, So off I trotted to his barracks. At the far end of the room a figure sat hunched over a magazine. He looked around when I entered. He could easily have passed as Herman Munster. I told him the guys had decided to hold a concert and I had been given the job of rounding up talent.

His eyes lit up, "And you want me and Albert, right?" He got down on his knees, reached under his bed and dragged out a large tin box. Fred patted the lid. "Have you met Albert?"

"Er, I don't think so, but I wonder if we could get back to ..."

He smiled and reached into the box. "Albert, I want you to meet Ben. Ben, Albert."

The dummy he held in his hand was, I believe, the ugliest one that has ever been made. It wore the clothes of a guardsman – a red jacket with shiny buttons and a black fur busby. I was speechless.

Fred grinned. "What do you think? Isn't he great? Say hello."

"Er, hello."

He frowned. "I was talking to Albert. So, what do you want us to do?"

I could not take my eyes off of the dummy and found myself speaking to it. "Well, I, er, of course we do need, er, what I mean is, we will need an audition."

"Well I'm not sure that I'll be okay, but don't you worry, Albert will cover if there's a problem."

"Yes, I'm sure. Could you do a little something?"

"Like what?"

"Well, like you do onstage."

"Right." Fred reached into the tin box and brought out a script that he fastened to Albert's back with a large safety pin. He smiled, Fred that is.

"That's just in case Albert forgets his lines." He sat Albert on the end of his knee, stared at the script on the dummy's back and launched into his routine. The words were clear enough, but Fred and the dummy were at complete odds.

"Say good evening, Albert," said Fred between clenched jaws while the dummy's mouth moved in a parody of speech.

"Good evening," a high-pitched voice answered although the dummy's mouth remained closed.

"Can you say bottle of beer, Albert?" said Fred.

"Bottle of beer, bottle of beer, bottle of beer ..."

Fred looked up from the script and turned to me. "If you bring me a glass of water, I'll show you how I can do that at the same time as drinking."

"Er, that won't be necessary, thanks, Albert, I mean Fred."

We never did hold the concert. Most of the guys were not interested, I heard later that Fred and Albert had put on a show for the kids, Apparently Fred and his dummy got into a shouting match onstage and were flinging such bad language back and forth that mothers dragged their children from the hall in disgust.

After two weeks of rehearsal, the bands were ready to move on to Seattle. Since most of our performances were in the evening, I had time to wander around the exhibitions during the day. On one such walk, I stumbled upon a large crowd gathered around a film crew. I approached the crowd and struggled to see over their heads.

"So what's happening?" I asked the nearest tall guy, who had a kid on his shoulders.

"They're making a movie with Elvis."

"Presley?" I gasped.

"No, Elvis the Elephant," he sneered. "Of course Presley."

I looked around for a good spot to watch the proceedings, deciding on the roof of a nearby building. Once inside the building I was soon completely lost. I found a fire exit and pushed open the door.

"For heaven's sake, come out if you're going to come out, and stop squeaking that door." The film director was sitting at the top of a long, straight flight of stairs. I stepped quietly onto the landing and found myself directly above the crowd I had just been straining to see over.

"Sit down and I'll be with you in a minute." He continued his conversation with a man standing at the bottom of the stairs and holding the hand of a little girl.

"Okay, let's try it again, Elvis."

The star nodded and waited for further instructions.

The director turned towards me. "Was there something?"

"Er, not really. I'm from England and was hitchhiking across America, and I wondered . . ."

"Sure, did the same thing myself as a kid." He turned to the script assistant. "Fix him up with a crowd scene or something."

"Yes, sir."

I got up to leave and the director turned. "Where are you going?"

"I was going to get out of your way."

"You're not in the way. Anyhow, I don't want anyone using that door until we've finished this scene."

"Yes, sir. Thank you, sir."

"Okay, Elvis, now pick up the little girl under one arm and start up the stairs towards us," he shouted. "Ready? Okay, roll 'em!" I watched, fascinated, as Elvis grabbed the little girl and began climbing up the stairs towards us.

"Cut! See if you can . . ."

I sat there for hours while the director repeatedly asked Elvis Presley to redo the scene and come up those stairs towards me. Each time he climbed, I got ready to stand and shake his hand and practised a different opening line to a conversation that would result in a lasting friendship.

Elvis never did make it to the top of the stairs. When the director was finally satisfied, a relieved superstar jumped aboard a golf cart and was quickly whisked away.

Meanwhile, back in Calgary, word had arrived from army headquarters that someone had suggested I would be of far greater use at a newspaper desk drawing cartoons than continuing as an army musician. Doreen and I agreed.

This time we didn't drive to Toronto. We decided that I should fly ahead and that Doreen and the children would join me once I had found us a good place to live.

It was September 1963 when I moved back to Toronto, a city

I had left just a few months before. The move felt different this time. I was about to join one of Canada's leading newspapers as a syndicated cartoonist. I felt I had won the lottery without buying a ticket. For the first time I had a full-time job doing what I enjoyed most. Although I was sorry to leave my Calgary friends, the reception I received at the Toronto *Telegram* quickly dispelled any regrets. Al Beaton, the editorial cartoonist, suggested I move in with him for a few weeks. This I did, and he and his family went out of their way to make me feel completely comfortable.

I was given a desk in the entertainment department of the paper, where I joined a remarkable group of characters: illustrator and cartoonist Andy Donato; theatre critic Ron Evans and film critic Clyde Gilmore. No new arrival could have asked for a more decent group of co-workers. Overseeing this happy gang of reprobates was Jeremy Brown, the large, affable and capable entertainment editor.

A room divider separated us from the large newsroom, which seemed to be constantly erupting over one crisis or another. The commanding chief and publisher was John Bassett, who looked to be straight out of a Broadway play about newspapers. "Big John" was well over six feet tall, and his voice could be heard in every corner of the newsroom.

I was pleasantly surprised to find out that Brown had decided to place my small drawings on the front page of the *Telegram*. Big John loved all my early cartoons with the exception of one. It infuriated him so much he fired off a memo to the executive editor, saying, "Stop the presses, as they do in the movies, and take that fucking cartoon out of my newspaper." His next memo was to the syndicate, asking who I was and how much money I was making for the newspaper. After being told that my cartoons appeared in more than two hundred newspapers in North America, including the *Chicago Tribune* and the *Los Angeles Times*, all of whom were paying big bucks, nothing more was said.

I was now drawing two cartoons a day, one for the American newspapers and one for the Canadian. Not all the American newspapers were happy. My strong opposition to the Vietnam War led many of them to threaten to cancel the feature unless I changed my thinking. One Detroit newspaper did cancel, saying, "To put it bluntly, we think the guy's a communist."

When Doreen and the children arrived in the city, we settled into one of a group of townhouses built along the edge of a ravine in Don Mills. The complex was full of newly arrived immigrants and, with a thousand children to scream with and chase, Susan and Vincent settled in quickly.

Within a few years the children started to attend the local school. Each morning they would set off together through a small wood and make their way to Brookbank School, where both of them appeared to enjoy their lessons. One day, Vincent burst through the door to tell us that an important experiment in class had reached an exciting result. After weeks of incubating, a number of chicken eggs had finally hatched. One was a duck.

When Vincent was six, like Canadian boys his age, he discovered ice hockey. Fortunately we were living in an area that boasted a kids' hockey league. Prestige Construction had gallantly stepped forward to buy sweaters for the children, and with the name of their sponsor proudly reaching across their chests they took to the ice. On the night of Vincent's first practice, I watched anxiously as the coach and some helpers grouped the two teams together, facing each other, in the centre of the outdoor rink. It was so cold I and the only other father in attendance stomped our feet and slapped our arms at our sides in an effort to keep warm.

At the sound of the whistle a whole mass of sticks flayed the air in an attempt to hit the puck. Someone must have connected since the puck suddenly appeared from the centre of the pack and made its way slowly down the ice towards an astonished goaltender. The boy was completely hidden inside his gear so all we could see of him was a frightened pair of eyes looking through the mask at the puck cruising towards him. Eventually it came to a stop ten feet in front of him. Despite all his efforts, the poor kid couldn't make his skates propel him forward.

Meanwhile the small army at centre ice had turned and with whirling legs descended on the stationary puck. Packed tightly enough to hold each other together, the mass of tiny flesh finally reached the puck . . . and passed it. On they went, unable to stop, ending up in the back of the net. The goaltender looked forlornly at a puck that remained, untouched, where it had originally stopped. Many years later I learned that an NHL star had emerged from the ranks of this talented band. Paul Marshall went on to play for the Pittsburgh Penguins.

Through the first ten years in Canada, Doreen had sorely missed her mum. In 1967 she decided to return to England with Vincent and Susan to visit their grandmother for a few weeks. During the time she was away, *Time* magazine decided to write a story on me and my cartooning. Serrel Hillman, the *Time*'s man in Canada, did the interview over lunch in a fancy restaurant. As we stood to leave, he asked me to come to dinner that Sunday evening. In that way, I would be close at hand if his editors in New York had any questions. ·

I was met at the door by Serrel's maid, who escorted me to the dining room. Serrel leapt to his feet to introduce me to the other guests at the table: movie actor Oscar Holmolka and his wife, Marshall and Corinne McLuhan and, of course, John and Eleanor Bassett. As we retired to the living room for after-dinner drinks, John took my arm and steered me to a corner.

"I've read the *Time* story," he said. "It's great. Starting on Monday morning, I want you in for morning editorial meetings."

I was astonished. "I'm sorry, Mr. Bassett, but I don't attend editorial meetings."

"And why not?" he glared.

"Because I draw for more than two hundred newspapers and interpret the news as I see it. I don't need outside influence."

"Do you have a bathing suit?" He continued to glare.

"Yes, sir."

"Then be at the house next Sunday afternoon and join me for a swim." He was a remarkable man who respected those who stood their ground.

The *Time* piece was a full-page article. If anyone else in Toronto read it, they must have been damn fast getting to a news agent, because Doreen and I tried to buy every available copy in the Metro area.

I had joined the Association of American Editorial Cartoonists, a group of leading North American professionals in the field. Since few newspapers could afford their own cartoonist and those that could employed just one, its members numbered less than a hundred, but of that hundred, twenty were Pulitzer Prize winners.

In 1967 the association held a four-day convention in Montreal, their first convention outside the United States. As Montreal was within easy travelling distance, Doreen and I went. We attended as many of the sessions as we could and met several people who would, over the following years, become close friends. The following year the convention was held in Washington and included a visit to the White House. Doreen was as excited as I was when the time came to meet the president. She had spent most of the morning getting her hair done and trying various beauty treatments on her face. Since she has always had a marvellous English complexion, this surprised me. But not as much as the price of her new outfit.

We entered the White House to see the Marine band playing at the bottom of a large, curving staircase. Shortly after we took our seats the band played "Hail to the Chief," and in he came. President Johnson was surprisingly handsome. Doreen thought he had tremendous sex appeal, but this escaped me. We joined the greeting line to shake hands with him. His hand shot out. I took it. He smiled. A camera flashed, and it was over. How did Doreen look in the photo, in her new outfit and makeup? No one will ever know. The aide leaning over to introduce us to LBJ completely blocked her out of the picture.

Although the afternoon had been set aside for our visit to the president, halfway through the proceedings he was called away. I later found out that another setback in Vietnam had caused his hasty departure. I was disappointed to see him leave early. It would be two years before I was once again in the presence of this remarkable Texan.

That summer we went back to Britain to visit our families. Doreen's sister and her husband suggested that we all take a trip to Newquay. Naturally we agreed. This wonderful Cornish seaside town had played such an important part in my life. We rented two trailers and had the most glorious of holidays. Two weeks of watching both Vincent and Susan playing on the sand and them watching me build sand castles. Each morning we would wake in the trailer to glorious sunshine and the sounds of the Beatles on the radio. "All You Need Is Love" was played over and over. We agreed.

8

AT THE *TELEGRAM* I BECAME good friends with one co-worker – Peter Worthington, a journalist of the highest order – and we got in the habit of having coffee together at any hour of the day when each of us found time. Over the years I have learned that he has a standard of ethics rare in most occupations, particularly the newspaper business. The *Telegram*'s "man on the spot," as he was known, had the reputation of being Canada's foremost foreign correspondent.

At some point each morning when he was not travelling, we would sit in the cafeteria, and through his eyes, I would see the daily events of a world that seemed to be in a state of constant madness. In 1967, one area, in particular, was on everyone's mind – Biafra. This area of eastern Nigeria, led by Lieutenant-Colonel Ojukwu, had declared itself independent. Nigeria warned Biafra its plans for a separate state were not acceptable and a vicious civil war had broken out. Completely cut off from foreign humanitarian aid, the population of Biafra became another example of man's inhumanity to man. The living skeletons that the Biafrans had become were shown nightly on television screens around the world, and viewers were horrified.

A Toronto church group decided to help. Using donated funds, they bought a secondhand plane to ferry supplies into Biafra. What was needed was money for fuel and supplies. John Bassett promised to do what he could to help by publicizing their mission. First he needed journalists to go into Biafra and report on the effects of the war on ordinary people there. He sent for two people: his star correspondent, Peter Worthington, and me, a syndicated cartoonist whose artwork from Biafra would be seen by a wide audience. As Worthington has often commented, "I was sent to report on the war and Wicks was sent to draw the funny side of the conflict."

Whatever the reason for my being chosen, I was excited. Doreen was not, but her argument that it was dangerous fell on deaf ears. I had decided that it was time I played the part of a real newspaperman. Besides, with someone like Worthington by my side, what could possibly go wrong? I did not tell her that it seemed wherever Worthington showed his face overseas, someone tried to take a shot at it.

We arrived in Montreal to board the church plane taking us to São Tomé, a small island off the west coast of Africa and a supplies collection point for Biafra. We were told that the church had paid $100,000 for the aircraft, but, after a quick tour, Worthington and I decided that whoever had bought it must have been carrying a white cane. It was rickety and its furnishings had been stripped to make room for supplies. The plane was loaded with a couple of spare aircraft engines and a number of crates containing food and medicines. The few remaining seats were for Worthington and me, a CBC camera crew of three and two church representatives. The crew was made up of volunteers headed by Pat Paterson, a wonderful pilot who had spent most of his time flying in northern Canada.

When we took off we were further reminded that this was not exactly Air Canada. We quickly ran out of runway, and to this day Worthington maintains that we made use of a piece of road that carried on past the end of the strip.

It was early morning, five days later, when, after many stops to refuel, we approached the coast of Liberia. At the time, Worthington was trying to beat me at chess. I felt a slight tap on my shoulder.

"Excuse me, Ben." It was the navigator (who was later killed when the plane crashed in Biafra during one of its runs). "It seems we have a bit of a problem, and Pat would like you and Pete to come up front for a meeting."

We followed him to the front of the plane. Pat was sitting with a map on his lap. He turned and grinned. "Good morning."

"So what's up, Pat?" I tried to sound calm, but it was not easy. We appeared to be flying about eighteen inches above the waves.

"It seems we have a bit of a fuel problem."

"What kind of fuel problem?" asked Worthington.

"We're running out of it."

"You've got to be joking," I said. "For the last four days we've done nothing but land where we could and fill up."

"True, but unfortunately the church group back in Montreal kept shovelling in more goods without placing them on the manifest. So the fuel can't hold the load we're carrying."

"How far until we reach land?"

"Too far, I'm afraid. We're a couple of hundred miles off the coast of Liberia and the closest I can see is this." He held up the map and pointed to a fly speck of an island, one of the islands of the Cape Verde group, all of which were in the middle of nowhere.

"What is it?" asked Worthington.

"Sal, a Portuguese island used for political prisoners."

"Can we make it?" I asked looking down at the water, which seemed to be getting even closer.

"I'm not sure. Hand me the manual, would you?" I passed him a small booklet that appeared to be on how to fly the plane. He started to flip through it.

"What are you doing?" I asked.

"I'm trying to find out how to land this thing on water."

Worthington turned and hurried back to his seat. I followed in time to see him make a move on the pocket chessboard.

"What did you just do?" I asked, counting the pieces to make sure all of mine were there.

"I'm castling. If we go down, I want my king to be safe. Now, hand me the cameras."

"I'm not taking pictures at a time like this."

"Not now," he answered. "It's for when we go down in the water." His face was flushed with passion. "I can see it now." He lifted his hands and drew in the air: "Aid Plane on Way to Mercy Mission Goes Down in Mid-Atlantic."

I began to load the cameras.

"Don't forget. Load one with colour and one with black and white." He was almost beside himself with excitement. I was praying.

It seemed to take forever to get to Sal. Finally, there was a shout up front. We hurried forward.

"There she is!" The navigator beamed as he pointed towards the horizon. A small piece of scrubby land lifted itself from the water.

"It's going to be close," said Pat glancing at the fuel gauge. There was not a sound in the cockpit, and even Worthington was biting his lip. The plane flew lower and lower, closer and closer. When it seemed the water must be licking the bottom of the plane, there was a bump. We had made it with just ounces of fuel left. Everyone was slapping Pat on the back. I turned to shake hands with Worthington, but he was already back in his seat.

"I've changed my mind," he said. "I don't think I'll castle after all."

We left the plane and strolled around the small island, followed closely all the time by a sinister character in a raincoat. At first glance he looked like Humphrey Bogart redoing the last scene of *Casablanca*. Never more than a few feet from us, he was silent the whole time.

Suddenly Worthington stopped at the edge of a cliff, took off his clothes and dove into an unknown depth of water. I marvelled at my surprising travelling companion. When he scrambled back onto land I asked why had he done this.

"Because I felt like a swim," he answered.

The refuelling took about an hour, long enough to feel sympathy for the poor devils imprisoned on this barren, isolated island.

Although we now had a full tank of fuel, and there was no danger of going down at sea, we were all still very relieved when we finally approached São Tomé. The island was busy not only with relief workers organizing supplies for Biafra, but also with the scum of the earth. Gunrunners were everywhere, working deals and trying to find ways of smuggling their arms into the tiny new country. I find it difficult to understand how those involved in the business of selling weapons can sleep at night. When they see a child who has lost a limb to a shell, does the arms-dealer open another bottle of wine, knowing the mortar he sold had reached the target area? The "business" disgusts me.

Getting into Biafra had always been difficult; now it was almost impossible. The only way in was over Nigerian territory, and for obvious reasons, it was a route best taken after dark.

It was common knowledge that the Biafrans had contact people in São Tomé and it didn't take long before Worthington found them. After several long discussions, they gave us permission to enter Biafra and promised that someone would meet us when we arrived. Worthington and I headed for the airport and joined the motley aircrews from a dozen various countries who were drinking in the bar. We began our search for someone to fly us in and finally hit the jackpot with a Norwegian pilot. Our initial excitement at the news that his would be the first plane to leave soon evaporated when we realized he intended to fly over Nigerian territory mostly in daylight.

We climbed aboard the DC-7, followed by one of the aid workers who had come with us from Montreal. We crossed the African coast and arrived over our destination as it got dark a nerve-racking one hour and twenty minutes after takeoff. Anxious to see what I had gotten myself into, I made my way forward and stared over the pilot's shoulder into the night sky. The Biafran forces no longer had an airfield under its control, and so we had to land on a small jungle road. As we began to lose height, a frantic voice came through the transmitter: "Land quickly."

I looked out of the window hoping to see a landing area and saw nothing. If someone was keen for us to land, I thought, surely they would light the landing strip and show us where. I glanced at the altimeter – a thousand feet. It was blacker than coal outside, and we were losing height rapidly. At three hundred feet I was wondering whatever had made me agree to come. Then suddenly I could see lights ahead of us. A line of flares was illuminating an incredibly narrow road. As our wheels touched the surface, the flares went out. With inches of space to spare on either side, we tore down the road.

The plane finally came to a stop. Astonishingly, we were still on the road. The pilot edged past me and made for the door. I could hear voices outside. The door swung back, a ladder appeared and hands reached up to help us out. "Welcome to Biafra," said a voice from the dark. I whispered a reply and allowed a small group of Biafrans to push me towards a car. As we moved off into the jungle, I glanced back, realizing that I had forgotten to thank the pilot. He was too busy to wave. A truck had already backed into position and he was beginning to unload the supplies.

Our car crept though the dense bush without the help of headlights. I couldn't see a thing and sat back listening to the sounds of plant life swishing against the window. Suddenly there was a shout: "Halt! Who goes there?" The car came to a stop and we climbed out into a well-lit clearing. In the middle sat a small hut – Biafran customs! We showed our visas and swore that we had nothing to declare. A young Biafran woman asked if we had any questions. She looked attractive in the dim light and, more and more, I felt like we were actors in a B movie.

We continued our journey to Umuahia, a large town an hour and a half away that was overrun with refugees from the outlying areas escaping the advancing Nigerian army. Luckily the Biafran authorities felt that we were important enough to give us a room in their propaganda centre. The cost was nineteen dollars a day, which included food at a nearby government centre and a driver-guide to accompany us wherever we went. It was beginning to look like the deal of the year.

There was no time to visit our room before we were whisked off. Like propaganda officials the world over, our hosts were anxious to show us the result of the vicious Nigerian bombing of innocent victims. A visit to a hospital was particularly disturbing. Many of the patients were children suffering from both malnutrition and injuries. As I walked between their beds, I was enraged at an enemy I had yet to meet.

At nightfall we got back to the propaganda centre. We hurried along a narrow outdoor landing and opened the door to our room. Worthington switched on the light. I had never seen a ten-watt bulb before and, frankly, did not think they existed. Its weak glow allowed us to find a bed on each side of the room. On closer inspection, I noticed that not only had mine been slept in recently, but whoever had lain down had left bloodstains on the sheet. I pulled it off the mattress and threw it on the floor. I was about to suggest to Worthington that we change beds, when I noticed that his was little better.

A rag hung across the window and on this swung the biggest spider I had ever seen. Even Worthington, with his vast experience of wartime conditions, was shocked. We stared at this monster, each of us hoping the other had an idea of how to evict it. Worthington suggested that I hold back the curtain while he hit it with a shoe. It seemed like a good idea at the time. I held the curtain back and Worthington swung. Nothing. Worse than nothing, the spider vanished. We dropped to our knees to hunt for the beast, but a frantic search of the room revealed no sign of it. Worthington, being a true journalist, unpacked a typewriter and, after setting it on one end of a box, began to type the events that had led up to our sharing sleeping quarters with the world's biggest spider.

I was about to doze off to the rhythm of Worthington's clacking fingers when there was a soft knock at the door. Worthington unlocked it, only to be pushed back as two young Biafran women crashed into the room. Giggling and joking, one threw Worthington on his bed and the other joined me. It took some time to explain that we were both extremely tired and, although we were sure that what they had to sell was of top value, neither of us were in a buying mood. It was only next morning that we found that the rooms upstairs were used as a brothel.

We were awake most of the night. At the slightest tickle we were convinced the spider, which we had named Albert, was back. In the morning our guide knocked on the door and, as he waited for us to answer, saw Albert scurrying across the landing. He casually raised his foot over our ugly friend and Albert was no more.

After a hurried breakfast, our guide led us to another nearby hospital to show us the real horror of starvation. During our tour of the children's ward, an air raid took place. The courageous nurses, forgetting their own need for cover, immediately raced around the wards grabbing the children and bundling them under the beds for safety. Luckily, the bombs fell a distance away. Later, when we left in the car, our guide, upset at the bombing, declared, "We will fight until heaven falls!"

For the next two days we were led from feeding stations to burial grounds. Everywhere we went we met death and horror – and wonderful Irish priests and nuns. I was astonished that they had managed to keep their sense of humour in this hellish atmosphere. They were some of the bravest people I have ever seen. Rarely did they show their anger at the world, but with their ever-ready wit were able to instil a sense of calm into the most dangerous situations.

One visit took us to a tiny makeshift hospital close to the front. It was so overcrowded with the wounded that it resembled the railway scene from *Gone With the Wind*. In a room set aside for twenty beds, eighty patients lay on the floors. An Irish priest greeted us at the door. Sensing our shock at the smell and at the overcrowding, he lightened the atmosphere by pointing out one patient on the floor.

"D'you see that one over there?" he asked. "'Tis tree times I've given him the last rights and if he doesn't go soon, oi shall kick him up there."

On our return to town we were told that Lieutenant-Colonel Ojukwu, the leader of the Biafran forces, had agreed to meet with a small group of journalists. We hurried to the State House and, after a thorough search, were led into a room set aside for the interview. Ojukwu, a large, black-bearded man dressed in camouflage fatigues, was sitting at a table. Worthington asked him questions as I circled the room taking pictures. In answer to one question, the lieutenant-colonel assured us that he would die fighting alongside his people. A few months later a helicopter would carry him to safety, leaving his people to fend for themselves as Biafra's struggle for independence collapsed.

Back at the propaganda centre we were told that those who wished to leave must leave that day. Worthington insisted on staying, feeling that to be in Biafra and not cover the fighting at the front was ridiculous. I cheerfully said I would go with him, but behind my show of bravado lurked the thought that the front would be an extremely dangerous place to be during a war. I began to have second thoughts about accompanying Worthington. As I grappled with the dilemma, a Nigerian plane swept down and dropped a bomb.

The others in the group ran for cover, but Worthington started to walk down the street. I hesitated a moment, then followed him. Looking up, we could see the plane strafing the street ahead of us. The bomb it had just dropped had turned over a car and a small fire was burning. It was impossible to get close. As we turned to leave, I stared in horror at a nearby wall. A man who had been sheltering there had been strafed. Only half of his body remained, splattered against the bricks.

The war was going badly for the Biafrans, yet Worthington was determined to do the job he had been sent to do. I had a problem. To go with Worthington could mean a lengthy and dangerous stay and I wasn't sure I wanted to risk my life. Yet I couldn't stay just a few more days or a week. If I wanted to leave, I had to leave now while there were still flights leaving Biafra. Back at the press room, we ran into two journalists from an American magazine preparing to leave. I decided to join them.

The three of us squeezed into a car that had obviously seen some action. I said goodbye to Worthington, feeling dreadful at leaving him alone in such a place to fend for himself. The two-hour drive took us through the bush and back to the same spot where I had arrived just three days before. It was my first sight of the road in daylight and I marvelled that we had been able to land on such a narrow strip.

Since we had a few hours before darkness and the arrival of the first plane, we made our way to a nearby feeding station, run by an Irish priest, Father Finucane. Early each morning this dedicated man made his way through the bush, finding families who, although starving, were too afraid to come to the feeding station. I asked him how he had the courage to stay where he was, close to a front line that was constantly changing. He smiled: "To be honest, son, I'm too much of a coward to leave these people in such desperate need."

By 6:30 P.M. it was dark and the bombing had started again. Despite this, the first friendly plane landed a few hundred yards from us. We introduced ourselves to the pilot, another Norwegian, who agreed to fly us back to São Tomé. As the plane began to climb, I leaned back and, for the first time in three days, slept.

In São Tomé, my problem was how to get back to Canada. If it was difficult entering Biafra, it was almost as difficult leaving an island crowded with what appeared to be half of Africa. There were regular flights to Europe, but getting on them was not easy. The two journalists I had left with were anxious to get back to New York. They decided that the only way to do this was to get on board the lone plane leaving for London.

They hunted down a harried official who appeared to be in charge and told him that they were with the CIA. Gripping my arms in bodyguard fashion, they insisted that I was an extremely important person they had to get to the States. Within minutes we were being shoved through the milling crowd and into the aircraft. To this day I'm not sure what my role was in all this — whether I was a diplomat or a prisoner. As the wheels left the ground and the nose of the aircraft pointed its way towards London, three very tired and relieved journalists sat back for the long flight home.

My trip to Africa opened up a whole new world. Back in Toronto, I offered the syndicate my work as a journalist. Those newspapers buying my cartoons could receive, at no extra cost, the odd story I would write. Not having the Worthington touch or journalism training, I predicted that most of my attempts to write a story would soon find their way into the

garbage of most editors. Fortunately, I had kept a diary of the
trip to Biafra, and it was this that the syndicate sent to many of
my clients. It appeared in more than eighty newspapers in
North America, and soon I found myself being invited to
appear on interview shows.

Peter Worthington was by now reporting the war from the
Nigerian side of the front, so I carried the ball for both of us.
Fortunately his absence allowed me to neglect to mention that
I had spent no more than three days in Biafra. Most radio and TV
stations were more than happy to go along with the omission,
anxious to suggest that finding someone from the war zone was
a real coup. The first of the broadcast interviews whetted my
appetite for more.

Two weeks after my return I realized that the tiredness I was
feeling wasn't normal. Then I started to have difficulty walking
and felt as though I had a bad bout of flu. A few hours after
going to bed one night, I awoke in a sweat. Doreen insisted on
taking me to the nearest emergency ward. The doctors there
could find nothing wrong, so we returned home.

By morning I was feeling no better. Doreen called our own
doctor. He was as puzzled as the emergency doctors, but felt that
some penicillin shots might help. They didn't and early the next
morning I was admitted to the hospital for observation. Doreen
held my arm tightly as I staggered to the car.

My recent trip to an African country suggested to most of
the doctors that I had some rare tropical disease. To be safe, I was
put in isolation. Within three days my condition was worse. I
was now floating in and out of wicked dreams. Doreen was
rarely away from my bedside. Little or no information was
forthcoming from either the nurses or the doctors.

She watched my skin turn yellow, but when I began to drift
into a coma, she could take it no more. She charged into the
nearest office and demanded that something be done. Her
action saved my life. Aware that this woman meant business,

they made a thorough search of the hospital and found a doctor who had worked in Indonesia. He threw back the sheets and, pointing to my enlarged spleen, declared, "This man has malaria." Within days of being treated I was much better, and was released two weeks later.

Not long after Worthington returned from Africa, the Biafran war was over. Perhaps to keep our minds off the terrible sights we had seen there, he reminded me of a discussion we had had about putting together a cookbook. At the time we had been sitting in the middle of one of the worst areas of starvation known to man, so I had felt it was just a rather sick joke.

Now he was serious. "Think of it," he said. "It will be like no cookbook ever written."

Since it was my impression that the millions of cookbooks already published covered every recipe in existence, I was intrigued to know what approach he had in mind.

"I've travelled and covered most areas of this world and eaten almost everything there is to eat. I'm in a perfect position to write about those foods that are not only rare, but exotic."

"And what will I do?"

"You can draw the pictures."

I thought it was a good idea, since it seemed to me that cookbooks were always popular. There was no question that Worthington was the ideal writer. He cooked for a survey crew in northern British Columbia, where he had prepared such delicacies as cakes, pies and goulash. When pressed, he did confess that most crew members would remember him for his ability to wield an axe and not for his culinary exploits.

We set out to find a publisher and finally persuaded Simon & Shuster in New York to take on *The Naked Gourmet*, a cookbook the likes of which had never been seen and likely will never be seen again. The recipes ran the gamut from Girl Guide cookies to the cooking and preparing of human flesh. During a television interview to promote the book, Worthington claimed that human flesh was a well-known *pièce de resistance* in certain parts of the world, and that once during a particularly festive evening spent around jungle fire, he had found a knuckle bone in his soup that resembled a human's.

The interviewer was quick to turn to another page of the book to discuss the cooking and eating of a boot. We had come well prepared. Worthington had insisted that we take an old army boot and a large pot. Now he filled the pot with boiling water, dropped in the boot and launched into a rapturous description of the flavour that could be expected from this kind of leather. I was given a stick and ordered to stir the boot and broth throughout the interview. The fumes became too much for me, so, despite my desire to be seen on television, I turned my head away from the camera and the pot. The interviewer was not as fortunate. Forced by Chef Worthington to look inside the pot as I lifted the boot on the stick, the interviewer caught the full stench of the oily, black, sticky mass. The show was aired on a Sunday morning, and I doubt anyone who watched it ate lunch that day. Certainly the interviewer seemed relieved to see us leave and neglected to say that he would be happy to see us again.

The number of newspapers carrying my cartoons continued to go up. I had an idea that I could get even more newspapers to sign up if I periodically supplied a free story to each of the newspapers carrying my drawings. I certainly enjoyed the pretence at journalism and was more than pleased to have the syndicate send whatever I wrote to my client papers. My position was ideal. I not only had the freedom to choose what story I wanted to write, I also had a captive audience. One of my stories was about that most noble of professions, the masseuse. Many media reports were claiming that a vast number of those practising the art were there to exercise more than a set of aching back muscles. I felt strongly that if something were being done behind the doors of these curative establishments other than the service advertised, I, for one, would ferret out the misdeed.

After extensive research I discovered that the ideal parlour to visit was not far from my office. As I was well known in the area, I waited until after dark before going up the poorly lit flight of stairs. As an extra precaution, I wore sunglasses.

"One, please," I said before remembering this was not a movie house.

The waiting room was full. All were men and all had found a spot on the floor that commanded their fullest attention. After a few minutes of staring at my spot I followed the young lady down a narrow hallway. She stopped. "Which room would you like?"

"Any room will do."

"Well, would you like France, Africa, Hong Kong or London?" I glanced into the rooms. Each had wallpaper depicting various scenes from the areas she had mentioned.

"I'll take Africa," I mumbled. Somehow the thought of being caught in a police raid while surrounded by lions and tigers appeared more decent than being caught naked at the feet of a group of can-can girls.

"Wait here, please." The room was small. A white sheet covered the kind of table used for medical examinations. I sat on the edge and began to swing my legs. Should I undress? Better not. I thought again of a police raid.

The door opened. "Hi, I'm Michelle."

"Hi, I'm . . ." I began, then stopped. Michelle had begun to remove her clothes.

She smiled. "What did you say your name was?"

"Ben," I answered.

"Okay, Ben, would you like to hang your scarf, overcoat, shirt, trousers and socks over there and put your dark glasses on the table."

I wondered if I should ask her to leave the room first. I

decided against the idea and turned my back. There was an uncomfortable silence as Michelle sat on the edge of the table watching me.

"First time?" she asked as I finally removed my scarf.

"Yes." She began to help. I was appalled and searched for something to say to get her to stop undressing me. At a complete loss for the right words, I told her that I was born in England.

"Does that mean you want something extra?"

"Well, I would like a nice cup of tea," I replied.

Maybe it was my accent. She was laughing so hard as she left the room that she forgot her clothes. I waited fifteen minutes and, when she failed to return, I replaced my scarf and sunglasses and quietly crept away into the night. The story was published and perhaps even resulted in increased business for those who have a special skill in easing the pain in tired muscles.

9

LONDON BRIDGE HAD BEEN SOLD. England had decided to sell the old lady when she could no longer take the weight of London's mounting traffic. The news brought memories of my childhood flooding back: watching the dockers loading and unloading goods from around the world, and waving at the boatmen in their tugs and barges to get them to hoot a greeting in reply before they vanished beneath the sooty arches.

Now it had gone. And to an American. Appalled at the news, most Britishers protested loudly at the sale, but none had been moved enough to place a hand in his wallet and save this heritage bridge. I had mixed feelings. As a Cockney I found it hard to believe the bridge would have been sold, but as a cartoonist struggling to find his way in the world of journalism, the story was heaven sent. Who else knew that bridge as I did? Who else had seen an enemy's bombers thwarted time and time again in their attempts to knock her down?

I contacted the *Los Angeles Times* syndicate and suggested that I write a story about the bridge in its new site at Lake Havasu City, Arizona. They agreed.

It was 110° as I strolled across the bridge in her new home.

Looking over the side, I watched the Colorado River gently ease its way through her arches.

"Well, it so happened I needed a bridge, so when London Bridge came up for sale, I was naturally interested." Robert McCulloch of chainsaw fame stood beside his private jet on the tarmac of the small airstrip at Lake Havasu. He had learned the bridge might be sold from a television interview with the Lord Mayor of London, who was visiting the States and suggested that the bridge was about to be replaced.

"I immediately ran to the phone and put in a bid," McCulloch grinned.

"How much did you bid?"

"Two point four million dollars. Then I figured, gee, everyone will be bidding two point four million so, since it was my sixtieth birthday, I threw in another sixty thousand dollars." What kind of way was that to buy the old lady, I wondered.

I left the airport and headed for the office of the chief engineer, Bob Beresford, anxious to find out how a structure the size of London Bridge had been moved.

"We had to take it apart." Beresford looked surprised at the question. "How else were we going to get it here? We took her apart stone by stone. Each stone was numbered and lettered, then put back together again over here."

It seemed a fair enough answer. I suppose it would have been difficult to move it in one piece.

"Any problems with the move?"

"Just one. We found a complete row of 10,254 stones missing when we got them to the American side. The row of the letter *w*. It seems that one of the workers on the London side was Spanish."

"So?"

"They do not have a *w* in the Spanish language, so he just missed it out. That accounted for the missing bricks."

I left Beresford's office and made my way back to the

bridge. I threw a pebble over the balustrade into the water and watched as the ripples circled their way outward. I thought about the sights the bridge would never see again: my mother rushing across, dodging the bombs at four o'clock in the morning, scurrying along like a little white rabbit for fear of being late for her lousy cleaning job at the bank. And what about Alf Smith, the undertaker? Many's the time he had crossed the bridge, his boozy breath cutting through the fog as he led another horse-drawn hearse to the graveyard. As I looked at the water below I could hear Dad's voice: "Alf was the greatest undertaker the world has ever seen. Many people committed suicide just so's they could have Alf give them a good send off."

The stones were the same and, sure, water was flowing between the old girl's arches, but how did the bridge feel about the strange people that now crossed her back? They would take care of her, I was sure. For us, she had been a part of our family and as such, we had taken her for granted. Now those surrounding her treasured her; they had carefully wrapped her and tenderly set her down in her new home.

I strolled on and stopped beside a small souvenir shop at the foot of the bridge. Two visitors stood inside.

"Can I help you?" asked Laura Cohen, one of the shop owners.

"Just looking . . . You've sure got a lot of things."

"We have enough stone in here to build another bridge," she laughed. "Let me take you around. As you can see, we make souvenirs from pieces of the bridge. Here we have cufflinks, desk sets, pen sets and, over here, we have our religious section."

I picked up a crucifix that had been stuck to a piece of stone. "How do I know that this is an authentic piece of old London Bridge?"

She smiled. "Because there is a small label on it with the signature of Mr. King, the City of London engineer."

"What's to stop me strolling outside and just taking a little chip off the bridge?"

"It wouldn't be authentic."

"Why not?"

"It wouldn't have Mr. King's signature, right?"

The ferocious sun, its reflection bouncing off the water, hit the underside of the bridge and shadows danced beneath her arches. I plopped another pebble into the water and stared at the ripples forming lines of the past. It was three o'clock. The bookie would now be taking bets close by the bridge. His limping lookout man would shout "Heads up!" and, too late to escape, would once again find himself in the arms of the law. Who will shout "Heads up!" in Arizona?

I looked at my watch. It would soon be time to leave the old lady. I just had time for a quick snack.

"Would you like something from our London Bridge Pantry?" a young waitress asked.

"What do you have?"

"The Regency, the Bond Street, Ten Downing Street or a Bonnie Prince Charlie?"

"I'll try the Bonnie Prince Charlie."

"Would you like mayonnaise on your Bonnie Prince Charlie?"

I began to smile. Oh, what the characters who had lived beside the bridge would have made of a line like that.

I strolled back to the centre of the bridge for one final look. A small boy stood gazing at the water.

"Do you know the song, 'London Bridge is Falling Down'?" I asked.

"Do you mean 'London Bridge is Going Up'?" he answered.

The plane banked as we crossed the bridge and headed north. The small boy's voice was still ringing in my ears: "London Bridge is going up, going up, going up, London Bridge is going up, my fair lady."

I had been home to Arizona.

The story was well received and soon after it was published I reworked it for the London *Observer* and for the Canadian magazine *Weekend*. Most important of all, a weekly CTV news program thought it would make a perfect item for them. I travelled back to the bridge with a cameraman and producer.

I returned home, and some months later, in early 1970, Doreen presented me with the best Valentine's Day present ever – a nine-pound baby girl we named Kim. Both Vincent and Susan were excited to have a new member of the family, and since they couldn't visit Doreen and Kim in the hospital, they were quite anxious to have them come home. I can still see Vincent and Susan barrelling down the hill in our townhouse parking lot, eager to greet their new sister, as we pulled up in the car.

Once our home life settled down a bit, I refocused on the story I had written on London Bridge, which had left me keen to take on similar ventures. *Weekend* magazine suggested I do a profile piece on Minnesota Fats. It occurred to me that, since my television piece on London Bridge had been successful, CTV might also be interested in an interview with the great pool player. Why not do them both at the same time? CTV agreed, and off I went with a cameraman and producer.

We drove through New York State to Minnesota Fats's home in Dowell, Illinois, in a blizzard. Luckily, it didn't take us too long to find his house. I pressed the bell and from somewhere inside a New York accented voice boomed, "Hey, Eva-line! They're here!" The door opened and a huge man in Bermuda shorts put out his hand. I was face to face with one of the world's greatest talking machines.

"Hi, Wicks. How you doing? Wanna cup of coffee? This is my wife, Evelyn." Rudolph Wanderone, alias Minnesota Fats, the greatest pool hustler of all time, had the build of Jackie Gleason and the voice of W. C. Fields.

Fats took our coats. We followed his waddling figure down three steps into a long, low, carpeted room with floor-to-ceiling

windows. There stood the other loves of his life: a refrigerator
and a pool table. The cameraman set up his lights and Fats
unbuttoned a leather pool-cue case stamped with his initials in
gold. I began to chalk my cue. Tired after our hellish four-hour
drive, I was hardly ready for pool.

"I love this place. I helped a lot of people here. They gave me
the highest award of the year, the greatest honour a man can
have – the humanitarian award of the year. See this shot, Wicks.
I wouldn't miss this shot in a thousand years. I made this shot a
hundred and fifty times in a row once . . . Missed it! I don't know
how I missed it. Let me have that ball back . . . Missed it again!
This is a very tough table. The ball I'm using is an extra heavy
ball and it ain't the best ball to play with, you understand." Fats
took the chalk.

"How come they call you Minnesota Fats?" I asked.

"Beat everyone in Minnesota by the time I was ten, playing
grown men. I was five feet eleven inches tall. Shorter now.
Shortened up with age. I've seen people you wouldn't believe
shrink two feet . . . See this shot? I bet a guy five hundred dollars
on this shot in Reno once . . . That's a beautiful shot, Wicks!" It
was. The champ was beginning to warm up.

"Ever work for a living, Fats?"

"Never worked a day in my life."

"Want to play a game, Fats?"

"Sure, Wicks, though I never play for fun." I agreed to play
him for a token dollar.

"Call it."

"Heads."

I hit the fifteen balls on the table with the cue ball. None
found their way to a pocket. I began to chalk my cue again. Fats
looked over the layout.

"When I play for money a guy has no chance on this earth. I
once played for a quarter of a million dollars, you understand?
In cash . . . Nine ball, end pocket."

"Ever feel any pressure when the stakes are high?"

"Never feel anything. This shot here is a mortal cinch for me. A jump shot. I make the greatest jump shot in the world. Make a ball jump like you've never seen, jump four feet in the air. See that? It's unbelievable."

I began to remove some of the chalk that was building up on the end of my cue.

"See, I use the diamond system. The guy that invented it died, and I perfected it. Take you fifteen years to learn it. I'm the only man in the world that can explain the system, let alone play it."

"Do you drink, Fats?"

"Never smoked or drank in my life . . . Two ball, kiss shot . . . Not that it would have affected me . . . Six ball and five ball, end pocket . . . Not like sex. Now sex will affect any living creature that has to do something where endurance is involved, you understand? Sex is a mortal sin to weaken you . . . Ten ball, two cushion bank . . . See, just to be around a woman is enough to weaken you. That's what they was put on earth for. To weaken a man."

"Ever lose, Fats?"

"Lose? What are you talking about? Lose? I beat every top champion that ever lived. I beat everyone all over the world. If I wanna win, I win, every time. You know how I lose? I'll tell you how I lose. When I don't wanna win, that's how. No money shows up . . . fifteen and eight ball, end and middle pockets."

The last ball drifted quietly around the table, rolled to the brink of the middle pocket, paused to look around and plopped its way gently out of sight.

I handed Fats the dollar as the phone rang.

"Hi there. Yeah. Got these guys doing a TV show on me. Can't make it next week. Going to Nashville, playing the governor of Tennessee, black-tie affair. Week after? Leave for Washington. Getting the greatest player that ever lived award. Yeah."

I enjoyed writing the story on Fats, and both it and the television item went well. My editor at *Weekend* felt sure I would be interested in doing another quirky sports story. I was.

"Then how about doing a piece on Bobby Fischer for us?"

Being a chess player of some mediocrity, I jumped at the chance. Before the editor could get off the phone, I asked where I could contact Mr. Fischer and was told that, since he was so often in the news, it should prove no problem. He was preparing for his world championship match with Boris Spassky, scheduled to take place in Reykjavik, Iceland.

I got on the phone to track him down. The obvious place to begin, I felt, would be the Manhattan Chess Club in New York City.

"Mr. Fischer does not take calls. You may leave a number."

I left my number. Five times. Apparently I was not the only person to leave a number. Unhappy with the arrangements for the forthcoming contest, Fischer was issuing daily bulletins threatening to take his pawns and go back to wherever it was he came from. In an effort to dissuade him from withdrawing, the White House phoned to remind him of his patriotic duty to beat the Russian. They may as well have saved their dime.

I decided to try again.

"Mr. Fischer does not take calls. You may leave a number."

I complained that I had been leaving a number for five days.

"Don't feel too bad," said the operator. "So has President Nixon."

I was beginning to understand why Fischer's lawyer had wailed, "He's harder to get to than Chou En-lai."

I reminded *Weekend* magazine of this fact.

"Maybe he doesn't like Nixon," said the editor helpfully.

I set out to find Robert James Fischer. I tracked him through the Catskills in upstate New York, furtively following his trail through the dense undergrowth of that wild, untamed region. Sometimes I lost him, but always I was able to pick up his tracks again. Relentlessly I hunted Bobby Fischer and, like a man caught in a knight fork at KB2, he never knew. I found him at Grossinger's Hotel, having read in the newspaper that he was there.

I insinuated myself into the inner workings of the impenetrable hotel by renting a room. I developed contacts. I talked to the tennis pro, a lifeguard and a waiter. They said Bobby Fischer was a good tennis player, swimmer and eater. I struck it rich with the waiter when I said to him, "Boy, I'd sure like to meet the great Bobby Fischer." My cover, you see, was that of the ordinary starstruck hotel guest, and this is the way you're supposed to talk when that's your cover. So well did I play my part that the waiter agreed to sit me at Fischer's table.

That very night I was seated what was supposed to be Bobby Fischer's table. Three elderly ladies were also there.

"And what do you do?" they asked me, in the manner that this question is always asked in dining rooms.

I was about to say that I was just an ordinary hotel guest, but I realized that didn't sound right, so I said that I was a travelling salesman. I sat there and played with my food and worried whether Bobby Fischer would show. They talked to each other about their former husbands.

Halfway through dessert, he arrived. Introductions were made. Before the ladies had a chance to ask Fischer what he did for a living, he ordered fish, opened a book and sank out of hearing. How could I open a conversation? I took a deep breath.

"Er, I have an advantage over you, Mr. Fischer. I, er, know who you are." He kept reading. "In fact, you're the reason I'm visiting Grossinger's." He turned a page.

"Hmmm."

At last. A breakthrough. I distinctly heard a sound. Throwing all caution to the wind, I let him have it between the eyes: "I'm a journalist!" Conversation at the table came to an abrupt end as all eyes turned to me. I stuck the spoon in my dessert and began shovelling ice cream into my fluttering stomach. Slowly the book was lowered to the table.

"You're a what?" hissed Fischer.

"A magazine writer. I'm here to do a story on you."

As if to protect himself from some deadly snake, he whipped the book up to his face. The women began talking again. Having compared husbands, they now spread their conversation to the merits of their various birthplaces.

"You were born in Chicago, weren't you Bobby?" I asked in my best one-big-happy-family voice.

"I'm not talking," he answered and retreated again behind the barricade of the book. The rest of the table excused themselves from our lively discussion and left.

"Do you play tennis?" I asked.

"Do you?" he asked back.

"No, I play table tennis."

"Any good?"

"I can beat the shit out of you," I answered and smiled. He turned and looked at me for the first time.

"Who's the story for?"

I told him and asked if he'd like to play ping-pong.

"Just one game," he said. We left the dining room and found the ping-pong table.

"Your serve." He threw me the ball.

"Is your mother still living in England, Bob?"

"I won't answer that. Zero, five, my serve."

"Ever play chess for fun?"

"Rarely. Eight, two."

"Why do the Russians produce all the great chess champions?"

"Four, eleven, your serve. Because they're subsidized."

"Any thoughts of marriage?"

"Won't answer that."

"Who's had the greatest chess influence on you?"

"Morphy, Paul, last century. Fourteen to six, my serve."

"How does the World Tournament work?"

"We play twenty-four games. One point for a win; half-point for a draw. As the challenger I have to make twelve and a half points. Get on with the game."

"Right. Er, what's the score?"

"Eighteen to seven."

"Are you at your peak?"

"Nowhere near."

"How do you compare yourself with Boris Spassky?"

Suddenly it was all there, a competitive animal waiting for the kill.

"Spassky!" He spat the name out. "I'm sick of being compared with him. 'What's Spassky like?' 'How does he compare?' I'll tell you how. He doesn't. He's not in my class and never will be."

The game ended the interview, but a chess match in Reykjavik still had to be played. In Bobby Fischer's mind, that, too, was already settled. And it soon was. He would soon be the world champion. He was and still is one of the best chess players who ever lived.

In Toronto, news at the *Telegram* was about the *Telegram*, and was not good. Rumours were everywhere that Bassett was ready to sell the newspaper. Certainly his enthusiasm had waned since a fierce strike a few years before. Few of his workers could forget the sight of the owner delivering a speech from the top of one of the newspaper trucks. The act had been dramatic to watch, but in retrospect many felt it marked Bassett's loss of love of the newspaper business.

The prospect of looking for another location to work from didn't concern me. Where I drew the cartoons was of little

importance to the increasing numbers of newspapers buying
the Wicks cartoons. All that mattered was that they arrived on
time and the readers enjoyed them.

Life on the home front was more settled. The whole family
continued to enjoy our new home. Doreen and I agreed that
three children was the perfect number for a family. Although she
had been one of eight children, Doreen had no wish to carry on
the tradition. Unfortunately, the pill had been giving her
trouble, so we decided that I would have to take the necessary
action.

Many men were opting for a vasectomy, and when I was told
that one of these incredibly brave men worked in the *Telegram*
news room, I swiftly hunted him down.

"It's the greatest thing since the first apple."

I asked him to lower his voice and steered him to a quiet
corner. "Er, does it hurt?" I asked.

"Hurt? Of course it doesn't hurt."

"But I thought you had to cut something."

"So does a barber."

"How long does it take?"

"Twenty minutes."

"Twenty minutes! Are you sure?"

"Of course I'm sure, though I did hear of one guy who did
it in five minutes, but that was in China."

"Isn't there a pill a guy can take?"

"It won't work. It's this . . ." he made a quick movement
across his throat with his finger, "or nothing."

I dialled the phone number of a doctor he'd recommended.
Why is it that whenever a man wants to discuss a delicate matter
with a doctor, it's always a woman who answers the phone?

"I'd like to speak to the doctor, please."

"Name?"

"Wicks."

"What do you wish to speak to him about, Mr. Wicks?"

"Er . . . a private matter."

"Medical?"

"Sort of."

"Do you have a pain?"

This was getting ridiculous. I took a deep breath. "I'd like an acupuncture . . . I mean I'd like a . . ." Good grief, I'd forgotten the name of the operation!

"Is it internal?"

"No!"

"Your stomach?"

"You're getting warm."

"Mr. Wicks, we're very busy and I wonder if you wouldn't mind . . ."

"It's my private parts," I blurted out.

"You want a vasectomy?"

"Er . . . yes, please."

"There's a rather long waiting list."

"How long?"

"Ten weeks. But I can recommend someone who may be able to fit you in sooner. He has just moved into the building and has started in the very same field."

I was shocked. A beginner? I mean it's not as if I was having a tooth out or getting a new pair of glasses.

"I assure you, Mr. Wicks, he is one of the best. He trained in England as a surgeon."

Convinced, I phoned this Michelangelo of the vasectomy world and made an appointment.

The steps in the medical building led to the lower floor. The smell of new paint filtered through the walls as I made my way to the doctor's office.

He sat behind a cluttered desk, a small East Indian man in a white coat.

"Good evening, Mr. Wicks," he said. "Please take a seat. I understand that you want a vasectomy. Is that so?"

"I do."

"Of course, you understand that we are very particular who we operate on."

"No, I did not know that."

"For instance, we do not do the operation on bachelors."

"I'm married."

"Happily?"

"Very!" I looked at my watch. Five minutes had gone. If my friend was right about this lark, it would be all over in fifteen minutes.

"I want you to fill out this form. And do you understand that when I do this operation there is no turning back?"

I had no intention of turning back and told him so.

"Maybe you do and maybe you don't. Some doctors do a temporary job. I don't! Do you understand?"

"I do!" I glanced again at my watch. For goodness sake. Ten minutes to go. Maybe he's out to break the Chinese record, I thought. I began to have second thoughts. That's what you get when you go to a "no waiting" guy. He suddenly stood and opened the door to a small outer room.

"Would you please step in here, Mr. Wicks."

I hurried in and stood by a couch covered with a white sheet. I looked at my watch. Five minutes to go. If this guy was going to keep within the twenty-minute limit, he was going to need some help. I unfastened my belt and was about to remove my trousers as the doctor entered the room.

"Please remove your shoes, Mr. Wicks."

I stopped what I was doing.

"Remove my what?" I asked in amazement.

"Your shoes, Mr. Wicks."

Had I heard right? I began to smile. My shoes? Isn't that a strange place to start? I began to giggle, and as my nervousness was released, I couldn't hold back. I doubled over with laughter. The doctor looked puzzled at my outburst for he was, of course, only worried about my shoes spoiling his clean white sheet. But it was too late for explanations.

The newsman had been wrong. The operation was not done that day, and the only reason for my being there was for a preliminary examination. A week later I attended the outpatient department of a local hospital, where my doctor made me a changed man.

The rumours that had flooded the *Telegram* came true. The newspaper folded on October 30, 1971, and although most of the employees retired with a severance package, as a freelancer I was once again on my own.

Fortunately this precarious position did not last. Peter Worthington had joined a small group that was planning to start its own newspaper. Peter tried to get me to become part of the new *Toronto Sun*, but I had been offered a job by both the *Toronto Star* and the *Globe and Mail*. I joined the *Globe and Mail*, feeling that as Canada's only national newspaper, it would give my work exposure across the country. Since the *Globe* did not have a syndicate of its own, I took the advice of an old friend, Jim Cherrier, the director of the *Toronto Star* syndicate, and joined.

More and more while I was drawing my cartoons, I was dreaming of working in other forms of media. The CTV pieces I had done on London Bridge and Minnesota Fats encouraged me to become more involved in television.

When I received an offer from the CBC to join their flagship current-affairs program, "Weekend," it seemed too good to turn down. George Robinson, the executive producer, convinced me that my humour could be used in a conversational setting. He explained that a light interview in the hour-long program would be a welcome break from its more serious items.

My first assignment was to interview Ivan Rebroff, an extraordinary singer with a range that would echo in the basement before soaring up through the roof of the house. I rendezvoused with the five-member crew at the Sutton Place Hotel in

Toronto one hour before his expected arrival. As we stood in his suite, I tried to figure out what I could do to make this interview a little different. I wandered into the bathroom, and suddenly it came to me. Of course, get him to sing in the shower. The crew thought I was crazy but, since this might be my one and only chance at the big time, I decided to stick to it. So we set up the lights in the bathroom and, not wanting Rebroff to notice, closed the door. My biggest concern was that when he entered he would need to use the washroom.

The door to the suite opened and in came a bearded giant with a broad grin. Without giving him time to remove the large leopard-skin coat he was wearing, I pushed Rebroff towards the living room, shoved him into a chair and began the interview. He was wonderful, everything an interviewer could wish for. Near the end of our chat, I leaned forward.

"It's been said that you have one of the greatest of voices in the world."

Rebroff nodded in agreement.

"I, like everyone else, love to sing in the shower, the one place that appears to do justice to my vocal cords. Unfortunately, I have no idea how I should sound."

He smiled and nodded.

"Now, I was wondering if maybe you could let us hear what we should sound like. Would you mind singing in the shower for us?"

He smiled and nodded. Then a puzzled look suddenly crossed his face. "Er, you want me to, er . . . sing for you in the shower?"

I nodded and pointed across the room to the closed door. Rebroff grinned as he stood up. "And why not?" With that he crossed the room and entered the most brightly lit bathroom he had ever seen. The camera continued to film him through the open door. He began to strip.

"No, no," I called out. "With your clothes on will be fine."

Rebroff smiled, snatched at the curtain and with a flourish swept it back. He stepped into the bath and began a series of scales that ended with a wonderful rendition of a song. Still in the shower, he bowed. As we applauded, he showed his natural sense of theatre by grabbing the open shower curtain and, with a final bow and "thank you," pulled it closed.

10

MY FIRST REMINDER THAT the *Globe and Mail* was a newspaper of some importance came with a phone call from Major General Richard Rohmer. A decorated Second World War flyer and now a civilian lawyer, Rohmer was in charge of Canada's Air Reserve. Concerned that the force was not equipped with enough two-engine aircraft to patrol the North, he had decided to publicize the fact by demonstrating how difficult it was to monitor the Arctic with single-engine planes. He was ready to begin in August 1972, with me from the *Globe and Mail* and three others from the CBC to record the journey.

Richard's idea was to carry out an exercise aptly called "The Flight of the Ancient Bird." Two single-engine planes would set out from Churchill, Manitoba, and fly to Eureka, on the northern tip of Ellesmere Island, farther north than any piston-driven aircraft had ever gone before.

I took a large Hercules transport plane from Toronto to Churchill. This important harbour of the North was unlike any port I had seen. The sheds that hugged the bay were just as scruffy as those that occupied most ports, but had none of the large cranes vital to the loading and unloading of ships. The port area appeared deserted, yet there were signs of life on the streets as the few inhabitants hurried to whatever it was occupied their time in this isolated town.

Huge flies swarmed overhead in the immense sky as I strolled to the briefing room. Squadron Commander Ron Richardson, an electrical engineer, was speaking of survival. Then pilot and lighting consultant Serge Holoduke spoke of survival. He was followed by pilot and stockbroker Bill Purdy, who also spoke – surprise, surprise – of survival.

I left the room as Rohmer began to describe ways to keep warm in icy waters. More survival. If survival was such a big issue, what shape were the planes in? It was time I had a look at them. The two de Havilland aircraft stood wing-tip to wing-tip in the vast, empty hangar. Both looked decidedly unsafe, and my first thought was that each was holding up the other. Both planes had one engine in the front, one wing on top, one tail at the back and two wheels. I kicked the wheels and returned to the briefing. It was short. Bad weather was coming. The Arctic would have to wait twenty-four hours.

The briefing the next morning brought more bad news. The air between Churchill and Baker Lake, our first fuel stop, was filled with highs and lows doing all manner of things. The Flight of the Ancient Bird would have to be postponed another seven hours.

Finally, at 4 P.M. we were ready to go. Crewman Doug Carmichael helped me into one of the tiny planes. Rohmer and Holoduke were at the controls, with Carmichael and me behind. I could not rid my mind of the fact that the men who would be flying us were a lawyer and lighting consultant first and pilots second. I made a quick check: life jacket, parachute, airsick pills, dinghy and flares. I fastened the seatbelt, crossed my fingers, feet and legs and waited for the take-off. The prop swung, banged, spluttered, kicked, groaned and stopped . . . then started again.

"Baker Lake here we come," said a voice from up front. Nothing happened. 4:05 P.M., 4:10 P.M. We hadn't moved an inch. "Everyone out." Was this a joke? It wasn't. The weather had caught us again. "Be back here tomorrow morning!"

The sun was up as *Ancient Bird One*, this bag of string, ran along the runway and left the ground alongside *Ancient Bird Two*. The warm sun emerged from a sea of blue under our wing and threw itself around the cabin. Far below, sickly looking greenery bordered the shoreline of Hudson Bay, and in the distance ice hung like a cloud on the northern horizon. Six white whales frolicked in the sunlit waters, miles from the polluted waters of the south. The hours passed. Trees had long since disappeared. Lakes and rivers looked like puddles in a rainswept city street, as two thousand miles of the oldest rock known to humans spread itself across a northern land. The spectacular Kazan Falls bent a river downward and cut a line through the virgin wilderness. What an incredible country it was!

Eventually, we reached the small settlement of Baker Lake. I was anxious to see more of this town, which sat beyond the reach of car or railroad. Here I would be meeting my first Eskimos. I knew that they were now known as Inuit, but for me they would always be the indomitable people that I had read about. As a child, I had watched as the Eskimo had crossed my local movie screen, and had been intrigued by this remarkable race who lived in one of the harshest climates in the world.

I strolled along the shores of Baker Lake while our planes were being safely stored for the night, ready for an early-morning take-off. High on a hill I could hear the sounds of barking ricocheting between snowmobiles and of clothes crackling on lines in the midnight sun. The small Catholic church of St. Paul held its head above the noise and pointed its tiny white steeple to the sky. Father Choque, the local priest, was a French Canadian with a slight frame that hid the strength of a person who had lived in the North for thirty-four years.

Mom and Dad in their eighties during one of my visits back to England.

Me at three years of age in a studio portrait.

Eighteen years old and ready to take on the Nazi horde.

The Roy Kenton Band at the Blue Lagoon dance hall in Newquay, Cornwall. I'm sitting second from the right.

Our merry band of musicians on board the *QE*. I'm in the middle, left of Tiny Clark, who didn't always look like this.

Me with Stan Kenton, the band leader, whom I interviewed for the *Record Mirror.*

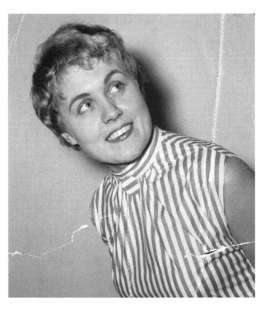

Doreen aged eighteen, the year I met her.

Our wedding. It was a perfect day, despite the haircut.

Our campsite at Two Jack Lake near Banff. The opening to the tent faced the winds off the lake, and we froze all night.

Susan kisses Vincent goodbye as he leaves for work during their regular "Mom and Dad" act.

A Biafran air raid was no place for a cartoonist, although I did my best.

The remarkable foreign correspondent Peter Worthington interviews Lt.-Col. Ojukwu, the leader of the Biafran forces, while I take pictures.

A playful time in an early Toronto home.

The Wicks clan: in the front row, starting at the left, are me, Dad holding Kim, Susan, Vincent, Nan, Mom, Doll (in the flowered dress) and Doreen.

In its new Arizona home, London Bridge was without water at first. Diverting a nearby river soon did the trick.

Lyndon Johnson welcomes Doreen and me to the White House. Doreen had spent a fortune on makeup and new clothes, only to have an aide lean forward and block her from the camera lens at the crucial moment.

Michael Caine insisted on a pint before I interviewed him in London.

Minnesota Fats at his home chalking his cue before taking on a new victim – me.

Raymond Cantwell, letter-writing champion of the world, looks anxiously for a postman to pick up his latest offering.

Rosemary Brown showing me Beethoven's tenth symphony, which she has just completed with the help of the dead composer.

It's eighty-four floors up and I'm seriously thinking of standing on the window ledge to do my interview with the window washer.

As the crowds close in, I raise my voice and plant my feet firmly on a soapbox at Speakers' Corner in Hyde Park, London.

The nicest of all five hundred interviews, Ingrid Bergman – the only one who asked for payment: one hundred pounds to be paid to her favourite orphanage.

Sir Edmund Hillary looked surprised to find a fellow mountaineer when I paid him a visit at his Toronto hotel.

Joseph explains to me why he wears women's clothing as he tours the streets of Los Angeles.

It's the only way up and down their mountain in Haiti. Sister Simone and Sister Janine go by donkey back to their clinic and tiny school.

My host in the Negev Desert kindly chewed my meat for me before passing it to me to eat.

Eritrean rebels rest long enough to chat before continuing their fight for independence from Ethiopia.

With no other means of transportation, and with vital medical supplies to deliver, I covered the last few miles of my journey in Eritrea by camel.

Madam Jeanne Sauvé presents me with Canada's highest civilian award – the Order of Canada. I still sometimes wonder what I did to deserve it.

Mom, in her nineties in this photo, relaxing in a nursing home in England.

Vincent and Susan, still close as adults.

Our grandchildren: Toran standing with a little help behind Rhia, Caleigh and Brittany.

Kim looking glamorous
in a studio portrait.

Kim's twins, and our latest grandchildren, Monty and Rupert.

This sad, bespectacled man told me of the white man's cruelty to this ancient tribe.

"There are six hundred Eskimos in Baker Lake," he said. "Many of them arrived in 1958. They were starving in the barren land. The dead were flown in with the survivors."

"Should they have been left to die?" I asked.

"Once fed, they should have been encouraged to leave, not bribed to stay. They were a nomad people of hunters lured into the twentieth century by a welfare cheque."

As I made my way back to the plane, I kicked the pebbles on the beach and wondered why decisions are always made by bureaucrats who live far from the people whose lives they affect.

It was decided at the morning briefing that we must follow the coast route to our second fuel stop, Shepherd Bay. This way we could avoid air uplifts over high ground, which causes rain and fog. The weather was not good, but Richardson decided that we had to make the DEW Line station at Shepherd Bay that day or abandon the flight to Eureka. We climbed back into our planes and once more headed north. The huge Back River split the land and a giant rainbow arched across the sky. At 3:30 P.M. we crossed the Arctic Circle. For me, there was only one word that suited the occasion: blimey!

An aircraft hangar broke the even line of the horizon. Banking overhead, we saw the rabbit ears of a nearby DEW line station.

"Welcome to Shepherd Bay," said John Sheldon, a short, stocky man in charge of this station. The five-minute truck ride to the living quarters did little to kill my initial impression of utter bleakness. After food and a shower, I went to bed early. Some of the crew decided to go fishing, and at 1 A.M. their excited voices eased their way under my door.

"Arctic char . . . Caught twelve. . . . Fish so hungry we had to hide behind a rock to bait our line."

I dreamt of mermaids.

The morning weather briefing was held in the pool room, with maps scattered over the table. As far as I could make out, we were heading for the middle right-hand pocket. Resolute Bay was the next stop and we decided to get away after lunch.

Both planes stared down the runway to take up their positions for take-off, then Holoduke said he could hear something squeaking. He should have sat where I was. I had heard nothing but squeaking since we left Churchill. We relayed the news of the squeak to the other plane.

"No sweat," said Richardson. And to prove it he took off . . . in the other plane. We tried applying full power. Nothing. Holoduke had an instruction book in his hand. Not for the first time, I wondered what was I doing there. Fifteen hundred miles from civilization and stuck with a lawyer and a lighting consultant. The trouble was a broken cable housing. Carmichael fixed it with tape.

"It's not as if we're driving to the local malt shop, Carmichael," I said.

"Don't worry, Mr. Wicks, everything will be fine now."

I closed my eyes and placed my hands together as we took off, heading north.

Beneath us a vast, uninhabited world of ice creaked and ground its way between the islands of the Arctic. As our aircraft banked, we could see hundreds of walrus lining crevices in the ice as they patiently waited for fish. Old heads leaned back and gazed up unperturbed at our winged intrusion of their magic world of peace and beauty.

Resolute lay ahead. Along the shoreline birds glided above a distant village. Landing was no problem and, as we headed to the lone hotel, I realized how good it was to walk instead of fly. Inuit families were crouching in the hotel's corridors, waiting for a movie to begin. Their village was two miles down the road, and my chance remark that I would like to visit their homes found a willing driver.

Our truck followed the hydro lines along a dusty road as the ever-present dogs barked in the evening air. Levi, a friendly bowlegged Inuit, invited us into his home. Tables, chairs and an old black stove filled the living room. Children ran to hide their giggling faces as Johnny, a twelve-year-old, told me how much he enjoyed his school. He was extremely bright, and I was not surprised to hear that he topped his class of fifty-five students.

Outside, the rotting remains of seals and whales lay on the shore. The Inuit had lost too many of his garbage collectors, the sled dog, and the snowmobile was no substitute when it came to dealing with carcasses. A light breeze from shore scattered litter along the crevices in the ice. Strange how ugly the smallest piece of paper becomes in the wilderness.

Late that morning our two shaky planes climbed into a clear blue sky and headed for Eureka. For the first time I began to feel that maybe these crazy flyers would make it.

But soon enough, the crackle from the earphones warned, "Close up! We're going into some fog. Close up. . . ."

"Are you receiving?" Richardson's voice from the other aircraft hit an irritating pitch.

Why didn't we answer? Something was wrong! Holoduke's and Rohmer's hands were flying everywhere. "Check the fuses," said Holoduke.

"Okay," answered Rohmer. "Push button to check battery . . . less than half . . ."

"Close up. Are you closing up? What the hell's going on over there? We're going into fog."

"Turn starboard eighty per cent. Last ditch effort to make contact. . . . Got it!" Holoduke found the trouble. A small switch under a seat had been accidentally tripped.

As soon as we cleared the fog, our planes flew together once more, each happy to find the other nearby. The Eureka weather-station waved us in among its small collection of huts. We were there! Six part-time flyers had punched and kicked two tiny

planes to the top of the world. "Welcome to Eureka," read the
sign. "Population: Not Many."

For Rohmer's purposes, the trip was a great success. The
Globe and Mail was happy to print the story and the CBC followed through with a half-hour television program. I had also
made a new friend, a decorated pilot and wonderful Canadian.

Earlier that year an opportunity to do a great interview had
fallen into my lap. "Weekend" wanted to know if I would interview Liza Minelli. She was arriving in Toronto the day after the
Academy Awards, where she had been nominated in the best
actress category. "Weekend" told her agent that it was the most
important current-affairs program in Canada and was interested
in doing an interview, but only if no other media were present.

Minelli won her Oscar. We watched the Academy Awards
and cheered as our exclusive guest stepped up to receive her
award. Her arrival in Toronto was a picture-taking event with
no interviews. Minelli went straight to her hotel.

"Weekend's" producer Ian Brimes arranged to film the interview at her hotel, and three hours before the agreed time we
busied ourselves setting up. First one and then another reporter
slid into the room. By six o'clock the room was packed with
media. So much for an exclusive.

An hour past our interview time, Minelli had still not
arrived, and everyone was restless. I was on my tenth cup of
coffee when Ian decided enough was enough. He would find
out what the hell was going on.

He returned with news. Minelli would agree to be interviewed only if her travelling companion, Desi Arnez, Jr., would
be included. I agreed. What the hell. We waited . . . and waited.
Ian went off again. More news. Yes, Liza would do the interview, but only if we agreed to ask Desi the same number of
questions.

The interview was a disaster. I smiled and asked inane questions that Liza and Desi answered just as inanely. It never made

the air, but every question and answer did make the morning papers. The dozens of journalists in the room taping the interview made sure of that.

Despite this flop, I was sure that a series of programs could be built around the style of interview I was filming for "Weekend." I approached the CBC with my idea and was turned down. Then I arranged to meet with John Ross, a brilliant independent producer, and explained to him the simple format of "The World of Wicks." Each week three interviews would be shown during a half-hour. John and I agreed that most viewers were sick of seeing the endless parade of stars flickering across their screens giving the same kind of boring chat. Surely there were other people in the world with more fascinating lives. These, it was agreed, would be our target.

First we needed to make a pilot. As he worked independently and did not have the vast sums of money that were available to the CBC, John rented a cameraman for the day and acted as his own soundman. We set out for Yonge Street in Toronto, certain that this was where we would find the kind of people we wanted to interview.

One strip joint seemed perfect. Someone with the largest bust in the world was performing inside. After taking a few notes from the poster material outside, we started shooting. I faced the camera and, with John holding an outstretched mike, began to welcome viewers to "The World of Wicks." After thirty seconds of nonsense about the wonderful performer we were about to meet, I turned and pretended to vanish into the theatre.

After three hours walking the streets of Toronto, we had enough material to return to John's office. Happy with what we had accomplished, we began to set out phase two of our new show. We agreed that the three interviews would consist of fascinating unknowns. Rarely would a star be included, but those that were would be major. Although I would need research material before interviewing any major star, the strength of the other interviews would be in their casual approach – just stop, chat and see what happened.

John agreed that my experience as a cartoonist would prove invaluable. Fellini was a great cartoonist and Hitchcock would draw hundreds of thumbnail sketches before filming a movie. The famous shower scene from *Psycho* involved more than seventy drawings. Although I am not comparing myself with these great filmmakers, I shared in common with them the fact that I had been successfully drawing small one-act plays for years. John and I felt we had the makings of a perfect team: a producer and cartoonist who, without the help of the CBC or government funds, could make a successful television show. We would tour the world and film the people we met. This would give the viewer the opportunity of travelling outside the confines of Canada to meet some of the thousands of characters that share our planet. Travel, we were sure, would be no problem. Most countries were anxious to have a film group visit and show what they had to offer potential tourists.

The Global Television Network was the new kid on the block and was ready to back any bright new ideas. They had succeeded in acquiring a television licence and were looking desperately for Canadian programming before going to air. They were also prepared to make decisions. No endless committee meetings or "We'll get back to you." One look at our rough pilot and that was it. "We love it. We'll take it." They agreed to buy thirteen half-hours of "The World of Wicks."

Another chapter in my life was starting, one that would occupy much of my time for the next three years. My new career dictated that I be out of the country for ten days each month, and, once again, the burden fell on Doreen. Although she gave me her support, we were both unhappy that I would be away from the children so much.

John and I decided that our initial filming of characters of the world should take place in London. Finding these people would require the help of an excellent researcher. We found her in Fiona Barrington, a tall, attractive Canadian with a constant smile. She had never arranged interviews before, but she was bright and had a determination that appealed to John and me. We instructed her to head for London and line up fourteen interviews.

"Oh, and one other thing, Fiona," I called out as she was about to leave the office. "I hear David Niven is filming in London. He should be good. He certainly falls into our category of major stars only."

She grinned, no doubt biting her tongue at the same time. Yet when we arrived, she had done a superb job. A whole slew of fascinating people, including Niven, were willing to talk to us.

In addition to the people we needed in front of the camera, we needed a British camera crew. Anxious to keep our filming costs to a minimum, we had decided to use as few people as possible. Unfortunately, this was frowned upon in unionized Britain, and on our first day of shooting we found a crew of five waiting at our hotel. We were dismayed by the costs, but soon forgot the seamier side of the business and enjoyed their company.

It seemed the whole first week was a series of infectious laughs. Our first stop was at a studio where David Niven was making a film. The setting was the inside of a castle. Since Niven was in the middle of shooting a scene, we quietly set up in the castle's large dining room and stared through a doorway at the action taking place in the bedroom. Niven was leaning across a bed occupied by a gorgeous female. Dressed as a vampire, he was about to sink his teeth into her neck. As soon as they finished the scene, Niven came strolling across the set.

"Hi, Cyril," he said to the soundman.

"'Ello David," said Cyril.

Obviously our soundman had been around. We sat around

the ornate dining table and laughed our way through the endless tales of this master storyteller. If this was the way all our interviews were going to go, then I for one would think about paying Global for time on the job.

As happy as we were with the David Niven piece, John and I reminded ourselves that there were a million other interesting people in Britain whom we could lure in front of the cameras. We were right. Fiona had made arrangements for us to interview all kinds of characters, the kind of people who appear at every turn in Britain. After a quick look through the *Guinness Book of World Records*, our researcher had discovered one such person living in a village in Oxfordshire.

Raymond Cantwell was a champion and he knew it. The friendly nods of the locals told him that as we strolled with him through the village to the post office. It was the obvious place to discuss his title. You want to interview a boxer? Go to a gym. A swimmer? Go to a pool. The letter-writing champion of the world? Go to the post office.

The picturesque village was right out of a British calendar, with a rustic bridge across a stream flowing past the church and graveyard.

"That's the dead centre of town," Raymond laughed. It was an old gag, but I laughed along with him. He was a happy man, the kind of person who makes instant friends.

"How did you get into the letter-writing game, Raymond?"

"I don't know. As early as I can remember, I wanted to put the world straight. One day I started writing to newspapers complaining about this and that. From there I started to think about the people I felt could do something about changing it. So I began writing to them."

"Now the *Guinness Book of World Records* says you're the letter-writing champion of the world. How many letters have you written, do you think?"

He held up the thick wad of letters he was carrying. "With these here, it will make 22,022."

"When did you write those?"

"This morning."

"But it's only nine o'clock. How many are there?"

"Eighteen. I got up early, since I knew you were coming." He took my arm. "We cross here. The post office is on the other side. Watch the traffic." We both laughed as a lone cyclist pedalled by. I liked this man.

We opened the door to the shop and overhead a small cowbell jangled, announcing our entrance.

"I want you to meet one of my best friends." Standing behind the counter was a man with a ruddy face and big grin. He held out a hand.

"This is Dennis," said Raymond, "the village postmaster."

"I'm pleased to meet you," said Dennis.

"This is Ben Wicks, Dennis, and he's come all the way from Canada to do an interview with me."

Dennis looked startled. "Do you want me to leave?"

"No, I want you to stay. I have some questions for you as well."

Dennis looked even more startled. "Shall I close the shop while you do it, Mr. Wicks?"

Raymond leaned across the counter and laughed. "It's for a Canadian television show, not the *News of the World*." We all laughed as he mentioned the famous racy Sunday newspaper.

As we waited for the camera crew to set up their equipment, the cowbell jangled again. An old lady closed the door behind her and came to the counter. I smiled and was soon into a friendly conversation. I was struck by her quick wit and twinkling eyes and was sure that a few minutes with her would be well worthwhile. As she left I asked Fiona to follow her and talk with her more. At last we were ready for the interview.

"Raymond tells me that you're the greatest postmaster in the world."

Dennis grinned. "According to Raymond, if you give him good service, you're a champion."

"How many letters do you write a day, Raymond?"

"Oh, I don't know. I reckon I go through about a hundred and fifty."

"When do you write?"

"Usually in the evenings. I get home from work about six. The missus has the supper on the table, and by seven I'm ready to make a start."

Dennis made neat piles of the new letters and began licking stamps.

"Now, who do you write to?"

"The newspapers, mostly."

"About what?"

"About anything."

"Who else gets your letters?"

"The Prime Minister gets one from me twice a month."

"Anyone else?"

"I write to the Queen regularly."

"That's good. What does she say?"

"It's from her private secretary. He says, 'I've been commanded by Her Majesty the Queen to acknowledge receipt of Mr. Cantwell's letter.'"

"Oh, not exactly the kind of letter to strike up a friendship. What do you think is the nicest letter you've ever received?"

"Well, I've had so many . . ." He leaned on the counter and looked towards the ceiling. "I can tell you the nastiest I've ever had."

"Fine, tell me about that."

"Well, I'd written a letter to the *Oxford Mail*. I forget what it was about, but somebody didn't like it. There was a ring at my

front door and a man stood there. 'Mr. Cantwell?' he says. 'Yes,'
I says. 'I've brought your manure,' he says."

"Manure? In an envelope?"

"No, in a lorry."

"What did you do?"

"What could I do? He'd already dumped it outside. We had a
good laugh about that, I can tell you."

"You and the wife?"

"No, me and the boys. The wife had to help me clean it up.
She wasn't too happy." He glanced at his watch, obviously
worried about the post.

"Well, I won't hold you up anymore, Raymond." I turned to
Dennis. "Is he still okay for the next mailing, Dennis?"

"He's fine."

We gathered up the newly stamped envelopes and went
outside to the mailbox.

"I enjoyed meeting you, Ben. Maybe I'll see you in Canada
some day if I ever decide on a visit."

"Sure, do that, Raymond. But just one thing. Write me a
letter first."

Fiona returned to the shop to tell us that the woman we were
interested in lived close by. I suggested that we bring her to the
centre of the High Street, where, with cameras rolling, we
would meet and strike up a casual conversation. She agreed. I
began my walk towards her. As she approached I was sure that
my idea had been a good one. She was the archetypal village
senior out to do her morning shopping.

"Good morning," I said and stopped to begin our chat. As a
handheld camera circled us, she talked and talked . . . and talked
. . . and talked. I asked her what she enjoyed most of all.

"Bingo. I loves me bingo. Can't get enough of it." She
switched her basket to her other arm and rested her free hand on
my arm.

"Have won a few times, too," she boasted.

"What else do you enjoy," I asked.

"Singing. I love to sing. Do it all the time down at the village hall on club nights."

"Do you have a favourite song?"

"'Roll a Silver Dollar,' that's my favourite."

"Would you like to sing a few bars for Canada?" I asked.

"Certainly." She placed her basket on the ground and adopted the position of an operatic star about to perform at Carnegie Hall.

"You can roll a silver dollar, down upon the ground and it will roll, roll, roll, and it will roll, roll, roll. . . ."

Neither the cameras nor the fact that she was singing on High Street seemed to give her the slightest concern as on and on she went. After four choruses I touched her arm.

"That was wonderful and I'd —"

". . . and listen to me, you will see that it will roll, roll, roll and it will roll, roll, roll. . . ."

"That was lovely. Thank you so mu —"

"So, you can roll a silver dollar. . . ."

I didn't know that song had so many verses. The camera continued to roll as she sang on and on. Fearing that we were in danger of using up a week's worth of film, I was finally forced to command in a loud voice, "CUT!" It did the trick. Our lover of music and silver dollars was also a film fan, and she instantly recognized the signal that her scene was over.

On the drive back to London I marvelled once more at this remarkable country that hid within its folds all kinds of warm, kind eccentrics. All that was needed was a smile to bring it all to the surface.

On the weekend John suggested that we head for Hyde Park and Speakers' Corner. This renowned landmark would surely give us the interview we were looking for.

The most famous meeting place in the world was going at

full blast as the various orators delivered their speeches and, in return, got some of the wittiest verbal abuse in the world. It was cold and damp as our miserable crew prepared to film the crowd around the soapboxes. I noticed that most of the men shouting and screaming from the boxes were black. I turned to John and protested. Although I was quite prepared to hassle and shout from a crowd at some "nut" on a box with strange ideas on where the world should be headed, I did not want to be seen as a goofy onlooker with racist tendencies.

John's eyes took on the sparkle that I had by now learned to recognize as trouble. "No problem. We'll get our own box."

"And?"

"And you can get up on it and deliver a speech."

The brief discussion that ensued was heated, but I knew that John was right. We were thousands of miles away from home to do a job. We were paying a full camera crew to shoot something.

John pointed to a corner of the park. "Ask that kid over there."

He stood off to one side, one foot resting on a large, empty wooden box.

"Wanna borrow a box, mister? Only a quid."

I'd always harboured a secret yearning to deliver a speech – to witness the roar of the crowd, to experience the screams of adulation, to bang a fist on the rostrum and hear the chants of a million people as they scream, "Wicks, Wicks, Wicks."

"I'll take it," I blurted out and handed over the one-pound note.

"Don't ferget ta bring it back in an hour."

There were five speakers, well spread out to avoid the mixing of the various audiences. The largest crowd had gathered around an old man who was advocating that all meat in England be banned since it was, by his thinking, the cause of a dangerous upsurge in crimes of passion. Obviously sex as a topic was a guaranteed winner.

I picked a spot and stepped up on the box. My lips were

suddenly dry. A recent survey had found that, of all human fears, number one was public speaking. I could believe it. I was glad of the rolled-up umbrella that I was carrying. At least it gave me something to do with my hands. But how to attract the crowd who were quite happy listening to others? I took a deep breath and pointed the rolled-up umbrella at the camera crew.

"... And another thing. I'm sick of you television people following me around everywhere," I shouted.

At the mention of television cameras, heads began to turn. Encouraged, I poked the umbrella into the air. "You probably think I'm going to reveal more sex scandals going on in Downing Street. Well, I ain't!" I screamed.

The heads that had turned now began to converge on me, anxious to hear a revealing story about Margaret Thatcher and an unknown lover. Within minutes a crowd had surrounded the box, including two policemen. One had a notebook drawn. Obviously, to continue with the sex in Downing Street speech could mean trouble. I tried a new direction.

"I am from a distant island that shall remain nameless," I shouted.

"Then go back there!" screamed a red-nosed character, a typical Cockney with a stud in his shirt and no collar.

I ignored the remark and continued above the laughter. "I have come to England because our island has been hit with a terrible tragedy."

"I would like to fink so if they've go' more like you livin' there," yelled Red Nose. Once more the crowd burst into laughter.

"Our island has been hit by the pill," I shouted.

A peculiar hush descended on the crowd. Even Red Nose was silent.

"This terrible invention of man has left us short of children."

"You're bleedin' lucky then, mate!" screamed Red Nose, obviously "blessed" with a large family.

"We have now banned the use of the pill, but too late we've found ourselves short of men who can help us rebuild the population."

A tall, skinny, well-dressed matron called out, "What are you trying to say, my good man?"

"I am trying to say that we have an abundance of lovely young girls, but a shortage of young men, mainly caused by a recent war with a nearby island."

"So?" shouted Red Nose.

"So, we need volunteers who will come to my island and breed with selected island maidens."

"Where is this island?" yelled Red Nose, obviously eager to sign up.

"I'm not telling you," I screamed, "because you're just the sort we don't need." The crowd roared with laughter and Red Nose's face took on the colour of his beak.

"Wot's wrong wiv me?" he screamed.

I pointed the umbrella down towards him. "You, sir, are English, and we don't need the likes of you." A quick rumble of dissent went through the crowd. I ignored it and carried on. "As part of my world tour," I yelled, "I have been in England for six days and I can safely say that never have I seen such a lazy, scrounging crowd of welfare bums in my life."

Boos, shouts and angry fists waved in the air as the crowd became ugly. Soon the box began to rock, as those in front of me were pushed by those at the back.

"Who in the 'ell do you fink you are?" screamed Red Nose.

"Get the bleeder down," shouted a pimple-faced youth.

"Shut yer mouth." A redhead waved her fist. As I called for order, a sudden shove from behind forced me off the box. Up jumped Red Nose to take my place.

"Are we a lazy lot of bums?" he screamed.

"No!" yelled the crowd.

"Let's 'ave a vote," shouted Red Nose. A roar of approval

went up. "Up on the box, you!" Red Nose glared down at me, and I was quickly lifted back on the box beside him. Red Nose lifted his hands for order.

"All those who are for this bloke and 'is island, 'ands up." I shot my hand into the air. Red Nose shoved his face into mine. "Not you. You ain't allowed to vote." I slowly lowered my hand, the only one in the air.

Red Nose turned to the crowd. "All those fer England?" The roar and the show of hands would have done justice to a balcony appearance by the Royal Family.

"I demand a recount," I shouted.

Red Nose turned and screamed in my ear. "You trying ta be bleedin' funny?"

"No!" I yelled back. "There's a man here who hasn't voted." I pointed to an unshaven man who stood silent in the front row. Red Nose looked down at him and screamed, "How do you vote?"

"I has a question," the old man shouted back.

"Are you voting or ain't yer?" screamed Red Nose.

"I has a question," shouted the old man.

"All right," yelled Red Nose. "Ask yer bleedin' question." The crowd went strangely quiet as the old man took a deep breath and placed his hands behind his back.

"Do you believe in sex after death?" A roar of laughter went up from the crowd. I looked down as I felt a slight tug at my trousers.

"Yer time's up, guv." The boy had one hand on his box.

I stepped down and pushed my way through the large crowd. As I passed two policeman I overheard one ask, "So who's the new nutcase this week?"

11

WE WERE FAST APPROACHING "The World of Wicks" deadline and, although we had plenty of interviews "in the can," we needed plenty more.

John and I had decided that each of the three interviews in the half-hour program should be from different parts of the world. Although this meant more travel, it made our programs unique. Since time was running short, we agreed that a trip to New York would not only prove fruitful, but also keep our travel costs to a minimum.

Once again Fiona went ahead to arrange the interviews. But this was not Britain. Although New York had its share of interesting characters, it was much harder to hunt them out. Then it occurred to us that although the city was full of skyscrapers, no one had ever taken the trouble to interview those whose job it was to keep the windows of these giant towers clean.

So it was that in the early hours of a dull, grey Monday morning we made our way to an office on the eighty-fourth floor of the Empire State Building. Few New Yorkers were bothering to look up. If they had, they would have seen a grinning window cleaner leaning half in and half out of an open office window. Inside, a television producer was busy organizing his camera crew.

"Okay, Ben, you step outside with the window cleaner and I'll get the camera fixed in the office above, so that we can get a good shot down on both your hands."

"Are you aware that we're eighty-four floors up?"

"Sure, sure, but you were a window cleaner once. Think of it as just another set of windows to be cleaned."

The window cleaner leaned out with his back against the open sky and tugged on his safety belt, checking that it was firmly locked in place. He smiled into the room as he watched the arrangements being made to put him on television for the first time.

"You know, I've never done this before," he said in a broad Brooklyn accent through the open window.

"Not to worry, you'll be fine." I smiled and leaned across the window ledge to get some idea of where I'd be standing. It was a very long way down. Thousands of ants below had heard a siren and were now crossing the street to where an ambulance and police car had stopped. In a few minutes I would be standing high above them. Would they suddenly begin to point and shout "Don't jump!" as I'd seen in countless movies?

My thoughts were suddenly interrupted by the producer. Would I go up to the office directly above? It seemed the camera-man there had taken one look through the lens at the street below and become dizzy. I followed them upstairs and fixed the camera into a position that would film our heads once we started the interview. We were ready to begin.

I was fixing the safety belt onto the sides of the window ledge when the superintendent of the building entered the room.

"Do you have insurance?" he asked. Not a very happy question when you are about to climb out on a window ledge of the eighty-fourth floor of the Empire State Building.

"I'm afraid not," I answered.

"No insurance, no safety belt." He took the belt from my hands and left the office.

"Well, that's that." I turned to the producer, who was continuing to prepare for the interview.

"No problem. We'll do it without his stupid old belt."

"*We* will?" I grimaced. "Who's the *we*?"

"Look, Ben, if we do the interview inside, it's boring. But you outside . . . now that's an interview."

I climbed out and stood on the ledge with our window cleaner friend. Fiona held my legs from inside the office. I was trembling, but carried on with the interview.

"Have you ever dropped anything?"

"Oh, sure. Once dropped a brush."

I looked at the heavy wooden brush he was using to clean the window. "Hit anyone?"

"Who knows? From this height it just went straight out somewhere out there." He released one hand and pointed across the city.

"Anyone ever drop things on you?"

"Oh, sure. Once had a window thrown open and someone threw a pail of filthy water all over me." He began to laugh.

"You love your job?"

"You kidding? I wouldn't do anything else."

We finished filming and made our way out of the building. I looked up at the small dot sloshing water on a window. Passersby stopped and began to look up, searching for something unusual. What they missed was a rarity. A happy man on top of the world.

Back at the *Globe and Mail*, it was drawing-board time once again. As a syndicated cartoonist, it was necessary for me to cover myself for any trips. This I did by preparing my work way ahead of time.

Since my story on the Arctic had appeared in the *Globe*, a few public-relations companies had offered me free trips in the hopes that my articles would encourage tourism. The reason for these all-expenses paid trips is obvious. The PR agent needs a positive story, and most journalists are quite happy to supply this in order to be in line for the next freebie. It's the reason Canadian newspapers' travel sections are full of wonderful stories. Few are going to bite the hand that feeds them. This is not to imply that I am against such free trips. I have once, or maybe twice, taken one myself.

One such invitation arrived by way of a phone call from Air Canada. Would I care to go to Los Angeles with a few journalists and politicians? The airline was anxious to promote the fact that it would now be making direct flights between Toronto and Los Angeles. Being an honourable man, I promised I would think about it. I thought about it.

The plane was full. The president of Air Canada told funny stories to the press sitting in the back as our merry band took off. The flight attendants served us champagne and caviar to ease the pain we all felt at leaving Canada in the dead of winter and heading for the sun. They also gave us press kits. I immediately placed mine under the seat for safe keeping.

When our plane arrived, a lone piper played as we made our way down the steps. Some of the journalists found it difficult to walk after enduring the in-flight hospitality and were convinced that the aircraft had yet to come to a stop. After a short welcoming speech from the mayor of Los Angeles, we were herded onto buses and whisked away to a luncheon held in our honour. More drinks and a boring speech followed and then we visited two Hollywood studios, saw the feet and hand imprints of the stars in front of Grauman's Chinese Theater and met at least three movie actors (since they were Canadian, no one in our group had the faintest idea who they were).

It was 6 P.M. before we finally saw our hotel (this hardly mattered, since more and more of our travelling group had difficulty seeing anything). When our bus stopped outside, half of its occupants were asleep. We staggered off and formed a group in the lobby.

A young woman welcomed us. "I'm sure you've had a hard day and will be anxious to get to your rooms. Everyone nodded. "Before I assign them, I would like to mention that we have set aside a hospitality suite for your . . ."

She got no further. It was, without a doubt, the fastest movement I have ever seen from a team of journalists. The same group who had ignored the mayor's welcoming speech, the same group who had listened with glazed eyes as "fascinating" stories had been told at lunch, the same group who had worn bored expressions during the tours of the movie studios, were now ready to give it their all. Pads and pencils appeared as if by magic, as the gallant reporters stood ready to receive vital information.

"The number of the hospitality room is . . ." She gave a number.

Those fortunate enough to be at the front and within earshot took off in a cloud of dust. Not me. I was ready to do my duty with the remaining dedicated journalists and ask my first question.

"Er, excuse me, Miss. What was the number of that room again?"

John Ross eagerly awaited my return to Toronto. There was filming to be done and where better to do it than Hollywood? With a mass of stars just waiting for the kind of publicity we had to offer, it would be a cinch. I headed back south.

"So what happened to the ordinary folk of the world?" I asked John, settling into my seat on the plane.

"If you mean the nutcases, we're heading for their headquarters."

John was right. We entered a world that was difficult to distinguish from a Disney theme park.

Fortunately, I was syndicated by the *Los Angeles Times* and so was able to introduce myself to the editor. I told him that I was looking for characters who may be a little unusual. He was right on the money with his first suggestion.

Joseph lived downtown. A tall, thin man, he was proud of his area of the city, so proud in fact that for eight hours a day he pushed a shopping cart around the block, picking up litter.

Since he wore women's clothes and high-heeled shoes, he was easy to spot. A half-hour with him proved to be an absolute joy. This kind man, who had often been beaten by louts, answered my question of why he wore women's clothes in a completely rational way.

"They're cool." Then with a twinkle in his eye, he added, "And anyway I like women, but I love my men."

An old friend who wouldn't know me from a hole in the ground was filming just out of town. The prospect of another interview with Michael Caine would, I knew, develop into a nostalgic one for us both. (I had interviewed him in London a few years earlier.)

"In fact, my best friend lived in the buildings where you grew up." Caine leaned across the table in the trailer. "We were sixteen at the time. He was an absolute master with the women. Whenever we would see two women, his first remark was, 'I don't think much of the looks of your one.' And he was right. I always ended up with the unattractive girl. When I read the script for *Alfie*, I immediately thought of him and played the same character."

It was 2:30 A.M. and he was making a movie in the middle of California. The bustle of a film crew in action outside could just be heard. It was hot, yet inside the large trailer it was cool. I remarked on this.

"Yes, it's very nice. It belonged to John Wayne. Unfortunately, we're just borrowing it during the making of the movie."

I smiled and said, "Now we're from the same background.

The only difference is that you've made a bundle. Has it changed your politics?"

"Well, I suppose I've always been emotionally a socialist, which, I suppose, goes back to where I grew up. But I've never voted. I have never voted in my life." He leaned forward. "I have never seen even the still photograph, or a moving one for that matter, of a politician that I would vote for. I don't trust any of them."

"Why is that?"

"Like you, I grew up in a working-class area. Everyone lied to us – the politicians, the church – and I figured very early in life that if I was going to do anything with myself, I was going to have to do it myself. It was no good relying on anyone else. So, I've spent my whole life just running my own life and family, as it were."

"How did you get out? How did you get over the wall?"

"I got out by answering an advertisement in the newspaper. It was for what is known as a repertory company in the Midlands. You know, the acting companies that tour Britain. At the time I was earning eleven pounds a week in the meat market, and I took a cut. So, from what would be twenty-two dollars, I went down to eight dollars a week to become a stage manager in a theatre company and to play little parts on the side. I would earn eventually not much more that I would earn in a factory, but my gain would be happiness."

"Now has that carried on now that you're a rich actor? I mean, are you as happy as you thought you might be?"

"Oh, my God. Never believe anyone that says to you that money won't bring happiness. It's brought me joy beyond belief."

"So, that's what's wrong with my life." We both laughed.

He pushed his famous glasses up on the bridge of his nose. "You know, I read those stories that appear in these magazines about money not meaning anything. That's true to a point.

Money doesn't mean everything. I am happy because I have a wonderful family. But, you see, money has helped to make my family happy. I can do things for them. But I should emphasize that I never became an actor to make money. I became an actor in order to be happy. But a lot of the money I've made being an actor has made me a much happier person."

"One thing that I've always wondered about. You have a job where you make love to some of the most beautiful women in the world, right? In some cases you undress and get into bed with them."

"Don't believe everything you see."

"Okay, but you get into bed with them and go through the motions of making love. Now then, you get home. The wife says, 'Hello, darling. How was your day?' Do you say, 'Well, not bad. Spent most of it in bed with Sophia Loren.' How does she feel about that?"

He chuckled. "Well, she knows it's a job and, er . . ."

"Do you tell her you've been in bed with Sophia Loren?"

"If she asks, of course I do. Okay, she couldn't care two hoots. She knows that's what I'm getting paid for."

"Blimey, what a job."

He laughed again. "But I will tell you one thing. If I as much as take a sly look at a strange woman in a restaurant, then watch out."

It was early morning before John and I arrived back at the hotel. Despite this we were more than anxious to get to the next interview. Although Charlton Heston and I were a million miles apart on the political scene, I have rarely met a nicer person. We had decided to take full advantage of the city by setting up in a large home that overlooked Los Angeles. The star arrived on time, fit and tanned and sporting the broad grin so familiar to millions of movie fans.

I suggested that, rather than talk about films, we make the interview into something bordering on an event. How did he feel about arm wrestling as we chatted? We could continue to talk as each of us strained to get the better of the other. He loved the idea and immediately took on the role of director, suggesting the best angles to shoot the scene. It took more than an hour. Finally in position and ready to film, my camerawoman, Carol Betts, told us that she had a problem. Without hesitation, Heston dropped down on one knee and fixed the camera. The piece we shot turned out to be very funny. As we drove away I was reminded of the adage that the bigger the star, the nicer they are. In Mr. Heston's case, it was dead on.

Christmas was on its way and the school holiday would provide the time we needed to get away as a family. Although "The World of Wicks" trips were enjoyable, none could equal the fun of being away with Doreen and the kids. She suggested that we travel to St. Lucia, in the Caribbean. I leapt at the idea. The thought of building castles with the kids on a sandy beach was irresistible.

To this day I can close my eyes and see us racing down to the water and digging with a tiny wooden shovel. The shouts and screams as the tide slowly approached the castle still ring in my ears as we made a desperate effort to hold back the water with more and more sand. Joy beyond compare. Ah, yes, it's true. I shall remain a boy to my dying day.

It was a wonderful week that, for the first time, brought us in touch with the friendly people that inhabit the islands. Throughout our holiday, hotel waiters and cabdrivers continually invited us to visit their families. Like everyone else, they were immediately drawn to Doreen, who so genuinely cared about them.

One cabdriver who had taken us to a beautiful beach invited us to see a cockfight. Doreen was appalled.

"Surely that's illegal?"

"It is, ma'am, but it's just a sport. There's no harm done."

He should have told this to the cocks.

I had a different reaction than Doreen. I felt I had no alternative but to witness and write about a sport that I had never seen. It was agreed that early Sunday morning the cabdriver and I would set out together.

On the appointed day, the battered cab rattled over a crumbling road and panted its way up the hill. Behind us, Castries, the capital, yawned, stretched and squeezed a small group of figures into a church.

"Surely this being Sunday, no one will want to get involved in an illegal sport."

"Dey don't care if it's Easter Sunday, boss. Da cock fights go on." The driver's ebony face split in a wide grin. I could see why they called him Speak Easy.

"How much further to the village?"

"About five miles. We should be dere in half an hour."

We drove in silence through the lush growth of this incredibly beautiful island. The road ahead narrowed and wound its way through a small rainforest. The cab stopped. Speak Easy stepped out and approached a roadside barber, busy cutting a child's hair. They spoke patois. After a few minutes, Speak Easy returned.

"He says dat de other village has not arrived yet."

I looked around. A group of six dilapidated huts surrounded a small tin shed held together by Coke signs. A group of tattered locals stood in the doorway. A dozen cockerels, anchored by a string tied to a tree, pecked at the dirt. I began to wish I had stayed back at the hotel.

"When does he think the others will come?" I asked.

"Maybe half an hour. De other village have a four-hour drive. Dey left at six dis morning."

"Can we get a drink somewhere?"

He pointed to the shed. Now I understood the reason for its popularity.

"I'll buy. What will you have?" I looked to Speak Easy.

Before he could answer, the crowd in the room spoke with one voice.

"Johnnie Walker!"

The sound of an approaching truck quickly emptied the bar. As if suddenly liberated, the bar group, laughing and giggling, helped the rival team as they jumped from the truck. Each of the visitors had a cockerel under his arm. The dozen birds quickly joined their rivals at the hitching tree. Their owners made for the bar. The drinking over, the group made their way to a rough piece of ground ten feet by ten feet. Everyone began talking at once and pushing money into the hands of a tall, thin man who was taking the bets. The fight was about to begin.

"What are the names of the first two contestants?"

"Dr. Fu Man Chu and John Brown."

Two short men stood facing each other. Each had a cockerel under his right arm. The pushing and shoving of the crowd suddenly brought me face to face with Fu Man Chu. His owner grinned.

"You wanna place a bet?"

"I don't know. What's the usual?"

"Five St. Lucian dollars." That was two fifty Canadian.

"He doesn't look so hot."

"I sprayed him wid water." Water ran down the bird's beak.

"He's a tough old bird," said the owner.

"How old is he?" I asked.

"Seven years."

"Where's the red comb that should be on the top of his head?"

"I cut it off. You want John Brown to grab it in his beak?"

I certainly didn't. "Is he a good fighter?"

"Good? Sure he's good! How come you think he's still living after seven years?"

I patted his head. The cockerel, that is. He pecked me. A good sign, I felt. I bet five dollars Canadian.

"Fit the spurs!" Thin Man pocketed the bets and looked to the two contestants. Each owner took an ugly, six-inch needle-like nail from his pocket and fastened it to the leg of his cockerel. The cockerel's heads were smeared with oil.

Speak Easy whispered in my ear. "That's to protect their eyes from pecking. For some reason a cockerel will not peck at a shiny surface. He'll use only his spurred feet to attack."

Both birds were carried to the centre of the square and then thrown to the ground. Round one had begun. There was a mad flurry of feathers. Both birds locked. Round one was over. A quick spray of water was spat over each bird, and they were back at it.

"*Malinna comme ravet!*"

"What are they shouting?" I screamed above the din.

"Cunning fox," called Speak Easy over the yelling crowd.

"Who at?"

"John Brown's owner."

"Why?"

"He stepped on Fu Man Chu's foot."

"Time out!" shouted Thin Man. Round two had ended. Round three was on.

"Rip his heart out."

"Tear his neck to ribbons."

"Claw de stupid, cunning monkey to bits."

"Time!" shouted Thin Man. The birds were grabbed. Everyone was on his feet.

"What's happened?" I cried, trying to look over the heads of those in front.

"It's John Brown. He's in trouble."

I looked across at John Brown's corner. In trouble was right. John Brown's manager had a filthy penknife in his hand and was about to cut the bottom of John Brown's foot. A quick nick and the bird's foot went into the owner's mouth.

"He's gone mad," I screamed.

"No! No!" yelled Speak Easy. "He's trying to draw the blood from behind John Brown's eyes."

"Surely he's got the wrong end of the bird in his mouth?"

"Would you like to put John Brown's head in your mouth?"

The birds were thrown together again. Round four was a disaster for John Brown. Suddenly there was a large cheer. A smiling Speak Easy came back.

"Guess who won?"

I didn't hear his answer. I was too busy throwing up.

On my return to Toronto, there was little time to rest. More interviews were needed if we were to be ready for the opening program of "The World of Wicks." Fortunately for me, a hero was about to visit Toronto: Sir Edmund Hillary of Mount Everest fame.

I thought it would be fun to dress as a mountaineer and be filmed attempting to climb into his room on the twentieth floor of the Royal York Hotel. By tilting the camera down a corridor, it would give the impression of my climbing the face of a steep cliff.

Things went well, and by 2:55 P.M. we were outside his hotel door, just right for the 3 P.M. appointment. The plan was that I'd knock on his door and, when he opened it, film him and joke around as I presented him with a small Canadian flag (you had to be there). The elevator doors opened and a woman stepped out into the corridor. She looked surprised and began to step over the television cables as she made her way to her door, next to Sir Edmund's suite.

"I'm sorry for the inconvenience," I said, "but you see we're about to do an interview."

"Really," she turned. "Who with?"

"Well, it so happens that you are staying next door to a living legend," I answered, moving the ropes from around my chest. "Behind that door," I pointed down the corridor, "is Sir Edmund Hillary."

"Wow!" she smiled and hurried inside.

Right on the nose of 3 P.M., the producer lifted his finger. I took the flag, ready to push it forward, and gave a loud rap on the door. There were footsteps and suddenly the door opened. My mouth dropped and I slowly lowered the flag. The woman I'd left at the door of her suite stood there grinning.

"Come on in," said Lady Louise Hillary.

After being introduced to the crew, Sir Edmund immediately let it be known that he preferred we drop the "Sir" and call him by his first name. He then poured drinks for everyone, and the interview began. Although I'm sure it was a story he had told a million times, he related his experience of making it to the top of the world's highest mountain in the manner of a first telling.

I had decided to use his voice over the footage we had shot of my climbing up the hotel. It worked beautifully, and I remember fondly this wonderful couple who made it possible. I was upset to read a few months after this meeting that Lady Louise had been killed in a plane crash.

The summer of 1973 was glorious, and John and I decided to give our filming a rest for a few weeks. Doreen and I felt that the time had arrived for a trip back to our original Canadian home, Calgary. We decided to drive there in a recreational vehicle, and searched the Toronto newspapers for one to rent.

The Winnebago camper was new and, after promising to take good care of it, we waved goodbye to the owner and set off towards the west. It was a wonderful change from the last time we had attempted the twenty-one hundred mile journey. The kids loved it. They had lots of room to move around and best of all, a toilet. The miles just drifted away in the rearview mirror. Four days later we reached Calgary and immediately visited old friends.

After a few hours, anxious to get to Banff and the mountains, we set off once more. As we approached a bridge over the Bow River, I glanced at a sign warning that there was a height restriction for vehicles. I paid no attention to it. We had just made it onto the bridge when a grinding noise followed by a bang and shudder brought us to a halt. While the traffic slowly manoeuvred around us, I began to step out of our camper to find out what had caused us to stop. But I had not even opened the door when I noticed Doreen and the children pointing to a hole in the ceiling. I could see clear blue sky. The hole was where an air vent had previously been.

The good news was that we had made it past the first of the iron girders that crossed the bridge. The bad news was that there was another one on the other side. Fortunately that end of the bridge was far enough over land to allow me to leave the road, drive up onto a grassy bank and bypass the girder.

We arrived in Banff only to discover most of the campsites full. Eventually, we found a spot and, after much effort, parked the camper. We did not sleep that night for the simple reason that it rained, and most of our time was taken up passing pots and pans to each other in order to catch the water pouring through the hole.

By morning the rain had stopped and, after a good breakfast, we were ready to enjoy the awesome scenery of the Rockies. I began to reverse the Winnebago from the site. Although I had my foot to the floor, the camper refused to move. Convinced that the wheels must be caught on a large rock, Vincent and I got out and looked underneath. It was bad news. I had driven the vehicle up onto a tree stump. We were firmly stuck.

A fellow camper was kind enough to bring an axe and, after swinging and chopping whilst lying under the van, I eventually freed the vehicle. Unfortunately the stump had pierced the bottom of the Winnebago and taken away our toilet system. We now had a hole in the top *and* a hole in the bottom.

The owner was far from happy when I returned his "almost new" camper and insisted on keeping our $500 deposit. Considering the damage, I couldn't argue. I was only sorry that I had not taken a camera on the trip. The kind of holiday we had experienced would have been a perfect item for "The World of Wicks."

One American city John Ross and I felt sure would produce the kind of material that would fit our program was Las Vegas. We had read that Frank Sinatra was about to give one of his many farewell performances. Unfortunately John was too busy editing the film we had already shot and was unable to fly there with me.

Flush with the success of our previous interviews, I was sure that I could just push through the crowd, stick a mike up Sinatra's nose and have my interview. I hired a freelance crew in Las Vegas and, with a few hours to spare before show time, decided to stroll around the area. The hotel lobby was quiet. The bell captain yawned and turned a page of the newspaper he was reading.

"So you're a journalist? And what brings you to Vegas?"

"Sinatra. I'm hoping to get an interview."

He turned another page. "Borrrrring."

"You don't think Sinatra would make an interesting interview?"

"It ain't what I'd wanna watch on TV."

I leaned on the counter. "So what do you want to watch?"

"Me? I'd wanna watch stuff about da Cotton Tail Ranch."

"I don't do horse stories."

"I'm talking about goils."

"Girls at a ranch?"

"Da Cotton Tail is a brothel."

All thoughts of Sinatra suddenly disappeared.

"And how long would it take me to get to this ranch . . . if I was interested, that is?"

"About five hours. It's way out in the desert."

He was lying. With my crew it took four hours. A red light

turned slowly on the roof of the long trailer that hugged the side of the highway.

"What do you call a place like this?"

"This is a legal Nevada bordello." Beverly, the owner of the Cotton Tail Ranch, had the kind of eyelashes that could force a man to his knees.

"And how many girls do you have working here?"

"Six to eight who are on duty twenty-four hours a day."

"It's so remote out here, I'm surprised you do any business."

She laughed. "Good heavens, this is Route 95, the main highway from Las Vegas to Reno. Truckers pass here all day and night."

"Truckers are your customers?"

"Sure. They stop to take a break from driving."

"Hardly the kind of pit stop to freshen a driver."

"Many prefer it to coffee." She lifted her long dress out of the dust and began to walk towards the ranch. "We also have a lovely airstrip." She waved her arm towards the desert behind the ranch. "It's two miles long and can accommodate a Lear jet. In fact, just a few weeks ago we had a lovely gentleman who chartered a Lear jet in Calgary and spent a few days with us."

The sun began to fade behind the distant mountains as we went inside. The door had the kind of peephole I had only seen in gangster movies. A huge black woman opened the door and went back behind the bar. I missed her name. The room was full of Playboy centrefolds; I would have missed an elephant.

"Girls, this is Mr. Wicks. He's from Canada."

"Hiiiiii."

I nodded and tried to get back to what Bev was saying. She was offering me a quick tour of the place. I took it.

"We have six rooms, all complete with TV sets, as you can see."

"TV?" I asked, surprised.

"You'd be astonished at how many of our customers are sports fans."

"Married or single?"

"Many of our clients are married. Most of them want us to show them how they can make their partners happy. We show them how."

"It's really a school?"

"Exactly. And it's not just the men. Although all my girls are professionals, I hold classes for them also."

"Teaching them what?"

"The correct way to make a gentleman happy. Then he can go home and show his wife what he has learned here at the Cotton Tail."

"I couldn't help noticing a porcelain jug and basin in each room."

"We're very conscious of hygiene here. The gentleman holds the basin and the girls clean them. This is why the basin retains the same name it had back in the times of the old West."

"Which is?"

"The Peter Pan." Her lashes flickered as in an oldtime movie as she laughed.

Although the crew was anxious to stay longer I was just as anxious to get back to town. I watched as the crew packed their equipment into the back of the station wagon. I felt a slight tug at my sleeve.

"Thanks for coming, Ben. The promotion will be good for us."

"Anything to help," I answered.

"How about a free sample before you leave?" she waved her hand towards the grinning girls.

"Maybe another time, Bev."

12

LIFE AT HOME WAS WONDERFUL. Doreen had decided the kids were old enough that she could go back to work. She found a job working with children who had difficulty coping with life. It was perfect for Doreen. It required patience and a great deal of love of little ones, both of which Doreen has in abundance. Clara Will had become a close friend, and with Doreen as her assistant, the pair of them worked miracles each day.

Vincent was becoming interested in music. A series of tests at school had revealed that he had a good ear and his teacher suggested he should learn a string instrument. I was amused to find that those with a so-so ear were placed in band and those with no ear at all were sent to the singing section of the music class. Most important of all was the fact that Vincent enjoyed his music teacher, Mr. Green, and through him developed a lasting love of music.

Susan had also become interested in music, and one day I was delighted to watch her arrive home with a clarinet, my old instrument. She had also taken to swimming, and at every opportunity was in the nearby public pool with her friends. Since Susan was extremely creative Doreen tried to encourage her by organizing arts and crafts sessions in the house. Susan and her friends were not impressed and the idea was soon dropped.

Our youngest, Kim, was growing more independent every day. At age three, she loved playing on her own, setting up "house" with her dolls. When we put her into nursery school, she made it quite clear that she hated it and would much prefer being at home with her dolls. After a few weeks, however, she adjusted.

John and I still did not have a full thirteen shows for "The World of Wicks" so we decided I should go back to Los Angeles with camerawoman Carol Betts.

During the three days we spent in the city I was surprised to receive a phone call from renowned columnist Cecil Smith of the *Los Angeles Times*. He had heard I was in town and wanted to write a column on this strange little man who travelled the world looking for interesting people. Unfortunately we left town before we could read what he had written.

Back in Toronto plans were being made to celebrate Susan's thirteenth birthday. She had grown into a beautiful young lady with a crush on Donny Osmond. His records filled her room as did his posters and a special pillow with a picture of his face on it. It was not difficult to know what the perfect gift would be for this perfect daughter. Donny was coming to Toronto to perform at the Canadian National Exhibition. Doreen rushed to get the tickets for both Susan and her best friend and succeeded.

Since Osmond was, at this time, a mega-star, I suggested to John that we attempt to get an interview with him. Our researcher, Fiona, spent a whole morning around the grounds of the giant stadium with dozens of other reporters, but came back with bad news. Gino Empry, the Toronto agent who was handling the Osmond family's Canadian tour, had decided on a select group of media. We were not among them. I decided to visit there myself that afternoon. Somewhere on the grounds a trailer was being used by the family so they could relax close to where they were to perform. The police cordon around this trailer made it impossible to get within a hundred yards. I turned and strolled away. A bus that obviously had been put at their disposal was nearby. I walked over and stood talking to the man beside it. He was American, and after I introduced myself he remarked that he had read the story on me in the *Los Angeles Times*. I was thrilled and asked him in return what it was like to be the bus driver for the Osmonds. He laughed.

"I'm not the bus driver. I'm their manager."

I could not believe my good fortune, and told him that I had been denied an interview.

"How long do you need?"

"Half an hour."

"I'll give you ten minutes."

I rushed off to grab our cameraman and together we made our way to the trailer. After the interview I explained that Susan was a big fan and that it was her birthday. He suggested that she come back to the hotel after the concert to meet him.

Doreen was excited as I was at the news. We agreed to keep it from Susan and make it a birthday she would really remember.

After dropping off her friend on our way back from the concert, I explained to Susan that unfortunately something had come up, and I had to go to the Inn on the Park hotel for a quick business meeting. Would she mind coming along and waiting for me?

Although Empry and Osmond's manager had attempted to keep Donny's whereabouts a secret, the word was out. The lobby was packed with screaming teenagers. We pushed our way through to the elevator and, out of Susan's hearing, I explained to security that Osmond's manager was expecting me. He met us at the elevator and I introduced him to Susan, who was completely unaware of who he was. We sat in the corridor and waited. Suddenly Donny's mother appeared and, after a brief hello, walked on. Susan explained to me who the friendly woman was.

The door opened at the end of the corridor and along he came. Susan's mouth dropped. I was sure she was going to faint and kept a grip on her arm. He chatted to Susan for a few minutes and she asked for some photos to be taken. Then Donny left to join his family. He could not have been nicer. Susan still has those photos.

Susan had yet to speak to us. Finally the elevator door closed and out came words I shall never forget: "Dad, that was the greatest moment of my entire life."

In January 1974 the Global Television Network and "The World of Wicks" hit the airwaves. The program was a smash hit. Well, not exactly a smash, but the television reviewers seemed to like the show. "Based on this one sampling, it looked like the best and fastest moving interview show ever to hit town," said Jack Miller of the *Toronto Star.* "It may not be the top rated of the new Global shows," said James Bowden of the *Hamilton Spectator,* "but it's the most unusual." My own newspaper, the *Globe and Mail,* felt the interviews were contrived. I counted that as another good review.

Our bosses at Global were delighted. "Great," said John. "Let's get packing."

"Where are we going to this time?"

"Not 'we'," John replied. "You. I've got stuff to do back here. How about a return trip to Britain? You can use the same crew and, with the number of nutcases roaming the streets, finding characters shouldn't be difficult."

I arrived in London on a Sunday and planned to begin filming the next day. A story in the Sunday newspapers caught my eye. It was about one of the world's leading psychics, Rosemary Brown. For years Mrs. Brown had claimed that she was being visited by her best friend, Liszt, who had introduced her to other deceased composers. She would be a perfect interview for our show.

The crew I had hired was keen on doing the item and

quickly loaded the car with their equipment. Fortunately Mrs. Brown lived in London and within a half-hour we turned into a street of rowhousing in Wimbledon. My only worry was our soundman, Cyril. He was a constant joker, and I was concerned about how he would behave in the upcoming interview. To forestall any funny stuff, I gave him a brief lecture before we knocked on Mrs. Brown's door.

"Now I realize that the woman we're about to meet is a little unusual, but I would appreciate it if you conduct yourselves as you would in any home." I looked sternly at Cyril.

"Absolutely, guv. You're the boss, and if you wants us to behave, then behave you've got." The rest of the crew nodded their heads in agreement.

The door was opened by a woman in her late forties. Rosemary Brown invited us in and led the way upstairs. She lived in a rented flat with her daughter, who was at school. There were two main rooms: a small living room and an even smaller bedroom. I decided to do the interview in two parts. We would start the first section in the living room and finish the interview in the bedroom, at her upright piano.

Mrs. Brown leaned forward and poured tea into flowered cups. "I was seven when I first met Liszt. I woke early one morning and he was standing by my bed."

"What was he like?"

"A very old man."

"Did he say anything?"

"He told me that in this world he had been a composer, and that when he returned he would bring some music with him."

He certainly kept his word. Mrs. Brown had a huge library of music dictated to her from the spirit world.

Happy with part one, we moved to the bedroom. The room was too small for all of us, so Ron, our cameraman, filmed while standing on the bed. Cyril set his equipment down on the little landing outside. As he fixed the mikes we would use for the piano, I glanced at the music Mrs. Brown was working on. I was astonished. Most amateur composers and arrangers are careful when writing each note. Not so the professional. He or she will scribble in a fast, rough form that covers the manuscript. The music on the piano was as professional as I'd ever seen.

We were almost ready to start when Mrs. Brown entered the room with more tea. She sat down at the piano.

"How did you meet the other composers?"

"Liszt introduced me. He acted as an interpreter. His English is impeccable. More tea?"

"No thanks, Mrs. Brown. Tell me about the other composers."

"Like who?"

"Well, how about Beethoven?"

"A crusty old gentleman."

"Still deaf?"

"Not now."

"Chopin?"

She smiled. "See for yourself. He's just arrived . . . there beside you."

Ron spun his camera towards the empty space she was pointing at. This was getting ridiculous.

"Er, why is he paying you a visit today?"

"He knew you were coming and has written a special piece in your honour."

She placed the sheets of music on the stand of her piano.

"I'm afraid I'm not very good." She opened the music and set her fingers on the keys.

"If Chopin doesn't mind, I'm sure I don't." I smiled at her and flung a grin at Chopin.

She was right, she didn't play very well. I wondered what Chopin was thinking or whether he was still in the room. I took some music from the top of the piano. "What's this?"

"Oh, that. It's one I'm working on. Beethoven's Tenth."

"But he only wrote nine symphonies."

"I know. Isn't it exciting?"

It was. And eerie.

"Did you ever study music, Mrs. Brown?"

"Not really."

"So how did you start?"

"It was Liszt really. I was sick and resting at home one day and decided to sit at the piano. He suddenly appeared and began guiding my hands over the keys. After that he just kept coming back and bringing his friends with him."

I got up to leave.

"You sure you won't have another cup of tea?"

"No thanks, Mrs. Brown. But there is one thing you can tell me."

"And what's that?"

"Did you ever meet Schubert?"

"Naturally."

"And what about his Unfinished Symphony?"

"I finished it."

I was happy. It had been a good interview. Mrs. Brown went off to the kitchen to prepare more tea and I made my way out to the landing. Cyril squeezed past me to get into the bedroom to retrieve his mikes. Ron stood with his back to the piano, dismantling the camera. As Cyril left the room, he gently struck a few notes on the piano. Ron turned at the sound. There was no one there.

On the landing outside the room, Cyril and I started to listen to what we had recorded. Ron joined us. "Did you just play the piano?" he asked.

I was surprised. "Of course not. Mrs. Brown played the piano."

"How about you, Cyril?"

Cyril, primed for the question, answered. "Me? What are you, a bleedin' joker? 'Course I didn't play the piano. I got enough to do, ain't I?"

Ron was extremely quiet as he later sat in the pub staring at his beer.

"Wot you lookin' so bleedin' miserable for?" asked Cyril.

"Well, I know this is going to sound ridiculous, but something happened in Mrs. Brown's house."

"Like wot?" asked Cyril, a broad grin on his face.

"The piano played on its own."

"What are you talking about?"

Ron explained how he had stood in the empty room listening to the piano play. Cyril kidded Ron but gave him no explanation.

Years later at a party a friend told me he had been filming a story on grizzly bears and had used Ron as his cameraman.

"We were sitting around a fire one night, and Ron told us about the incredible thing that happened ten years ago when he was filming with you."

I had completely forgotten the incident and asked the journalist to explain.

"Well, Ron told us how you were filming this woman, and when she left the room, he stood astonished, watching the piano keys going up and down on their own."

The mind is a strange and wondrous instrument, and loves to elaborate.

This latest trip to London was turning up a real feast of characters. The newspapers were full of stories begging to be filmed. One that caught my eye was about a new art gallery that had opened a few days before. The Fake Art Shop was the brilliant idea of two students. Fed up after two years of art school, they had decided to go out on their own and paint pictures. The only difference was that the pictures they produced had already been painted before.

They would reproduce whatever you wanted. You want a Turner? Come back in four days. Need a copy of *The Sunflowers*? Come back tomorrow. Although they had only been open a few days, they were backed up with six weeks' worth of orders.

I strolled around their shop while they pointed out their copies of famous paintings. I could understand why the London *Sunday Times* had said it was impossible to tell which was the original without a chemical analysis.

"We work an inch at a time," said one of the entrepreneurs. "We start in the top left-hand part of the canvas and slowly work our way down."

I leaned towards a painting I recognized and read the familiar signature: "Picasso."

"Big demand for Pablo?"

He smiled. "Sure, and the best part about it is that he's easy. It's the older stuff that gets a little tough."

I thought about paintings by forgers who have tricked the experts. "Any problems with the law?" I asked.

"We're not breaking the law. As you can see by our sign, we're the Fake Art Shop. The only problem we did have was with the neighbours. They were hoping it was going to be a fish shop."

I made my way to the cash register.

"Would you care to order something before you leave, Mr. Wicks?" He took out a pen and pad.

"Well, I wouldn't mind a little *Mona Lisa*, if that's okay."

"With or without the smile?"

I was relaxing in my hotel room when a phone call from Cyril alerted me to a story.

"It's perfect, Ben. Fiona Richmond is just back from her world tour."

"Great. Who's Fiona Richmond?"

"A British actress and . . ."

I began to yawn. "Yes, that's interesting, Cyril. Why don't we discuss it in the morning?"

"You don't understand, Ben. Fiona is a pinup as well as an

actress. She was at a party and met the publisher of a well-known British men's magazine. Fiona suggested it would be a good idea if she went around the world and experienced the act of love-making with fifty men from fifty different countries and grade them. He thought it was a great idea, and that's what happened."

Cyril had seen the story in the *Daily Mirror* under the head-line, "ROUND THE WORLD IN FIFTY LAYS." I made a quick call to friends at the paper to confirm the story and, even more impor-tant, to get Fiona's phone number.

"I'd love to see you and your camera crew," answered Fiona's husky voice over the telephone.

Fiona Richmond, known by many Englishmen as the first porn princess, looked striking with her thick mane of hair and sparkling eyes. She was well spoken, so well spoken that an English magazine once described her as "the kind of naked girl you would get at Sainsburys, if Sainsburys sold naked girls." Since Sainsburys, the most famous of Britain's grocery stores, does not sell naked girls, I found Fiona in a luxury apartment overlooking the Thames. In her forties, married with a young daughter, Fiona was now a successful writer.

"Do you miss the stage?"

"I was always happiest on the stage."

"You were rarely dressed."

"It's true that most of my parts were not sensitive character portrayals, but I did have fun."

"Now you're a successful traveller. Did you actually do what you set out to do?"

"Do you mean travel to fifty different countries?"

I didn't, but I let her carry on.

"Sure, I travelled. I wasn't going to let them set up phony backdrops of Hawaii and Moscow, or whatever. You look sur-prised."

I was.

"Look at it like this. Most girls go off on their once-a-year holiday with a girlfriend and hope to find romance, be it with a Spanish waiter or whatever. The difference between them and me was that I had my holiday paid for."

"I suppose they were all young, good-looking men."

"Not at all. I prefer older men. Over thirty. They're like a good wine; they get better with age." She crossed one shapely leg over the other. "And so do I."

"Er . . ." For some reason I had lost my train of thought. "What's wrong with younger men?"

"They're terribly preoccupied with themselves. They're constantly trying to prove something. Older men don't need to."

This was a very intelligent lady.

"Older men have probably gotten somewhere in life or are going somewhere. Anyway, some younger men are so pretty, I can't stand the competition."

"Was the, er, survey successful?"

"Very."

"You travelled to the fifty different countries and, er, carried out your assignment?"

"I did."

"And what were the results?"

"I had a very good holiday."

"No, I mean the grading results. Who were the most disappointing?"

"Gosh, the Russian, I think, with the Australian a close second."

"And the best perform–, I mean, er, nicest?"

"The nicest? The Englishman."

The Englishman? To say I was shocked was to put it mildly. The Englishman! The twit with the bowler hat and umbrella? The man who, we're told, hates sex?

"I'm sorry, did you say the Englishman?"

"I did."

"Can you tell me why?"

"He was the only one of the fifty who turned out to be a gentleman."

"In what way?"

"He not only thanked me afterwards, but helped me remake the bed."

On a typical grey London morning we drove to the spot where we had agreed to meet our next interview. We parked next to what looked like a tank. A closer inspection revealed it was a bicycle with a large box covering all but the wheels. I placed a hand on the side of the box and spoke into one of its slots.

"Good morning."

"Good morning." The ruddy figure inside was fiddling with a camera.

"My name's Wicks."

"Commander Boakes, ex-Royal Navy."

"Would you mind if I ask what it is you're doing?"

"Certainly not." The voice came back through the slot with the kind of bark that had sent many a German U-boat scurrying for its home port. "If you read the sign on the outside of the turret, I think it should answer your question."

I stepped back and stared at a large sign. It read "ONLY ONE PUBLIC SAFETY PREMIERSHIP CANDIDATE."

"What does it mean?"

Before he could answer, a double-decker bus turned the corner and narrowly missed the bike and its driver. The Commander glared and shook his fist through the small front window.

"Damned road hog. Now, where was I?"

"You were going to tell me what it is that you're doing."

"Let me start at the beginning. At one time I ran a naval concert party. We had two hundred members in it, and one of the things we had to remember at all times was this: If you can amuse them, you can hold them." He smiled through the slot.

"I see. But what has that to do with this?"

"Well, this bicycle is not boring, right?"

"Right."

"So, if it's not boring I can deliver the message."

"What message?"

"The road safety message. I'm trying to remind drivers that they must, at all times, show consideration to others."

"But why the bicycle with the box on top?"

"To creep up on them."

"You creep up on a driver hidden inside this?"

"Well, sort of. What I do is pedal to the nearest school, then I sit and wait."

"For what?"

He placed his face close to the slit. "For the driver, of course."

"What driver?"

"What the hell is wrong with you? The inconsiderate driver, of course."

"Okay, let me get this straight. You pedal to the nearest school hidden on your bicycle. You park by the school and wait for a driver to come along."

"Right. And if he doesn't stop to let the children cross, I let him have it."

"With what?"

"With the camera, of course. I poke it through the front slot and, click, he's had it."

"What do you do with the pictures?"

"Send them to Scotland Yard."

"Is it very successful?"

"Very."

"And you do that all day and every day?"

"No, most of the time I'm working on my campaign."

"What campaign?"

"To become prime minister."

"You're going to run for Parliament?"

"What do you mean, going to? I have."

"You've run before?"

"Eleven times."

"What makes you think you're qualified?"

"Anyone who has been the captain of a ship can certainly run this country."

"What's the first thing you'll do when you get in?"

"I'll eliminate party politics."

"You don't have a party?"

"No, sir, I do not."

I was suddenly aware that passersby were staring. I was not surprised. I was standing on the corner of a busy street talking to a box. I lowered my voice.

"How about a policy?"

"None. But I can tell you this. When I get in I certainly intend to stir things up. Now, if you'll excuse me, it's time for work." He began to pedal the box away from the curb.

"Goodbye, Commander," I called out and heard a muffled cry in return. I felt good. At last I had found the kind of candidate that would get my vote any day of the week.

When I got back from that trip I found that Doreen had fallen in love with a house for sale close to where we were living. It was a beautiful, low bungalow with a gorgeous Japanese garden at the back. But what had the children leaping around was the pool. I liked it. But at $125,000 it was way more than I thought we could afford. But with Doreen and Vincent and Susan all enthusiastic, I finally agreed. We eventually sold the house eight years later for $230,000, proving once again that the smart one in our family wore a dress. Our new neighbours, a Chinese family of husband, wife, son and ninety-five-year-old grandmother, could not have been better. Every weekend in the summer their extended family gathered around their pool. The garden would be packed with laughing people. How we envied them.

After we moved, Doreen and I attended a charity dinner and auction, although I had tried my best to avoid it. After we had eaten, we sat back to watch the bidding. The wine flowed freely and, after an hour, I began to feel rather pleasant and silently congratulated myself on the good fortune of successfully missing out on each and every item that I had absolutely no use for.

Suddenly, the auctioneer began to speak about soccer and introduced a former soccer player in the audience. His name was Stanley Matthews, one of the greatest players of the sport. Just the mention of his name sent my mind spinning back in time.

I could see myself leaning out of a window and looking anxiously down to the alley below for a sign of my sister Nan's boyfriend. I was ten and waiting for John, who, in order to impress Nan, had agreed to take me to a football game. It was Saturday afternoon and game was the talk of the neighbourhood. The greatest player in the history of British football was appearing. I couldn't wait for Monday morning to arrive when I would regale the school with the story of how I had leaned across the fence and touched the shirt of the great Stanley Matthews.

Almost thirty years later, when I joined the *Telegram*, sports editor Doug Creighton and the publisher's son, Doug Bassett, were kind enough to take me with them to an evening sports reception. I had found myself face to face with the great Stanley. To the amusement of everyone around, I blubbered like an idiot as Matthews placed an arm around my shoulders and grinned. Now, ten years later, I was once again sharing a room with my hero.

My idol was invited to the stage and, as he stood shyly facing the crowd, the auctioneer reached into a large box and held up a pair of football boots. They were the boots that Stanley had worn during the greatest game of his career, a British Cup Final that will continue to be talked about as long as football is played, a game that had seen Matthews, almost singlehandedly, bring his team back from almost near defeat to victory. I turned to Doreen.

"Can you imagine, they're the actual boots he wore during that game." I leaned back and started the bidding at $200.

Doreen smiled. "You'd really like those boots, wouldn't you?"

I nodded and continued to flick a finger in the air as the price began to climb. I think it was at the $800 mark when I remembered I had an old pair of football boots in the house and really didn't need another pair. Unfortunately, Doreen was not of that opinion and took over the bidding from me. At $950 I tugged her sleeve.

"What are you doing, my love?"

She smiled. "I was wondering what to get you for Christmas, and now I know." Once again she flicked her finger and, with a nod from the auctioneer, the price went above $1,000. More and more I could see problems with the boots. They were certainly beat up and, let's face it, were they really the boots that Stan had worn?

The bidding was down to two people and up to $2,000, when a gentleman stood to request a recess. It was Doreen's rival bidder and, after taking the mike from the auctioneer's hand, he stood facing Doreen.

"Madam," he began, "I can appreciate your wanting these boots, but I feel it only fair to warn you that however high you go, I shall bid above you. I saw the great Stan win the Cup Final wearing these boots and I come from the same town he represented on that wonderful day. Being a gentleman, I would like to make you an offer."

Doreen, her face flushed with wine and a sense of determination to get the boots at all costs, glared back.

"If you will agree to stop bidding, I shall be more than happy to send a magnum of champagne to your table."

"I'm sorry," said Doreen, "I want those boots."

He shrugged and began to turn away.

"Wait," I almost screamed. I took Doreen's arm. "Look, darling, I know you want those boots for me and, of course, there's nothing I want more." I did not add that I had no wish to mortgage the house for the scruffy footwear. "But this very nice gentleman actually saw Stanley wearing these boots."

"So? We can see Stan wearing the boots." She lifted an arm.

"But he's from Stan's own home town," I protested.

Doreen's face fell. "But it would be such a wonderful Christmas present for you."

"I know it would, and I would have loved you to have got them for me —" I crossed my fingers "— even if you went to $10,000, but we have to think of others."

She looked up at the rival bidder standing anxiously by the table and said, "Well, okay, if you really want them."

I breathed a sigh of relief.

I am not a lover of champagne, however I did enjoy the magnum that arrived at the end of the auction.

Since that night Stan and I have become good friends, and he has reminded me of the auction many times. He is now in his seventies and in incredible shape. As modest as ever, he has been recognized as few of us ever will be by his native country. He is now Sir Stanley, but never uses the title, and in the centre of the small town where he kicked a tennis ball against the wall as a boy, you'll find a bronze statue of my boyhood hero. And although I never did get to hang his boots in my closet, I have something of far more value. A friend.

13

IN THE FALL OF 1974, John and I learned that our television program had been renewed. We were delighted and sat down to plan the coming 1975 season. Most of the characters we hunted out appeared to live in England, which made our show expensive to produce. We had used some Canadians but, to our minds, they had not been eccentric enough. Both of us agreed, however, that with a little more effort we should be able to find fascinating people in Canada. It would be a whole lot cheaper for us, especially if they were living in Toronto. We set out to find them and, fortunately, the search paid off. There were indeed strange people living in Canada. Even more important, these people were not only willing to appear on television, but anxious to be seen.

Eddie Diijon was not a tall man. Close to forty, clean-shaven and with a broad grin on his face, he carried a small case. What he had to offer had been advertised in the local press. It was perfect, the kind of show I had read about but never seen — a flea circus.

We started the cameras rolling. Eddie opened his case.

Having satisfied himself that all was in order, he reached in his pocket and placed a small box on the table.

"Inside this little matchbox I have a trained flea," said Eddie as he tapped it with a pair of tweezers. "Her name is Donna Domingo, and she's the only flea in the world that can do a triple somersault into a glass of water from a high platform."

He set up a tiny circus on the table – wagons, hoops and a ring. In the centre was a wee ladder leading to a platform that reached over a glass filled with water.

"Where do you get the fleas?"

"The only kind you can use for the circus are human fleas. The original ones I had came from Afghanistan. They were trained in Hong Kong, and I brought them from there to Canada."

"This one is from Hong Kong?"

"No, Donna is an offspring."

"Are females the best fleas to train?"

"They're bigger, so they're easier to work with." He began to open the matchbox.

"Before we see Donna, let's talk about training. How do you start?"

"First you've go to stop them from jumping. You can't train something that's jumping all over the place."

"Right."

"What we use is an old flea-training trick. You take a small, ordinary test tube with a cork at one end." He showed me a tube. "You place the flea inside and recork the tube. Every time she jumps, she bangs her head. After two weeks, uncork the tube and out she walks."

"With one hell of a headache."

He ignored my remark and with his tweezers lifted a tiny red dot from inside the matchbox.

"A red flea?"

"No, that's the red dress I made for her."

"What happens now?"

"I'm going to place Donna on the end of the platform, and when I give her the cue to jump, she'll do a triple somersault into the glass of water." He gently placed a barely visible Donna on the end of the platform. "Okay, Donna . . . Jump!"

Nothing happened.

"Jump, Donna!" He began to tap the table with the tweezers. "Jump! Jump! Donna, come on, girl."

"Maybe she's afraid of heights."

"How stupid of me. I know what it is." He began to roll up his sleeve. "I've forgotten to give her a feed." He took Donna from the platform and placed her on his arm. "There you are, old girl. Sorry about that. Okay, easy does it. Not too much." He replaced her on the platform.

"Now, old girl, jump! Jump! Jump!"

"Maybe she's got stage fright."

"Come on, Donna. Do it for me. Jump!"

"Are you sure she's feeling up to it?" I suddenly had a worse thought. "Maybe she's dead."

"Dead? What are you talking, dead? She's probably still a bit hungry."

He took Donna and placed her back on his arm. "There, you see. She was hungry." I could see nothing but a tiny red dot.

"Okay, old girl. This is it." Donna was back on the platform. "Now, jump! One, two, three, jump!"

This was getting embarrassing. "Are you sure this is Donna and not another flea?"

"Are you suggesting I don't know Donna when I see her?"

"I'm sorry."

"Come on, Donna. This is it. Jump!" His taps on the table were becoming bangs. Everything was jumping but Donna.

"You don't have a little whip?"

"Are you trying to be funny?" He turned and glared. "Come on, Donna, let's go. Jump!"

"I think I saw her move." I leaned in towards the platform. "I'm sure she moved."

"That's it, Donna. You can do it." Now we were both shouting and thumping the table. "Jump, Donna, jump!"

Suddenly it happened. Whether it was from the banging on the table or the shouting I'll never know, but Donna left the platform and, plop, she was at the bottom of the glass. Eddie seemed as surprised as I was and sat stunned, staring at the glass.

"Can she swim?"

Eddie continued to stare. "I don't know."

"You don't know?" I was horrified. "For heaven's sake, get her out." I grabbed the tweezers and lifted Donna from the glass. She wasn't moving.

"Come on, Donna," yelled Eddie. "You can do it. You can breathe."

It was, I believe, my suggestion that Eddie give her mouth-to-mouth that finished the interview. I am still unsure whether there ever was a Donna. But the Eddie Diijons of this world do exist, and the world is a better place for them.

Things at home were as hectic as any flea circus. Much of our attention at the time was on Kim, the youngest. She appeared to be very bright, so bright that when a new form of schooling, French immersion, was offered, we immediately made inquiries. The idea was that a child would be able to cope much more easily with French if he or she were taught early enough. Kim could hardly have started any earlier. She was five and, although the teacher convinced us that one hour of English a day and the rest in French would be no problem for her, it did not stop Doreen asking the obvious question, "What happens if she wants to go to the bathroom?"

French immersion is not for every child, but for Kim it was a lottery win. So good would her French become that during her later years at a British university, she earned extra money as an interpreter.

Kim was not alone in adjusting to a new school setting. An open-concept method that had invaded the high school Vincent and Susan attended concerned both Doreen and I. Children were left alone to study as they wished and, having finished whatever the assignment was for that day, were free to leave. It seemed that every day I was trying to find out what had happened to Vincent. He'd complete whatever was required, then he'd go off and not appear until suppertime. Doreen and I were anxious. A visit to the school produced this explanation from a principal who, I'm sure, had no idea what was happening to his students. He said that the new method prepared the young students for university and encouraged a feeling of self-confidence. I replied that I thought it was the most ridiculous idea I had ever heard, and furthermore, as a taxpayer paying for my children to stay at school and be taught until 3:30 P.M. I would appreciate it if the school made sure my children did just that.

For Susan, the mix of grades in one large area, with everyone attempting to complete his or her assignment, made it impossible for her to concentrate. I have no idea whose bright idea brought about the new changes, but whoever it was should look back in shame on a scheme that did immeasurable harm to a number of great kids, and at the same time gave teachers never-ending headaches. To our great relief, the whole idea was eventually sent to the scrap heap.

At home, our two cats, which we had had since they were kittens, were causing us a problem. Kim had suddenly developed allergies, the worst being to cats. Of all the family members, it was Susan whom the cats really loved. Each morning she would walk to school and they would follow her to the end of the block before returning home. Susan was heartbroken when we told her they had to go. We finally gave them to Pierre and Janet Berton, who made sure they got a good home in the country.

Weeks later Susan was still moping about the cats. For this reason, and this alone, I finally agreed to get a dog. I had resisted the constant pushing to do this from all the family, especially from Doreen, who regularly reminded me that she had grown up with a dog and everyone she had ever known had grown up with a dog. I gave in.

Peter Worthington mentioned that his sister had a Jack Russell terrier that was about to give birth, and she was looking for families who would care for and love the pups. So Rosie joined our home and settled in for sixteen years. She was a wonderful friend and family member. Luckily, Kim wasn't allergic to her.

Our pool was very popular with the children during the weekends and summer holidays. All were good swimmers, and the regular exercise helped them improve their techniques. Thanks in part to the pool, the children's friends gravitated to our home, something that Doreen and I had always hoped for. It was wonderful to read in the garden, listening to the yells and screams of happy children.

John and I received an offer to take our film gang to Portugal, and we leapt at the chance. All expenses were to be paid by the Portuguese Tourist Board, which figured that our program would remind people that there were other places to take holidays than Florida.

Armando, our contact who was waiting for us at a Lisbon hotel, was a disappointment. It's true that he could speak English, but as for setting up interviews, he was in a complete fog. We settled into the bar after unpacking, hoping to hear something about all the interesting people he'd located for us. Instead he asked us what it was we intended to do in Portugal. We explained as best we could that finding people to interview was, in fact, what he was being paid for. Nodding his head, he shook our hands and went off to arrange what he felt would make fascinating stories.

Within three days we had conducted only three interviews, all boring. After a day of filming around Lisbon on a particularly dull grey day, John and I went back to the hotel for afternoon tea. The face across the lobby looked familiar. Surely not? I nudged John. "Isn't that James Mason?" John agreed that he certainly looked like the famous British movie star. I signalled to a nearby bellboy.

"Is that James Mason, the movie star?" It was.

At last an interview worth the trip. "What is he doing here?"

"Oh, he was filming, and they're just checking out."

"Who is *they*?"

"Oh, Mr. Mason and Gregory Peck. They've been here filming *The Boys From Brazil*."

We could have killed Armando.

"Why didn't you tell us that two of the biggest movie stars around were staying in the hotel?" we asked.

"Movie stars?" he answered. "Who cares about movie stars. I have a king for you to interview."

All disappointment vanished. "A king? A real live king? King of who or where?"

"Why Italy, of course."

"But they don't have a king."

"Sure they do. He's the ex-king of Italy, and he lives in Estoril."

I was ecstatic. I'd never met a real king before. Sure, I'd met Al Waxman, the King of Kensington. But a real live king?

"Will he agree to be interviewed?"

"I'll phone and see." He strolled off, and we sank back in the hotel lobby armchairs. Armando was soon back. I stood up and grabbed his arm.

"Well?"

"It's fixed."

"When?"

"Sunday at eleven."

"How did you fix it?"

Armando lit a cigarette and blew a stream of smoke towards the ceiling. "I told his secretary that there were many Italian-Canadians who wanted to see their king again, if only on television. Until Sunday." He bowed, turned and was gone.

The road to Estoril that Sunday was quiet. Most people were in church. I leaned back and enjoyed the beauty as we wound our way along the coastal road.

"Where has he agreed to meet us?"

"Outside his church."

"On the street?" I had a vision of interviewing a king as a man-in-the-street interview and shuddered. "Why not at his house?"

"His secretary said no."

"How much farther?"

"About ten miles."

"We're going to be early."

"*Si.*"

"Let's drive to his house first, just to make sure that he's left for church."

"If you wish." He shrugged and turned the wheel. We drove into the town of Estoril, with its clusters of white houses scattered along the sandy shoreline. Rich and poor alike shared the beautiful coast. Our car turned into a narrow tree-lined avenue and stopped at the entrance to a long, winding driveway.

"Is this it?"

"*Si.*"

We sat and stared at the iron gates.

"Are we driving in?"

"I don't think so." For the first time Armando looked uneasy.

"Why not?"

Armando pointed at a sign with a figure of a dog, the kind of dog that was popular with the commandants of concentration camps.

"What does it say?"

"What do you think it says? Beware of the dog, of course."

"Well, it's not as if we're on foot, for heaven's sake," I snapped.

"I think we should go to the church."

"But if he's here, it will save us speaking on the street," I argued. "Drive in!"

We drove in. It was the wrong house. A short, chubby cook waved her arms and, by her manner, it appeared she was threatening to call the police.

"I told you we should've gone to the church," yelled Armando above the screeching wheels as he backed down the driveway.

We stopped outside a small church nearby.

"Wait here, and I'll see if I can spot the king inside." He vanished inside the church, reappeared within minutes and climbed back inside the car.

"What's up?"

"It's the wrong church," he mumbled.

I glanced at his sullen face and, out of pity, resisted asking him whether we were in the right country.

We set off again and pulled up outside a white church. Armando hurried inside. Once again he came out to report.

"I can't see him."

"Are you sure you know what he looks like?"

"Are you telling me that I don't know what a king looks like?" he shouted.

"Well, he sure as hell won't be wearing his crown," I shot back.

"Anyway, his secretary told me he was thin, tall and bald." He strolled off again and began to make his way down the rows of cars. He rushed back.

"I've found the king's car. He's in the church," he laughed.

"Which car?"

"The one with the chauffeur sitting in it reading the newspaper."

"The small Fiat?"

"*Si.*"

"Are you sure? Let's go and chat to the driver."

We started towards the car. "Why do you want to talk to the driver?"

"I'd like to get some information before the interview."

"Like what?"

"Like how many children the king has."

"He's a bachelor," sneered Armando.

"How will I recognize him?"

"He's wearing a T-shirt."

"A T-shirt? A king in a T-shirt?"

"Of course."

The chauffeur lowered his newspaper and smiled as I approached the car. I turned to Armando.

"Ask him something about his boss."

A flood of Portuguese went back and forth.

"Well?"

"The king is married with four children and is wearing a dark suit with a dark tie. He says he's surprised that the king would grant an interview."

"He's surprised? What about all this stuff about being a bachelor?"

Armando was already heading back in the direction of the church. People were beginning to come out. I started to run as I spotted a tall, distinguished man surrounded by a group of elderly people.

"Excuse me, Your Majesty," I puffed. He turned and smiled. "My name is Ben Wicks, and I'd like to ask you a . . ."

I got no further. A swift shove from behind had me stumbling to one side. Armando grabbed the king's hand and had already begun kissing it.

"Er, Armando . . ." I tapped his shoulder and, at the same time, smiled at the king, who was trying to retrieve his hand. "Armando, would you like to introduce me, please. I'm Ben Wicks, Your Majesty, and I was wondering if . . ."

The king turned and, with a sharp tug, pulled his hand from Armando's lips. He was in the car before I could push my way through the elderly throng, all muttering words of adulation. I lifted the camera. At least a good picture would be something.

Armando's hand blocked the lens as he waved goodbye. It was with great difficulty that I paid Armando for his "help" at the end of the day.

We went to London. We knew that somewhere in that great city we would find what we were looking for. When we arrived, Fiona told us she had arranged an interview with Ingrid Bergman. Of all the interviews we did, and there were over five hundred, Ingrid Bergman was the only person to ask for money: One hundred pounds to be sent to her favourite orphanage.

Although there were more than ten interviews lined up for us in London, John and I were most excited about this one. Anxious that the interview be to her liking as well as ours, I hunted out a friend who worked for the BBC, and he helped me to get me into their research library. There I could find everything that anyone could possibly want to know about anyone. I spent the morning with a large file on Miss Bergman and prepared my questions in the order I intended to ask them. I had been so absorbed in my work that I did not realize that the time of the interview was fast approaching. I dashed onto the street and frantically hailed a cab.

I was late, and by the time I ran into the theatre, John and the crew were set up in Miss Bergman's dressing room. She was there preparing for that night's performance wearing a casual dressing gown and no makeup. She was the most beautiful woman I had ever seen. Unlike the Hollywood stars we had met, she had little need to cover her beautiful skin, a skin the sun had had no opportunity to wrinkle. Her smile sent my knees wobbling, and by the time John was ready to roll film she had captured another fan.

I had decided to open with an unusual question to get things going on a fun note.

"Do you still have the pig farm in Nepal?"

She stared at me, grinned, then suddenly burst out laughing.

"Wherever did you get such a piece of information? And the answer is, no, we don't. We sold it."

From then on the interview went easily. Naturally, I asked her those questions she had been asked a thousand times about the making of *Casablanca*. She said it was true Bogart was a very nice man, but he kept very much to himself. Yes, they did keep rewriting the script, and both stars would appear each day never knowing with whom Miss Bergman would finally leave Casablanca.

We spent an hour with her, and the time flew. She was as gracious and kind as we had hoped. It is difficult to describe what makes a major star, but I can tell you that of all the famous people we met in the course of doing "The World of Wicks," Ingrid Bergman was the only one whom John asked to pose in a picture with him. The resulting photo shows him gazing starry eyed over her shoulder. My photo was much more refined.

Now all we had to do was the other ten stories that Fiona had lined up for us. Many people have asked how we found our stories. Much of the credit should be laid in Fiona's lap. She was brilliant at spotting quirky items in the newspapers that others overlooked. And not just in the news section.

It seemed an odd place for the Second Coming, yet the ads in the newspaper had been very explicit. The Maitreya, who is said to combine the best qualities of Krishna, Buddha, Christ and the Imam Mahdi, would appear in a London restaurant soon. I phoned the number listed, and asked for Mrs. Patricia Pitchon, the Maitreya's social secretary.

"Have you seen the Master lately?"

She answered my question with a gentle yet enthusiastic voice. "Not for two years," and we went on to explain that, two years earlier, a similar ad had sent journalists from around the world scurrying to a curry place in London's East End in the hopes of getting the page-one story to end all stories. Media types from Yugoslavia, Canada, Los Angeles and even the BBC's Bengali service crowded into the back room of the Clifton Restaurant. One reporter from Japan lost his interpreter and was completely mystified by the whole evening. Mrs. Pitchon had insisted that the journalists order only one drink, feeling that more would impair their spirituality once the Master arrived.

"Did he show up?"

"I'm afraid not."

"Why do you think that was?"

"I blame it on the fact that certain members of a London television station consumed more than their quota."

This was not completely accurate. I later found a newspaper report of the evening that stated the main problem was that Mrs. Pitchon did not have the faintest idea what the Saviour looked like. Most journalists had spent the whole evening looking around the room. Could it be one of their own? Then a man of distinction had walked in, described later in the *Times* as "aloof, yet sympathetic." He was from the *Observer*.

By 10:30 P.M. they had ordered their last coffee. As the same reporter from the *Times* mentioned, "While grateful for the custom of 22 journalists, the management was more interested in a second sitting than a Second Coming."

I asked Mrs. Pitchon to tell me about the last time she saw him.

"I was having dinner with my journalist friends in Brick Lane, and I looked up and there, staring into the restaurant window was a man dressed in a long white gown. I looked into his face and suddenly I was blasted."

"Blasted?"

"His face. It exploded and a bright glow burned for about ten seconds then it disappeared."

"Then what?"

"He just looked at me and smiled."

"I thought his face had disappeared."

"It came back and he smiled, turned slowly and walked away."

"Did you grab your journalist friends?"

"I was too shocked. I couldn't move. By the time I'd recovered and we'd raced outside, he was gone."

"Did you ever find out why he never arrived the night the world press showed up?"

"As far as I know, he intended to come but changed his mind. Right up to 5:00 P.M. that evening he was coming, but he began to feel that there were too many who opposed his visit. He felt that at another time he will be received without the fear and trepidation. As far as we know he has decided to make the trip again and make a direct approach to the press."

"Has he said when this will be?"

"Probably in February."

"Brick Lane again?"

"I think not. It's my understanding that it will be a direct approach to a newspaper office."

"You mean it could be my office back in Toronto?"

"It could be. What kind of staff do you have?"

"Mostly nondrinkers."

"Sounds good."

"And the day in February?"

"The sixth. Mind you, there could be a change."

"If there is, will you let me know? Or, better still, let my producer know?"

"Whatever the time of day or night?"

"Absolutely. Er, one other thing. Just phone collect."

Although John Ross waited, the phone in Toronto did not ring.

John and I agreed that part of the charm of "The World of Wicks" was that it gave viewers an opportunity to travel to places they would otherwise not see. Objective number two for us was to give them interviews with fascinating people. The one place in North America that fitted both these criteria was Hollywood. Fortunately the title of the program and the fact that the network was called Global gave us a great advantage. Most stars' agents were convinced that our interviews would be seen by millions around the world. We decided that to tell them otherwise would be a mistake. Certainly Tony Randall's agent was thrilled to think that his client would join the likes of Ingrid Bergman and others whom we had interviewed.

Even though neither John nor our regular camerawoman, Carol Betts, was able to make the trip, I felt quite confident that filming would be easy in the centre of this world of entertainment. The crew I hired when I arrived in Hollywood was cheap, local and nonunion.

I left the crew on the sidewalk and entered a large building where they were filming the television show "The Odd Couple." Jack Klugman nodded as he passed by on the way to his dressing room, and I turned and followed him feeling sure that this was where I would find Tony Randall. Long before I reached it, I heard the sneezing and sniffles of someone with a very bad cold. Tony Randall was not happy. He held a Kleenex box in one hand and held the other up to warn me that to shake hands with him could result in pneumonia.

I said it was good to meet him, and he proceeded to show me where he thought the cameras should be set up for the interview. To avoid having to explain that I had a nonunion crew and to bring them into the building would result in shutting down production throughout Hollywood, I took another angle. I told him that we were filming for a worldwide audience that enjoyed seeing the locations of the interviews. To film outside would give them the added pleasure of seeing a piece of Hollywood.

He stared long and hard at me and slowly plucked a tissue from the box and blew his nose.

"You want me to go outside with this illness bordering on critical? You must be joking."

I assured him that I wasn't and that, provided we stay in the sun, he might, in fact, feel better. The discussion went on and both our voices began to rise. Eventually with a shrug that only his character, Felix, could give, he consented.

We left the building. I introduced Tony to the crew and explained what I had in mind. He and I would walk up to the top of the hill, turn and, with the cameras rolling, stroll back towards the crew. Tony listened politely, said nothing and continued to blow his nose.

With small receivers in our pockets and wearing radio mikes, we had no need of wires between us and the camera. The one disadvantage was that, although the cameraperson could see us through the eyepiece, he could not hear what we were saying.

Tony and I began to walk up the hill to take our positions.

"What are we going to talk about?" he asked.

"I never discuss what the interview is about. We're just going to chat."

He nodded and blew his nose. We turned at the spot and waited for the cameraperson to lift his arm in a signal for us to begin. He signalled and we began a slow walk towards him.

"I know you're a tremendous fan of Laurence Olivier," I began.

"Great actor." He blew his nose.

"I understand that he always places a little makeup on his face before he performs. He thinks this helps him project."

Tony blew his nose again. I watched, waiting for an answer.

"I know you're also a great fan of Robert Morley."

"Another great actor." He blew his nose.

"He's large and no doubt feels that his size helps him project."

Tony blew his nose once more. I suddenly realized that he was determined to get back at me for forcing him into the chill air of a 90° California day. I had to do something. I stopped walking and, taking Tony by the arm, stared into his face.

"Let's be honest. I mean, you're not all that big and you're certainly not handsome, so how do you project?"

He blew his nose, stared into my face and, as he calmly plucked another tissue from the box, said, "It so happens, Mr. Wicks, that I have a very large cock."

I must admit that that wasn't quite the answer I was looking for. When we aired the interview, all we used was that last exchange – with Tony's naughty word "beeped" out!

14

DAD'S HEALTH WAS NOT GOOD. Doreen and I had taken frequent trips to England and each time he appeared a little more tired. Mum and Dad no longer lived in the centre of London. Like many Cockney families, they had swopped life in the grimy East End for life closer to the country. Although they liked their cosy flat on a suburban estate, they missed Southwark and, even more important, the friends of a lifetime they had left behind.

The effects of the gas attacks Dad had suffered in the First World War had slowly disappeared, yet although he was no longer in pain, it was quite apparent to us all that he was coming to the end of his life. Tired as he was, he never ceased to take his grandchildren on his knee and read to them during our visits. Now at eighty-six years of age, he was finding it more difficult to get out of bed, not from any visible handicaps but because, as Mum said, "'E seems to 'ave just given up."

Some months after we arrived back in Canada from this visit, Doll phoned to tell me that Dad had died. I was devastated that I had not been there to hold him or tell him how important he had been in my life. As I write, tears are streaming down my face. Do we ever recover from the loss of those who are so close? Obviously not.

After the funeral, while we were grieving for Dad, my sisters and I were also very concerned for Mum. They had been together for more than sixty years. How would she cope alone? Fortunately, Doll lived just a few blocks away and could visit Mum regularly. Still, it seemed a good idea to all of us to bring Mum to Canada in the hopes of persuading her to live with me. None of us were sure it would work, but we thought it worth the try. At the very least, she would have a wonderful holiday. She was eighty-nine years old, and this would be her first trip out of Britain. It was 1976 and the world had changed since her travelling days.

We stepped aboard a giant 747. Mum stopped and looked down the length of the plane. "Blimey," she said. "It's like a bleedin' city." I laughed and steered her to her seat. Soon after take-off the attendant brought our meals. Mum took one look at the full tray, then leaned towards me and whispered, "'Ow much is this going to cost you?" I explained that it came with the ticket, and she tucked in.

Within a few days in Toronto she felt comfortable and was soon regaling us with stories of her life with Dad. The children were enthralled, it sounded so foreign to them, and sat around her on the floor listening as I prompted her with questions.

"How do you actually know you're eighty-nine?"

"'Course I know, don't I? I got me birth certificate . . . somewhere."

"Were you born in the centre of London?"

"Well, I was born at Bow, which I suppose is in the centre."

"What about your mum and dad?"

"Oh, I was given away when I was six months old to some woman I 'ad to call aunt."

"Did you ever know your mother and father?

"I knew me mother. Never did know 'im or who 'e was."

"Why did she give you away?"

"She 'ad no time for girls. Only liked boys. Funny thing was that the woman she gave me to never liked girls either. 'Ad a strap hanging on the door which she'd belt me wiv." She grimaced at the thought. "When I got to fourteen, she threw me out. A year later she were dead."

"Where did you meet Dad?"

"Met 'im in a little factory I was working in. A year later 'e went off to France in the war. Yer sister Dolly was already free months old. 'Course after 'e came back we 'ad yer sister Nan, then you and yer twin brover."

"Was I a good-looking baby?"

"Well, a bit better than you are now."

The children laughed.

"That's not very nice. Then what about my twin brother, William?"

"Oh, 'e was the best-looking one of the bunch. 'Ad a mop of thick black 'air, 'e did."

She looked down at her lap as the memories flowed back. "'E was buried between some woman's feet when 'e was twenty-six hours old. 'Course, it was nofing like the time yer uncle Steve, yer dad's brover, died."

I listened fascinated as she spoke and was suddenly aware of how constant death had been for the poor of London in her younger years. She took her handkerchief out and began to rustle it in her hands.

"There was this man, Billy the wreath-maker. I asked 'im to make me a wreath fer your uncle Steve. He said, 'I'll make a nice one wiv a white dove on top,' or pigeon or something. Anyway, I know it were a bird. I picks it up and am coming down the street wiv it, and as I turns a corner a gust of wind comes around and takes the bird right off the wreath." She began to howl with laughter and the children joined in.

Through the tears of laughter she continued her story: "So

I . . . So I . . ." She wiped her eyes with the hanky. "I went to this pub fer a drink and said to the man behind the counter, "Ave you got an old newspaper you can let me have?' So I shaped another bird out of the newspaper and stuck it on the wreath. When I got to the church, I put the wreath in a place where few people would notice it.

"When yer Dad got to the church, 'e said, 'Where's our wreath?' I pointed it out and thought 'e was going to 'ave a fit. 'I ain't sticking that on me brover's grave,' 'e says. Then he reached down and grabbed it and threw it and . . ." Once more she dissolved in a fit of laughter. "When I picked up the wreath, I found that only the three top flowers were real. All the others were made of paper, which Billy the wreath-maker had thrown in for real ones."

Eventually Mum began to miss England, and although we tried our best to persuade her to stay, she went back. She died five years later at the age of ninety-four. She was a tough, solid, loving mother who had endured terrible hardships, a woman who was unwanted as a child simply because she was a girl. I miss her. I wish she was alive today to see her great-grandchildren.

Vincent's musical tastes were changing. He was still learning the violin at school but rock music soon took over his life. He persuaded a few friends to join him in a band; he was the lead singer. Memories of my own group and our regular weekly practices came flooding back, as Vincent and the band closeted themselves in the basement each week to play what they called music, although to my ears "music" was hardly the word for what they were producing. I was glad that Susan was now playing the clarinet in her school band and Kim taking piano lessons.

Vincent's band, Curious December, began to get jobs and, although they were promised payment, they were regularly cheated out of their money through one excuse or another. Doreen and I supported him in doing what he obviously loved, and when we could we went to the various clubs that had booked the band. Most of these were below ground, which gave the noise little opportunity to escape. Although the crowds obviously enjoyed them, Doreen and I had to confess that, had it not been our son on the stage, we would have been in bed hours before the final song.

A phone call from New York interrupted my preparations for the next trip John and I were planning. A major American syndicate had been told that I might be interested in developing a new cartoon strip for them. A political strip called "Doonesbury" had become a hit and the *New York Daily News* and the *Chicago Tribune*, which did not carry it, were frantically searching for a rival. Would I be interested in producing something that would attract newspaper buyers away from "Doonesbury"? I said I was, then added that, since I had never seen the strip, could they send me some samples and give me a week to decide. They agreed.

The cartoons arrived and, after studying them, I phoned back. I thought the strips were interesting, I told them, but that, perhaps because I was still in many ways very English, I did not understand the appeal they had for editors or readers. The syndicate was sympathetic, but determined to follow through with using me. I agreed and within a few days had drawn six samples.

I had decided to draw the president of the United States on a small island. In the cartoon, he had won the leadership of the islanders by promising that he would eventually get them off. Each day the reader would see the problems they were facing, and each day they would see the leader promising to correct the situation. I called the strip "The Outcasts." Within weeks the answer came back from New York. They loved the idea and asked me to come to New York for a high-level meeting.

The lunch was held in an impressive room obviously reserved for the top executives of the newspaper syndicate. Along with the president were others involved in the business of selling newspaper features. Fancy waiters hovered around.

Everyone at the table was convinced that I was about to make millions of dollars. "Peanuts" and every famous strip cartoon of the past hundred years was about to sink without trace once "The Outcasts" hit the stands. First, the sales staff would need six weeks of strips, then all that remained was to sit back and wait for the Brink's trucks to arrive outside.

Delighted with the news, I ventured to ask how much I would be getting for the six weeks' work. Talk around the table stopped. The president explained that he was surprised that, as a cartoonist who had worked for the likes of the *Saturday Evening Post*, I was unaware that such work was executed and introduced as samples for use by the salespeople only. Without them it would be impossible to sell to any editor. I was aware of that fact, I explained, but still did not see what that had to do with payment for work received. The atmosphere became chilly.

"What kind of payment do you have in mind?" asked the president, a smile slowly making its way across his frowning face.

"Well, since we're all about to make millions, why not a little upfront?"

"How little?" asked the president.

"I don't know. How about fifty thousand dollars?" I smiled, picking a number from the air.

There was a clatter of soup spoons around the table. Then, it seemed, everyone started talking at once. Mainly they wondered out loud just who the hell was this Canadian cartoonist who had the audacity to expect to get paid for work? I explained that since I was busy enough already, I would just as soon get on the next plane home and put the whole lunch down to a fun experience.

It was finally agreed that, since this venture was, after all, a potential gold mine, they would pay me $10,000. I agreed.

For three months their lawyers discussed the contract with my lawyer and friend, Norman Griesdorf. He, knowing nothing about the newspaper business, asked what I wanted. I told him I wanted a cheque. Numerous calls from New York asking where the strips were were met with the same reply: "Where's the cheque?"

In the meantime I began to draw the strip as a Canadian feature, with Prime Minister Trudeau in charge of the island. Distributed by the *Toronto Star* syndicate, it had found its way into more than fifty Canadian newspapers by the time the cheque from New York arrived.

Unfortunately I was not as successful in the States. Despite the efforts of the syndicate's sales staff, very few newspapers were interested. Some time later I received a letter from the syndicate president asking me to return the money. I explained that this would be difficult since it had already been spent. With my letter I enclosed a statement detailing my expenses for the trip to New York. Their reply was not polite.

Released from the burden of what to do with the millions of dollars I was supposed to make from a daily U.S. newspaper feature, I once again concentrated on the jobs that were delivering a cheque each month – cartooning and "The World of Wicks."

John thought that a trip to Paris should pay us rich dividends. Although I could not speak French, he could and would be happy to step in when need be.

The Sunday evening meeting with our French crew went well. Although no one had the slightest idea what we were doing in Paris, each of us agreed that there must be dozens of stories here. If the crew would be at our hotel at 7:30 A.M., our merry band would set off to discover the life that throbbed along the streets of one of the most famous and beautiful cities in the world.

The next day it rained, hard. The drops thumped against the hotel window as John and I ate breakfast in silence. Now what? We could wait for it to clear, then set off, but the arrival of the camera crew was imminent, and when it showed up our meter would begin to tick.

We had no solution and temporarily avoided the issue by burying our heads in our newspapers. I turned a page of the European edition of the *Herald Tribune* and there in bold letters was our answer. The French Open Golf Tournament was about to take place, and Arnold Palmer was in town to kick off the event. Not only was the great golfer in Paris, but that very morning he was planning to hit a golf ball off the Eiffel Tower as a publicity stunt. It was perfect. John and I leapt to our feet and, grabbing our raincoats and the camera crew, who had just arrived, we raced through the lobby and into a cab.

It was still raining, the worst possible weather for filming, when we got to the Eiffel Tower. We sheltered in a doorway with dozens of other journalists to await the Palmer arrival. Within a few minutes a car slid to a stop, a smiling Arnold Palmer jumped out and vanished inside the tower. We followed along and, after showing our press cards, we joined the other journalists in the restaurant on the tower's first level. The great American golfer was presented and spoke the usual half-dozen words about how nice it was to be wherever he was.

The public-relations people had been sure that if Palmer hit a golf ball from the Eiffel Tower, the media would care enough to show themselves. It had worked. Ready at last, Palmer strolled onto the platform outside, followed by a pack of cameras. With the rain blowing in our faces, everyone pushed, scratched and kicked to get the pictures they wanted, us included. Like Foreign Legionnaires heading upstairs to a brothel, our crew clawed its way to the front of the mob. For the sake of our program, it was vital that I be seen beside Palmer, to give the impression that the whole ridiculous exercise was being played out just for my benefit. Obviously this was not going to be easy. Fortunately I did not understand French and ignored the words thrown my way as I twisted and elbowed past every-one between me and Palmer.

Eventually I stood beside him. He was having just as much difficulty being understood as I was, and when the ball was blown off the tee for the fifth time and I offered to help, he was obviously delighted to hear English. I knelt down and held the ball steady to the last second of his swing. With a swish, the ball left the tower and vanished into a blustering cloud. Within minutes we were back inside the restaurant drying off.

I joined John at our table and watched as the PR man and the *gendarme* barricaded off a small corner of the room to protect Palmer.

"There will be no interviews," the PR man said. Behind him we could see Palmer rubbing his hair with a towel and grinning.

"We need an interview with Palmer," John whispered. "Without it, what have we got?"

Of course he was right, but how could I get near him, let alone speak to him? What was needed was the brazen approach of a barrow boy. I waited for the PR man to move off, then approached the *gendarme*.

"World Syndicated News," I lied and flashed my Global press card. He looked at me and then at the card, amazed.

"Grab that chair and bring it here," I said. "And give me a hand with this table." We set up the small table beside Palmer.

"What would you like, Arnold," I asked the astonished golfer. "Tea or coffee?"

"Er, coffee will be fine."

I signalled a waiter and at the same time waved the camera crew into position. John followed behind, wearing a big grin, and began to instruct the crew.

As I sat waiting for Palmer to settle and the waiter to bring us both coffee, I suddenly realized that I knew nothing about golf or Palmer. I began to wonder what I could possibly ask the man.

Then I had it. It has been a discussion for as long as sport has been around: Is it bad to have sex before an event?

"Rolling," called John.

"Er, I must confess I know very little about golf," I said.

Palmer grinned, "Who does?"

My mind in a whirl, I blurted out, "Do you believe that sex is good before a game?"

He stared, then roared with laughter. "I believe that sex is good any time."

That cracked the ice, and the rest of the brief interview went well.

Among the letters and bills waiting for me when I got home was an invitation to travel with a group of journalists to San Antonio, Texas. Twenty of us from around the world were being invited to a glorious four-day bash. In return, it was hoped, we would write enough about San Antonio to cause a stampede of visitors to the city.

After a day of touring San Antonio's attractions, we were wined and dined in a small, expensive restaurant. A German journalist named Gunther sat beside me. Although I'd noticed him earlier, it was the first time we'd spoken. After the usual polite nothings, we found ourselves discussing the Second World War.

"And what did you do?" I asked.

"I was a Messerschmitt pilot."

I lowered my fork and stared at him.

"You flew Germany's Spitfire?" I asked.

"I did until I was shot down by a Spitfire in the English Channel."

"You were a prisoner?"

"No, no, I was picked up by a German torpedo boat."

I put a forkful in my mouth. He started to talk again.

"I met him later, you know."

I swallowed fast. "Met who?"

"The fellow who shot me down."

"You met the guy who flew the Spitfire?"

"*Ja*, thirty years later, in 1971. I had taken my family to England for a holiday and met some English ex-pilots in a pub."

"And one of them was the guy?"

He held up a hand. "No, no, they told me that there was an office in London that kept records of all flights made during the war."

Naturally. It was typical of England. A cluttered office in the bowels of some government building housing an Alec Guinness character with nothing to do but dust files.

"So you went?" I asked.

"Sure I did. An old man gave me a form to fill in."

"What kind of form?"

"Oh, where I was shot down, time, day, things like that."

I smiled. It was just as I'd imagined it.

"He took the form and vanished behind a stand of files. In ten minutes he was back. 'There we are, guvnor.'" We both laughed at Gunther's impersonation of a Cockney accent. "'The guy you want is a squadron leader, Bennett. Here's his log. Says he was flying over where you was that day and shot down a Messerschmitt.' I asked him if he had an address. He did."

"So you called?"

"There was no phone number, but by Sunday I knew I had to try to find him. I left my wife and children in London and set off for Kent."

"Have you finished, sir?" The waiter bent over to take my almost full plate.

"Er, yes, thank you. I'm not hungry." I turned to my companion.

"Then what?"

"Where was I?"

I leaned forward. "You were knocking on the door."

"Ah, yes. A woman opened the door. It was the right house. She explained that her husband was at the local pub."

"You didn't say who you were?"

"No, no, I just set off to the pub. It was crowded."

Naturally, I thought. Wife in kitchen, husband beering it up. England at noon on a Sunday.

"I made my way to the bar and asked the barman for Mr. Bennett. He pointed to a man beside a dart board, surrounded by friends. I pushed my way towards him and tapped him on the shoulder."

"Coffee, sir?" It was the waiter again.

"Er, no, no thank you," I said and turned to Gunther. "So you tapped him on the shoulder?"

"*Ja*, and he turned and I said, 'Are you Mr. Bennett?' He nodded. So I said, 'You shot me down in June 1941.'"

"You said it just like that?"

He laughed. "Sure."

"And?"

"His mouth opened. I thought he was going to faint. Instead he threw his arms around me and began to laugh. Soon the whole pub was laughing at his story. He insisted that I go back to London and get the family. So I did."

"Have you seen him since?"

"Regularly. Our families visit each other in Germany and England. We are now close friends."

Some months later Doreen was planning another trip to England. The children were growing and she and I were anxious for all of us to see England again. We rented a car at London's Heathrow airport and headed for Bristol, Doreen's home town. This historic city on the west coast was an ideal jumping off point to many areas of beauty, not the least of which was the home of the great Welsh poet, Dylan Thomas, in the village of Laugharne.

We drove out of Bristol on the Severn Bridge and had no trouble finding the little fishing village where Thomas had grown up. We made our way to the bar of the Brown's Hotel, had a pint and spoke to the manager.

"We're fans of Dylan Thomas and . . ."

"You are, are you?" he frowned. "You wouldn't be if you owned a pub in these parts." He turned and pointed to a small board with pieces of paper tacked in place. "They're the customers who still owe me for drinks. Most of them are your precious Dylan Thomas's." He smiled. "What the hell . . . it's too late now."

We finished our drinks and I asked him the way to the Thomas house.

"Go down the winding hill. At the bottom is the Corporation Arms. That's right, another of Dylan's hangouts."

"Where's the Sailor's Arms that was featured in *Under Milk Wood*?"

"That's the one. He changed the name for the book or poem, or whatever they want to call it. Anyway go past the Cross House Inn, that's right, another Dylan 'home,' and you'll find a narrow lane . . ."

Within half an hour we were hopelessly lost. We came to a small stream, took off our shoes and waded across. We walked down a country lane and came across a sign saying "Dylan's Walk." We followed the path across the top of a cliff until we came to a short wooden gate. It was locked. We could see down the garden path to a cottage, practically at sea level at the base of the cliff. It had to be the home of the poet.

We returned to the pub. "You should have said you wanted to go inside," said our friendly innkeeper. "Turn right when you get outside and go to number forty-three. It's where Dai Evans lives. He was Dylan's drinking buddy. He has the key to the house." We did as he said.

The small cottage was as Dylan described it in "Prologue":

234 ♦ BEN WICKS

"... my sea-shaken house on a breakneck of rocks ..." There wasn't much furniture and it was dusty. A piece of rope nailed to the wall replaced the missing banister on the staircase. Upstairs, there was a bed in the small bedroom, with a mattress leaning against the wall.

"Where did he write *Under Milk Wood*?" I asked Evans.

"D'you mean where did he work? He did that in the shed next door."

The wooden garden shed had a magnificent view of the estuary and rolling green hills. A rickety wooden table stood by the shutters, with a broken chair beside it. I touched the table.

"So this is it," I whispered in reverence.

"This is what?" said Evans, looking around the shed for something of value.

"Where he wrote," I said.

"That's right. Though it's a good job you didn't come a few months ago."

"Why's that?" Doreen asked.

"It was a mess, that's why. See that section of wall by the table? Old Dylan really went to town there. Wrote all over it, he did ... scribbled words and crossed them out ... real messy. Bit of paint soon straightened that out. Only took a quarter of a tin ..."

We were not listening. We were too busy staring at the white wall and trying to imagine what had been buried forever.

As we walked back to the village, Evans made an astonishing statement.

"If you like the cottage that much, why don't you buy it?"

He explained how the cottage was for sale. Dylan's wife, Caitlin, was anxious to sell and had yet to find a buyer. As soon as we could, we tracked down the real-estate agent who then passed us on to the lawyer. He lived in Cardiff, some miles away. A quick phone call was answered by an angry man who on hearing that we were from Canada was convinced that our only reason for wanting the home was to move it lock, stock and mattress to North America.

I tried my best to persuade him we had no such intention. We were motivated simply by a love of his work and an opportunity to own a piece of property in Wales. The answer was a phone thrown violently back on its hook.

We were back in the car and driving through the beautiful countryside of South Wales when Doreen had an idea.

"Weren't you evacuated to South Wales?" she asked.

It was true. We were in the very area I had called home almost forty years before.

"Let's try and find where you lived," said Doreen. It was a brilliant idea. As my excitement began to build, I explained to my children for the first time how, long before they were born, I has been sent away from home to live with strangers.

The village was not easy to find, but eventually a sign appeared with the magic words: "Cross Hands." We drove slowly into the village, which now seemed strange to me. The mountains of slag that formed its backdrop were now covered in grass.

We crept along the main street as I looked for the cottage in which I had lived. Suddenly, there it was, still lying in the shadow of the working-man's club.

I pulled up to the curb. The cottage was much smaller than I remembered. While Doreen and the kids sat looking at it, I walked up the short path to its whitened doorstep and knocked.

A woman in her fifties opened the door and stood staring at me. I explained how I had lived in the house during the war and had now returned to show my children.

"But I'm Rachel," she cried, "the daughter of the house. We were playmates."

We hugged each other and laughed. Then she held me at arm's length to get a good look at me.

"If only your mum and dad could be here, it would be perfect," I said.

"But they are. They're in the kitchen."

"But I was sure they'd be . . ."

"Not them, boy. They're too tough for that, though they're over ninety apiece."

I rushed back to the car to fetch Doreen and the kids, and we followed Rachel into the dark kitchen where I had spent so much time. Mr. and Mrs. Roberts sat at the table staring at us, as Rachel explained to them, in Welsh, who we were. We hugged, although to be honest, I don't think they remembered me. I had occupied such a small part of their long lives. Rachel bustled about, making a pot of tea as we caught up.

We didn't stay long, not wanting to tire Rachel's parents. As we stood at the door, the old man reached into his pocket and, as is the custom in Wales, pressed a coin into the hands of each of my children. As I watched Vincent's hand close over the coin, my eyes began to fill with tears. So many years ago another boy's hand had closed over a tiny horseshoe as he hugged and said goodbye to two wonderful Welsh parents. I have the shoe to this day. Along one side is written "Good luck and love, the Roberts."

15

THE CITY OF PORT-AU-PRINCE stank from the open sewers that twisted and turned through the narrow streets of its filthy and overcrowded neighbourhoods. Unashamed, the capital city showed its squalor to the rest of the world.

It was 1978 and I was in Haiti to film a television commercial for a nonprofit agency that wanted to encourage North American viewers to sponsor children in a foster home run by an American Catholic sister. I had happily agreed to this job, not knowing the shock in store for me. Now standing in Port-au-Prince, it seemed that the modern world had passed the city by, leaving its people in the darkness of a nightmare. Haiti was so close to North America, yet so far. I felt profoundly glad to be living in Canada.

I set out straightaway to find the remarkable sister who ran the foster home we would be filming. Within a ten-minute walk of the president's gleaming palace, École St. Vincent was a dilapidated building, with open sewers running around it like a castle moat. I rattled the iron gate. A shutter slid to one side and a child's face appeared. I introduced myself and was told to wait. The shutter was closed firmly. After a few minutes, it opened again and a chain that had been holding the door was released.

I followed a severely limping boy through a dark entrance-way to the sister's office. The iron gate did little to shut out the bustle of Port-au-Prince. From behind a cluttered desk a small, roly-poly figure in white lifted herself out of a chair with the help of two canes.

Sister Joan was seventy-three years old. In 1944 she had been sent by her Mother Superior in Boston to visit Haiti to comfort the sick. In her first week she found an abandoned, blind three-year-old girl, whom she took to the convent. There, under a large tree, she began to play with the child. A deaf two-year-old girl and a lame three-year-old boy joined in the game. They, too, had no homes. This was the start of Sister Joan's incredible mission.

"Before we start the tour of our school and clinic, there's a few things you should know." She spoke firmly. "One, I'm allergic to newspapermen. I threw out one who said he was from the *Reader's Digest*. Said he wanted to write about me. Told him I hadn't time for that nonsense. What are you going to write about?"

"The children," I lied.

"Good. Let's go."

I followed Sister Joan through a courtyard filled with giggling deaf, blind and crippled children. All were hurrying to their classes. I reached down to help a blind boy around an obstacle.

"Leave him alone." Sister Joan took my arm and began to walk. "Here my children are made to help themselves. They must learn to be independent. I want to tell you something important. These children are first just that – children. Secondly, they're handicapped. But first they're children."

We stopped at one of the many open classrooms. A nine-year-old girl without arms was busy writing with her feet. She looked up and smiled.

"You should see her sew and even brush her teeth with her feet," said a beaming sister.

"Why are the blind children and the crippled in the same class?"

"Why wouldn't they be? One group reads with their hands and the other with their eyes. What's the difference?"

She was already moving off. I hurried behind.

"How many children are there in the school?"

"Two hundred and fifty."

"Helpers?"

"Quite a few. Three doctors, a dentist and his wife and some Americans, plus some Canadian and English youths and a few Haitians."

"Any interference from the government?" Jean-Claude Duvalier was currently the president for life and, although he did not have the infamous reputation of his father, Papa Doc, Haiti was still a dictatorship.

"The government has been helpful in many ways," Sister Joan replied ambiguously.

She turned and was off again, swinging her two canes ahead of her as she clicked her way towards the hammering coming from across the courtyard. She swung a cane in the direction of a shed.

"That's our brace and prosthesis shop. It's the only shop in the world completely operated by deaf people."

A six-year-old boy on wooden legs hurried by, obviously late for class. Something was odd about his legs. Then I realized what.

"Surely that little boy has his legs on backwards."

The sister laughed. "You probably think that's the result of the kind of work we're doing in the shop."

"But why are his feet pointing backwards?" I persisted.

"For balance. It's the idea of the late Dr. Kessler from the Kessler Institute in New Jersey. The idea is that the boy has his arms in front of him to counterbalance his body."

"So his feet are pointing backwards to stop him falling back?"

"Right. But we'll be turning them around to the front in about a year from now."

We resumed our walk.

"Obviously you need money. How do you go about getting it?"

"Various people hear about us," she laughed, "from people like you. One group of Americans visit us each year. Most are teenagers. They bring medicine and clothes and return with Haitian souvenirs. Then they sell the goods for a profit in the States. With the money they buy more medicine and clothes ready for the trip back to Haiti and begin again." She smiled. Obviously the idea of such a simple scheme appealed to her.

"You like that idea?"

"I like any idea that will stop my children from begging."

"Aren't you begging?"

She stopped walking, turned to face me and leaned heavily on her canes. Her eyes twinkled and she smiled. "Never overtly."

I accepted Sister Joan's invitation to stay the night at École St. Vincent. At one minute to eight on a hot, smelly Monday morning, I was standing on a narrow balcony that wound its way around the school's courtyard. The day was about to begin as it had for the past thirty years, with a flag-raising ceremony. A crippled boy was holding the string to send the flag of Haiti creeping slowly up a white pole. The courtyard was filled with children, divided into groups. I looked down on a group of ten deaf children. Two of the smallest – about five years of age – had just been rebuked for "talking." Their arms were folded to stop their hands from communicating.

Across the yard I could see Sister Joan sitting behind her desk in her glass-walled office. The seats outside her office were already full of mothers and children, some of the eight hundred outpatients that visited this indomitable woman each month. She appeared a little tired. She should be, I thought. She had already been up for hours.

Sister Joan's itinerary would put the strongest to shame. Her day began at 3:30 A.M. with two hours of prayers. At 6 A.M. it was time for mass, and from there it was off to school for the 7:15 A.M. start. Yet this smiling woman was moving energetically among the outpatients, gently cradling each child in turn as its mother described the problem.

A blind eighteen-year-old boy lifted an accordion and began to play. The sound slipped around the yard, stilling the shuffling, impatient feet of the children. The ceremony began with the national anthem of Haiti. The group of deaf children joined in, signing along with their swiftly moving fingers. The two children whose arms had been folded were now allowed to unfold them. They joined in the song enthusiastically. Meanwhile, the others lifted their voices in joyous pride for their land and country, which had abandoned them to the care of a nun from Boston.

Before I left, I asked Sister Joan what she needed for the home.

"A machine that's used for duplicating braille," she replied.

"How much would it cost?"

"About a thousand dollars." She placed a hand on my arm and smiled. "I'm not begging, you know, or, at least, not overtly."

Back in Toronto, I wrote a story about Sister Joan, which was widely published, and it caught the imagination of my elder daughter, Susan. She was eighteen years old and had worked hard at school. I had often had to tell her to stop studying and go to bed, but she was determined to succeed. Unfortunately, despite her efforts, she had difficulty passing exams. Her frustration finally forced her to take action. She decided to quit school and go to Haiti to work with Sister Joan.

The fact that the story had moved her was no surprise. Susan was a lot like her mother, and her love for children had already manifested itself in many ways. There was something about her that made young children instantly recognize that she was a friend. But Doreen and I were worried at the idea of her going to Haiti. It was not a resort. We tried to explain to her that it was one of the ten poorest areas of the world, and a very dangerous place. After two days of fruitless argument, Doreen and I finally gave in. I phoned Sister Joan, who was overjoyed at the prospect of a young volunteer.

Once again I set off for Haiti. We arrived and took a cab to the mission. I glanced across the back seat at my daughter, whom I loved and whose safety was constantly on my mind. She was looking out the window, obviously shocked at what she saw. The stench was appalling, and as we stepped over the open sewers to reach what would be her home for six months, I could imagine what she was thinking. This was not what she had envisioned from reading my article. The reality was far worse than words could ever describe.

After being shown her room, we walked to my hotel. As I washed up, Susan sat on the bed. I heard a faint voice saying, "I want to go home."

I finished washing and returned to the room. "So what would you like to eat?"

"Did you hear what I said, Dad?"

I sat down on the bed and put my arm around her.

"Susan, I know how you must feel, but there's something you should know. Life is not full of exits. When you decided to drop out of school and work in Haiti, you made a promise to us all."

Her eyes filled with tears.

"Tell you what," I said. "I'll arrange for an airline ticket that you can use any time you want. Give it at least a two-week trial. If you're still missing home, then you can jump on a plane. If not, try it again for another two weeks, and so on. How about it?"

She grinned and wiped her eyes.

It was not easy saying goodbye to Susan at the airport, knowing that I was leaving her in a dangerous country.

"You what?" Doreen was furious.

How anyone could permit their daughter to go a place like Haiti was difficult enough to understand, but how a father could say goodbye to a daughter who had asked to come home was beyond belief. The phone calls were fast and furious. It seemed that each night Doreen would be on the phone to Port-au-Prince. As the days passed, Susan appeared to be settling in, although not well enough for Doreen's peace of mind.

"I'm going to Haiti."

This was no surprise. The only surprise was that it had taken all of two weeks for Doreen to decide. Now she had to persuade her employers at Sunnybrook Hospital that she needed time off. But her bosses were sympathetic, and within days mother and daughter were reunited.

Doreen's first visit to the developing world changed our lives like no other event. Susan had now adjusted well enough to be able to tour the island. She had seen the best and the worst of this dreadfully poor country and was anxious to show her mother something of how the rest of the world lived. Although the deaf and blind children, whom Susan had formed into a choir at the school, were happy enough, life on the outside of Sister Joan's compound was unbelievably grim. As she and Susan visited the slums, Doreen repeatedly stopped to examine the children.

"I saw children who were so full of worms that they were hanging from their rectums," she said on her return. "Although I've nursed for almost twenty-five years, I'd never seen a case of tetanus. Now I've seen a dozen, all babies."

She had been off the plane just a few hours and the sights and sounds of Haiti were still with her.

"And do you know how a baby gets tetanus?" she leaned forward resting a cup of tea on her knee. "Because the mother has delivered it in a field and cut the cord with a machete. And, as if that's not bad enough, the mother first wipes the blade of the machete with cow dung to keep away the evil spirits."

Ironically, the next day we were invited to attend a luncheon in honour of the visit of Her Majesty the Queen to Toronto. Almost fifteen hundred people sat and stared at the head table, waiting for the Queen to begin eating. In the meantime I watched Doreen. Although the rest of our table were animated in conversation, she said little. As each dish was served, it seemed to surpass the previous helping. Unable to watch this opulence any longer, Doreen wiped her eyes with her napkin and left the table. The wealth of food served at this gathering had been too much of a reminder of those who had nothing. As a journalist I had often seen sights that had been shocking, but unlike Doreen, I had pushed them aside.

"I'm sorry, I just cannot go on like this," Doreen said. It was her third night without sleep. "I have to do something. I'm going to quit my job and work to help mothers and children in the slums of the world."

If anyone else had made such a remark, I would have shrugged it off. But I knew better than to do that with Doreen. Whatever it was she had in mind, she was going to do it.

Of all the medical conditions that Doreen had witnessed in Haiti, none bothered her as much as the infestations of intestinal worms. Convinced that something could be done to cure this condition, she spoke to various doctors and was told that two of the best experts were in London, England. So she went there and met with both of them. A drug called Vermox produced good results, she was told so, back in Toronto, her next call was to the company that made the drug. In what was the first of many such donations by numerous companies, it agreed to give her the drugs for use in Haiti.

Within months my remarkable wife had set up a pilot program in Haiti. At a small clinic in La Coma, each child was first weighed and measured and then given a dose of Vermox. The obvious success of the pilot program was easy to see. Volunteer schoolteachers working in Haiti began to complain jokingly that classes that once had been full of sleepy children were now alive with laughing, energetic kids, feeling well for the first time. Pleased with her achievement, Doreen handed it over to another nongovernment organization to run.

After six months in Haiti, Susan had come back. Her time there had given her tremendous confidence, and she was determined to succeed at what she loved best – caring for children. She immediately signed on for a two-year course in early childhood education at Seneca College and, at the end of that time, was top of her class with three jobs waiting for her. I do not know what this says about the education of our children, but I do know that a young woman – who had failed at school, no matter how hard she had worked, had, on her own, found something at which she could excel.

Vincent had now taken such an interest in music that he decided to quit school and play full time with his band. We were not happy at this decision. Unfortunately, I was hardly in a position to complain, having left school myself at fourteen and having wound up playing in a band. Like father, like son. Vincent began travelling with his small group throughout Ontario. He was obviously happy and, although Doreen and I were worried, he did seem to know what he was doing and was planning a future for himself. He rented a cheap apartment, which reflected its price. All of us missed him around the house, but not the band's regular rehearsals in the basement.

Susan had made some good friends at her college and was

now enjoying her job at a day-care centre immensely. She loved it, but hers was the least appreciated job in our country. She was directing youngsters through the most vital years of their lives, yet all she received for her dedication was the most miserable wage. Most preschool teachers enjoy children so much that they would do the job for nothing, and an ungrateful government pays them just that.

Kim was now eleven. We had decided to send her to the finest school available, regardless of the cost. One program at Havergal College in Toronto was particularly instructive. Students would spend three months in France with a French family and attend the local school. It gave Kim an experience she would never forget. She lived in a tiny village in Brittany with a family that consisted of three daughters, an unemployed father and a mother who worked in the market. They loved Kim, and Kim loved them, and it was not easy for her when the time came to return to Canada.

Doreen continued to monitor the aid program in Haiti and was realistic enough to know that Vermox was only a temporary solution. The drug may rid a body of worms, but they would return quickly without clean water and improved health conditions. There was much to be done. She quit her job at the hospital and was now at a dangerous stage. She knew exactly where she wanted to go and nothing was going to stop her.

First she needed a name for her organization. Global Ed-Med Supplies (the Ed-Med stands for educational and medical), better known as GEMS, was founded in 1983 and hundreds of thousands of people from Bosnia to Ethiopia, from Brazil to Haiti, owe a better life to this special woman.

To her it seemed so simple. There were millions of people in this world without medical care. Without the means to get the simplest of medical supplies, they were left to die. We in West, on the other hand, had so much that a lot was wasted. Hospitals were discarding perfectly good medical equipment in order to replace it with the newest version. Why not collect these supposedly outdated supplies?

A space in the corner of a warehouse, measuring twenty square feet, quickly proved insufficient. Doreen discovered that there were many generous people in this world, ready to give. The hospitals were first to leap at the opportunity to put their obsolete medical supplies to good use.

But how do you get a dozen beds from Vancouver to Toronto free of charge? Easy. Just go to a moving company and ask. Allied Van Lines said yes. They would use their empty vans returning after deliveries to pick up equipment across the country. So GEMS grew and, as the word of its existence spread, requests for help came in from around the world.

Much as we wanted to help everyone, GEMS was too small to do without some assistance. Air Canada and British Airways were flying our medical supplies at no cost, but transporting larger items by sea was expensive. Running the organization was costing more money than we could afford. We needed to raise funds, and puzzled over how to do it. Then Doreen had an idea.

"What we need is a big-name sponsor," said Doreen.

I buried my face in a newspaper.

"Someone like the Governor General of Canada."

I continued to read the paper.

"You know him. Ask if I can meet with him and have a chat."

I had met His Excellency Ed Schreyer twice, both times at large gatherings where he had shaken my hand and passed on. I explained this to Doreen.

"Okay, so you don't know him all that well. He'll know you from your cartoons. Just ring him up and say that I'd like to meet with him."

I phoned and was surprised that I was easily able to arrange a meeting between the Queen's representative and Doreen, if only for ten minutes. Doreen was overjoyed. What was she hoping to get from the meeting?

"Simple. I'll get him to be our chief patron."

I explained that she should not expect too much from such a busy person and hoped in my heart that the trip to Ottawa would not be too much of a letdown.

"How did it go?" I asked when she returned.

"Fine."

"Did you get your ten minutes?"

"We spent two hours together."

I was amazed. "And?"

"And he's agreed to be our chief patron."

Why I ever thought that it would be any different I don't know.

The next morning the phone in my office rang. It was Government House. The Governor General's "whatever" wished to speak to me. It seemed there had been a terrible mistake. Certain rules had been broken. It was impossible for the Governor General to be the chief patron of GEMS for a variety of reasons. First, there was a strict rule that any organization he sponsored had to have been in existence for five years. Second, the organization had to be seen to be in a firm financial position and . . .

I promised I would pass the message on to Doreen. I did and she jumped to the phone. I would not have wished to be in the shoes of the Governor General's "whatever" for all the honours in a queen's cupboard.

"The Governor General promised me that he would be the chief patron of GEMS, and whatever it is you have to say, I suggest you say to him."

Once again the phone rang in my office, and once again the pompous "whatever" to the Governor General was on the line. A mistake had been made. The Governor General had indeed promised to support GEMS and had no intention of backing down. In fact, His Excellency wished me to pass on his sincere thanks for the honour of being associated with the organization.

While Doreen was busy establishing GEMS, I became involved in operating a chain of pubs. One day in 1981 I arrived at the office to find John excited at the idea of opening a number of pubs called the Ben Wicks. Because the exercise proved to be a huge flop, he has since suggested it was my idea in the first place, but I'm sure it was not.

The plan was simple in the extreme. First, we would gather a group of doctors and dentists who, as everyone knows, are constantly looking for ventures to invest in, and persuade them that the place to unload their loot would be our pubs. Second, we would open one pub and then a chain of them across Canada. Third, each partner would sit back and count the lolly as it flooded in. There was only one slight problem − none of us knew the slightest thing about running a pub.

If I had only listened to Doreen. She felt that running the pub, or a chain of pubs, would interfere with our lives. She was right. It was the worst move I have ever made. She suggested that I speak to my agent, Matie Molinaro. Matie thought it was a lousy idea. Why not speak to Norman, my lawyer? she suggested. I did. He thought the idea was dumb. So I went ahead.

"Okay, so it could be tricky," said John. "But we'll get a group of consultants to advise us. Like this we can continue to travel the world, filming our program, fully confident that back at the ranch a brilliant staff, handpicked by experts, will be on hand to look after the shop." The result of this clever strategy is so painful that originally I was all for leaving it out of this book entirely. However, since I am covering all aspects of my life, it is only fair that the disasters are included.

The consultants came well recommended. First they told us that we needed the right location. The location they suggested was in the Cabbagetown area of Toronto, named after the number of cabbages that were grown in the backyards of the immigrants that had settled there. The neighbourhood was a mixture of poor, very poor and would-be poor people. Our venture would leave John and I knowing what it felt like to be part of all of those groups. (Today the neighbourhood consists of the very poor, the poor and the filthy rich.)

Our original idea had been for a small bar catering to fifty customers. The food would be British, and my cartoons would be displayed on the walls. The consultants went along with the idea of the bar, then convinced us that what was really needed in the area was a French restaurant. We were amazed, yet stupid enough to go along. Four hundred thousand dollars later we had a British pub serving French cuisine, a French chef who refused to allow ketchup on the tables, a menu in French (which I could not understand), abstract watercolour paintings hanging on the walls and a room that could seat one hundred and fifty patrons. That we kept the business going for three years had nothing to do with our ability to attract customers. It was impossible to find a buyer sooner.

I do not miss it one iota. I do not miss grabbing a customer and slowly lowering him into a chair, fearing that the butcher knife sticking out of his stomach would be jolted into piercing a vital organ. I do not miss the regular who shot himself in the foot while showing a friend a new gun he had recently "acquired." I do not miss the frequent visits from shoplifters taking orders for clothes they were about to steal. "What colour shirt? Neck size?" I certainly do not miss the man who was very big and very annoyed.

"I've lost my overcoat," he said. "And not just any overcoat. This was a velvet overcoat and cost me six hundred dollars."

"When did you lose it?"

"I hung it up last night and left without it. I've just come in and it ain't there."

"I'll ask around and see if anyone has seen it."

"You don't have to ask. I know who took it."

"You know who took it?"

"I do . . . him!" He pointed to the other end of the bar

where an unshaven stranger was nursing a pint sat staring at his glass.

"How do you know it was him?"

"Because he was staring at my coat all night."

This hardly seemed the kind of evidence that would stand up in court. Nevertheless, I decided to have a chat with the accused.

"Good evening," I smiled.

He looked up and said nothing. I sat beside him.

"Mind if I sit down a minute?"

"Do what you like. It's your place, ain't it?"

"True," I nodded. "We seem to have a little problem and I'm asking everyone in the bar if they can help."

He lifted his glass and began to drink.

"It seems there's a coat missing from the rack, and we're asking if anyone can help find it."

"I never took his fuckin' coat. I got a coat."

"Of course you have." I immediately saw a court case looming and me answering a lawyer's questions. "Just asking."

"It's no good," I told the velvet-coat loser. "He says he hasn't got it, so what can I do?"

He was about to turn ugly when our wonderful manager, who had stayed with us through the thick of our problems, asked what was happening. I quickly explained. Before I could stop him, he went back to face the accused. When he returned, he was smiling.

"He'll bring it back tomorrow."

"He admits he has it?"

"Not exactly, but I told him we were bringing in the police to question everyone, and that if he knew of anyone who might have it, he should warn them."

"What did he say?"

"He said he thinks it might have been a friend of his who took it by mistake."

The next day he brought back the coat and I gave him a

twenty-dollar reward I'd promised. Somehow I couldn't see him in a velvet coat and couldn't help thinking that I was out twenty bucks.

Finally, we managed to find a buyer. We sold to him so rapidly I forgot to make the stipulation that he should not use my name for his new establishment. The Ben Wicks is still there on Parliament Street, but I have nothing to do with it. I don't miss it a scrap. I never have.

I was mowing the lawn one day when Susan said she had something to tell me. The lad she was seeing had asked to marry her. She wanted me to know that she was about to say yes. Doreen and I were delighted. Mark McLelland was a high-school teacher and a fine young man. The only drawback to the arrangement was that they settled in Cambridge, an hour's drive from Toronto. Doreen and I felt it was an hour's drive too far.

In 1985 the international news had once again settled on the troubled continent of Africa. Although newspapers everywhere were carrying stories of Africa's longest war, it took a BBC camera crew to lift the curtain on the mass starvation in Ethiopia. A celebration in the capital city of Addis Ababa inadvertently allowed this wake-up call to the rest of the world. Local officials from across the country were in Addis Ababa to attend the ceremony. Their assistants left in charge were not aware of the efforts that had been made to keep out the foreign press. One group allowed a BBC camera crew into an area of the country that was strictly out of bounds. The result was an eight-minute piece of film that shook the world. For the first time, around the world, hundreds of thousands of Ethiopians were seen dying of starvation.

An Anglican minister phoned Doreen. He had received two visitors from Ethiopia. Would Doreen meet with them?

The lobby of the hotel was quiet and the two Ethiopians stood out. After introductions, we went to a meeting room where the visitors explained why they had travelled from Eritrea to Canada.

"Excuse me. I thought you were from Ethiopia."

"We are," they said. "Eritrea is a district in the northeast of the country."

I moved a blackboard into place and asked them to draw where they were from. I was fascinated, especially when they said they were at war with the government in Addis Ababa. I interrupted.

"You're at war with the government?"

"We are and have been for twenty-five years."

"Are you telling us you're part of a rebel army?"

They nodded. "We're members of the EPLF, the Eritrean People's Liberation Front."

I turned to Doreen. "I think we need to talk."

"About what?" Doreen was obviously more anxious to hear from the Eritreans than I was.

"About these two gentlemen." I turned to the two, who stood passively looking on.

"I'm sorry to say this, but this presents a problem."

"What problem?" asked Doreen.

"The fact is if these two gentlemen are part of an army that's trying to overthrow their government, GEMS' involvement with them becomes very much a political situation."

Doreen ignored me and turned back to the men standing by the blackboard. "Do you have women and children starving and in urgent need of medical supplies?"

Both men nodded. "By the hundreds of thousands. Because of the war, no supplies are getting into our area, and we're desperate."

Doreen immediately took charge of the situation. "We're going to get supplies through and we don't care how we do it."

Both men smiled.

"How do you propose that we get supplies into a war zone?" I asked.

"You're going to take them, that's how," she grinned.

16

AS MANY AS TWO MILLION starving people in Eritrea, a vast area of barren land, were trapped in Africa's longest and most bitter war. A twenty-four-year struggle for independence from Ethiopia had left tens of thousands killed or maimed. Whole towns and villages had been blasted from the map.

After news of the starvation in Ethiopia was broadcast, millions of tons in food aid had been sent to those places in Ethiopia controlled by the Russian-backed government in Addis Ababa, but none had reached Eritrea, one of the hardest hit areas of the great drought. Appeals from the rebel army for a truce to allow safe passage of food to the north had been ignored by the government in Addis Ababa.

"And how do you propose that I get into this hellhole?" I asked the Eritreans visiting Toronto.

"By the back door," they grinned.

And so I left for the most gruelling journey of my life, flying from Toronto to London, on to Khartoum and from there to Port Sudan on the Red Sea. There, I was promised, friends of the EPLF army would take me across the Nubian Desert. Once over the Sudan–Ethiopia border, I would be safe in rebel-held territory.

GEMS had collected seven hundred kilograms of medical supplies, packed in thirty-three large cardboard boxes. Drugs, such as streptomycin (a powerful antibiotic) and anti-malaria pills, as well as syringes, sutures, sheets and laboratory equipment had been donated chiefly by Leslie Dan, owner of NovoPharm, a Toronto pharmaceutical company. British Airways flew the cargo from Toronto to Khartoum. From there the medicines were flown to Port Sudan. And it was there that l watched our supplies being loaded onto a truck before setting out on the final leg of my journey – the perilous drive to the Eritrean front.

We waited three days at a village in the Sudan for the rebels to show up. They finally arrived in a small Land Rover. Three young rebel soldiers sat in the front, joyfully whistling along to the Eritrean music on the tape they had jammed into the dashboard stereo.

Although the Sudanese government had given the EPLF free passage through its territory, the journey was far from easy. We left at night. The tar road we took out of the village stopped abruptly and we faced a trackless desert. Eighty kilometres out, we were down to a crawl. Another forty kilometres and we were scrambling under the truck most of the night, clawing at the sand that gripped the vehicle. A blinding sun rose above a distant mountain range as we limped across a crumbling border post, deserted since EPLF soldiers had overrun the Ethiopian garrison six years before. The desolate mountains closed around us, and boulders and shrivelled thorn bushes hemmed us in.

We had bounced and rattled for fifteen hours when the driver began to search for a concealed trail built by the rebels into a hidden valley. Suddenly, from behind a huge rock, a rebel soldier dressed in shorts and sandals appeared, a Russian rifle slung over his shoulder. He grinned, shouted a welcome to my driver and waved us through. This was Orota, the base camp of the EPLF. From here the rebels claimed to control 85 per cent of Eritrea, an independent country annexed to Ethiopia by Haile Selassie in 1962.

The valley stretched for five kilometres, and on every side of us bandaged men and women were shuffling along in the morning sun, grenades hanging from their belts. Soon all would be quiet. From sunrise to sunset nothing moved in Orota, but once the sun went down, a small city came to life. Generators hummed and truck engines barked in the darkness. At all times, the rebels scanned the skies for the Russian-built MiG jets that swept down over the mountains from Ethiopian airfields.

Victims of the war – soldiers and civilians alike – came to this valley to be treated in an amazing medical complex of tents and mud huts, which hugged the mountainside under a camouflage of rocks and trees. Talented Eritrean doctors, many trained in Europe and America, performed complicated heart and plastic surgeries, a rifle never far from their hands. They worked after sunset, when the generator could run the lights and their equipment. It was sometimes 2 A.M. when the last patient was treated and the lights went out.

At the entrance to a small tent pitched in the shadow of a tree, London-trained surgeon Dr. Nerayo Tekle Michael paused. "I want you to see something."

Inside, a boy of fifteen was lying on his side having his dressing changed. He was a victim of a napalm bomb. Blind in one eye, he turned his pitiful face up towards the roof of the tent. Dr. Michael said the boy was playing in his village when the MiG struck. He was burned over 35 per cent of his body. He had been carried more than one hundred and twenty kilometres, village to village, until ten days later he reached the Orota clinic.

As a woman removed the old bandages, blood poured from the boy's blackened skin. I shall remember his screams to my dying day.

"Are you a nurse or a fighter?" I asked her.

"Both," she replied. "I have two hands. I can hold a rifle in one and a bandage in the other."

There were happy stories in Orota. Dr. Michael pointed out a seven-year-old girl, now recovered, who was found in the bombed-out wreckage of her village marketplace, still suckling the breast of her dead mother.

"Please do something for me," pleaded Dr. Michael as I prepared to leave Orota. "Tell the people out there that we need help . . . not doctors, but specialists to teach us new techniques."

We unloaded half of the Toronto supplies for use in the Orota clinic. The rest we were taking into the country, where I was told the need was greatest. I hitched a lift with two British doctors through the hills to the trenches at Nacfa. Here the Eritrean rebels met their enemy face-to-face, in places throwing insults across the no-man's land that separated the two lines.

We sat in a bunker as the Ethiopian army fired barrage after barrage of mortar shells. The rebels, squatting safely in the trenches, laughed at the wasted fire. A particular weapon, known as the "Stalin organ," fired a shower of forty shells that straddled the trenches. "Every time they push the button, it costs them one hundred and fifty thousand dollars," grinned one soldier.

The rebel troops were highly disciplined, firing only on the orders of their section leader. Almost one third of them were women, and the section chief here was twenty-three-year-old Marza. She calmly asked me if I would like some tea.

She had been at the front for seven years. Her husband was a soldier in another section. They married in a civil ceremony at the front. Friends stood in for their parents and a member of the rebel government's social affairs department asked the couple to sign a card.

"And if you no longer wish to stay married?" I asked.

"Then the same man comes and takes back your card," Marza laughed.

The next day as I trekked along a dry riverbed that was buzzing with a million flies, I came upon one of the most desolate sights I had seen. Sitting dejected and despondent on the valley floor were three thousand Ethiopian prisoners of war, dressed in the ragged remnants of their khaki uniforms. Rebel guards, perched in rickety towers, looked on as a group of twelve prisoners played a silent, desultory game of volleyball.

Ghebru Haile, aged thirty, had the job of caring for this pitiful band of men, mostly peasant conscripts.

"They share everything we have," said Haile. "We have the same. It's a major problem for us. We've appealed to the Red Cross. They came to see the prisoners three months ago, and we've heard nothing since. We've offered to exchange them for the men of ours that the Ethiopians have, but they refuse. They say we have no prisoners of theirs. Only traitors."

I talked to one prisoner, Pafessa Taimere, aged twenty-nine, of Addis Ababa, who said he had been captured eleven months earlier. He told me he shared a blanket with a fellow prisoner and slept on the floor of a mud hut. "I have no problems," he said. "If I were set free, I would be killed."

That night we set off again through the mountains with the remaining medical supplies, stopping at dawn to rest in a mud hut. But before I could sleep, my guide, Gabriel, arrived at the door.

"We're going to have to move," he announced.

In daylight we drove across an open plain, anxiously scanning the skies for enemy aircraft. We left the road and began to cover ground fit only for travel by tank. In a small clearing sheltered by rocks, two Jeeps stood beside a group of huts.

"You're about to meet a very important man," said Gabriel. "He's our vice-secretary general, Issayas Afewerki. He has asked to meet with you."

I was surprised. This was the number-two man of the EPLF. Few journalists had had the opportunity to meet him.

We entered a hut containing two beds. I sat on one. It was as hard as a rock. Afewerki made a sudden dramatic entrance. Over six feet tall, he was a striking man in his mid-thirties. For a half-hour he answered my questions about the political aims of the EPLF. Then, glancing at a gold watch, he rose abruptly, thanked me and strode out.

After eight days on the road we were getting close to the place where I was to deliver the rest of the precious cargo of supplies. In an effort to provide relief to the estimated two million civilians living in this vast, isolated area of Eritrea, the rebel army had recently established its first settlement camp. From there they distributed the meagre food supplies they were able to secure. The food was stored at a camp near Zara, a two hours' walk from the settlement and protected by huge thorn bushes.

Our medical supplies were strapped to the back of a camel, the only form of transport now possible. A young female "barefoot" doctor, so called because of the maximum eight weeks' training most of these fifteen hundred volunteers received, led the camel. We plodded slowly across an arid wasteland strewn with the carcasses of camels awaiting the swooping vultures. Humans, in their desperate search for any food, had even stripped the trees bare of the leaves that once kept the camels alive.

Only two weeks before, word of the new camp had begun to spread. The promise of food was now drawing thousands of people to the area. Six thousand had already arrived after a three-day hike, and many more were on their way from more remote areas. They crouched along a clay-baked river bed, huddling for shelter under improvised tents of rags and branches. A few EPLF soldiers were attempting to direct the newcomers. A young rebel shifted his gun from shoulder to shoulder, shouting to a group of new arrivals, telling them where to set up.

"We must have discipline or we're finished," he explained. "Everyone will be treated equally and get their share of the little food we have."

I lifted the flap of a tent made of rags. Crowded inside were a mother and her four daughters. One baby hung from a dry breast. A three-year-old girl lay on her back, desperately sick with malaria. Her sister, aged four, lay across her, her face in the dirt, dribbling diarrhoea and blood from her rectum as a five-year-old girl looked on.

"My God," I heard myself crying. "They're dying. Can't you rush them to the clinic?"

"Why?" asked the young doctor.

"To give them treatment."

"With what?"

I lowered the flap. For one stupid moment I had imagined I was living in a sane world.

"Before the week is out, she will lose three of her daughters," the doctor said as she stomped away, her face grim. "She lost her son last week. Lift any other flap and you'll find the same." She waved her arm at the sea of tents, bringing the horror vividly to life.

The clinic was almost hidden by crouching mothers. All held tiny bundles, babies they had once carried inside them only to deliver into a man-made hell. Those women who could struggled to their feet and pushed their dying children towards me. I was white. I must be a doctor. One mother stood to block my way, her long, ragged cloak trailing to the floor. She suddenly swept it open. One hollow-eyed child clung to her leg, another lay lifeless in the crook of her arm.

Conjunctivitis was everywhere. The pus that oozed from the children's eyes made a nesting paradise for thousands of flies. Without treatment, most of these children would be irreversibly blind within six days, the doctor said, then added, "We have no ointment." All this for a fifty-cent tube of ointment? For the want of pennies, thousands would grope their way through Africa for the rest of their lives.

We unloaded our supplies. To my eyes, it was a miserable amount, and yet to the doctor it was the answer to her prayer.

We made our way out of the area. Our mission was over. I had faced a new truth – politics and war were a winning combination. Both were slowly pushing us towards the greatest natural disaster in the history of man. Who was to blame? The Ethiopians? The Eritreans? The Russians? The Americans? The United Nations? Or all of the above? I don't think so. For, in the words of the late Walt Kelly, "I have seen the enemy. And it is us."

It was 5 A.M. The sun had yet to make an appearance. Only a strip of light was visible over distant mountains as I made my way out of the small hut where we had taken shelter for the night. A steady stream of traffic was already on the nearby road. After saying goodbye to my hosts, I headed off in the direction of the Sudan border, glancing over my shoulder as I did, hoping to hitch a ride. Within minutes a battered truck pulled to a stop. The Arab truck driver smiled and pulled me into the cab of a vehicle that already held a crush of human bodies. Six of us were packed into the front of the truck. A baby's head nudged into my shoulder as the child attempted to feed from its mother's breast. Soon the baby's eyes closed as we rocked to the sway of the truck heading west from Eritrea into the Sudan and the ancient Sudanese city of Kassala, a hundred kilometres away.

As in all conflicts, the astonishing numbers of victims had begun to spill over into surrounding areas. Africa's largest country, Sudan, was reeling under a human load so pressing that the country was in danger of being swamped by more than a million people staggering across its borders in search of food – more than three thousand every day, mostly from the war-torn areas of Eritrea.

Within an hour's drive of Kassala, the first evidence of this massive migration of starving people loomed shockingly on the sun-scorched horizon. Huddled around a sea of makeshift huts, eighty thousand refugees sat patiently on the hot sand waiting for food. Then a swirling funnel of dust and dirt suddenly appeared, racing across the barren plain. It rose in a hideous twist and zigzagged through the camp, tearing down the meagre shelters and scattering debris. For these suffering people, the dust-storm season was just one more misery in a life full of tragedy.

Diane Mackie, a young nurse from Toronto, had been working in this refugee camp for four months.

"Many of the refugees are nomads," she told me. "They have lost everything – their loved ones, their camels, their goats and a way of life that goes back for thousands of years."

We ducked inside a large tent bearing the sign "Children's Hospital." There were beds for only thirty children and forty adults.

"Please tell the people back home that their help has made a fantastic difference," said Mackie. "We are beginning to hold our own, but if once their aid slows down or stops, we shall be back to where we were."

She recalled with horror the days of the previous December, when children by the thousands perished for want of food and medical supplies. All that Mackie and the other nurses and doctors could do was go from tent to tent making agonizing choices over which children had the best chances of surviving if they were treated.

Even so, she recalled sadly, "Every child we admitted to our tiny hospital died. Thirty to forty a day. U.S. Senator Teddy Kennedy arrived at Christmas, our worst period. He had been told in Khartoum that things were under control, and when he arrived he was appalled."

Within weeks of Kennedy's visit, however, conditions improved as fresh supplies began to arrive from the Sudanese ports. And the oddest items sometimes turned up. I noted with incredulity that each of the children I visited was sucking on a lollipop.

Mackie laughed. "I was scrounging around the camp and

found a couple of cardboard boxes. Inside were dozens of lol-lipops." Even stranger, the boxes bore the label of the Canadian drug-store chain, Shoppers Drug Mart.

We stopped beside the bed of a three-year-old Arab girl, Asha, whose father grabbed Mackie's hands in his, smiling and bowing. She explained, "Her father carried her into the camp three weeks ago. Her mother was dead and so were her two sisters. She was the only one left of the old man's family. Her case was hopeless. She weighed just five kilos. One doctor took a look at her and said, 'I'm afraid this little bird is for the cat.' But there was something about her that made everyone want to fight."

She reached down and gently took Asha's hand. "Asha is now seven and a half kilos," she said proudly. "And she's going to make it. One little bird that had a golden cage."

We left the old man playing with his daughter. "He never leaves her side," said Mackie. "Day and night, he's always there."

It is true that, amid the terrible suffering, there were many stories here and in other camps that had happy endings. Millions of people throughout the world had poured their hearts into Africa and their help had gone to save thousands of Ashas in every corner of this famine-stricken continent. And it was not only the children who were being saved. So, too, were some of the elderly who, in the turmoil of refugee life, had been left alone to starve and die, as fitter relatives began their desperate trek in search of food.

"There is no more tragic sight than that of an elderly strag-gler who has been left behind," said Ian Robbins of the British-based Help for the Aged Organization. "Provided these people are living in their own communities, the family plays a large part in taking care of them. Unfortunately, once these groups are forced to move, it is the elderly left on their own who are in dire need."

There was no end in sight to the human exodus.

"In the next three months we are expecting another three hundred thousand refugees," the commissioner of refugees for the Sudan had told me in an earlier interview. "And we are a country that is desperately short of food ourselves."

The commissioner had opened his arms wide. "The incredible thing is that the Sudan has kept its borders open. We are doing what our president, Colonel Jaafar al-Numeiry, feels should be done – invoking the Arab tradition of hospitality towards strangers. If you see an Arab family sitting down to eat, and if you have no food, they will expect you to join them. The Prophet Mohammed teaches us this." But it is one thing to join a family in a meal; it is quite another to stay for months and maybe years.

The fact was that the camps were a temporary answer. Like people everywhere, home was where the refugees wanted to be. As one of them told me. "I don't know why I came. I'm going to die here. If I'm going to die anywhere, I'd rather die at home."

I directed the cabdriver in Kassala to take me to a hotel and asked him where the bus station was and the times of buses to Khartoum. He laughed. The few buses that did set off across the desert left when the driver could find sufficient gas. This could take a few hours; then again, it could take days.

I quickly made this friendly driver aware of my need to get to Khartoum and told him that if he helped me, great riches – well, some riches – would come his way. Three days later, he excitedly informed me that he had found a bus driver. This driver had been touring various back streets, and, with the aid of a long piece of tubing, had transferred sufficient gas from parked cars into his hungry bus.

We hurried through narrow streets and were fortunate to find the very bus. The driver was sympathetic to the pleas of the cabdriver and allowed me to step on board. Considerably lighter in the wallet, having satisfied both drivers, I took my place on the only seat available. Once again the woman beside me was breast-feeding. Chickens and various animals appeared to take up the rest of the space and, after a series of bangs and other loud noises followed by thick black smoke, we began to move.

With water so scarce, I had been forced to neglect the usual rules of sanitation for eating abroad. At the hotel I had searched my salads for anything moving, but on the road I had had to ignore the fact that much of the food was likely home to a million varieties of bacteria. Within the first fifteen minutes of the ten-hour journey across the sand, a strange rumbling began in the pit of my stomach. Hoping that the woman beside me would think that these embarrassing noises were the result of her baby's need for food, I turned and smiled. She glared back. The baby was sleeping. Within the hour my pains had spread and now danced around my lower stomach. I needed a bathroom and quick. I tried gripping my stomach in the hopes that a tight squeeze would hold off an even more embarrassing situation. It was hopeless. I had to stop the bus.

I struggled to my feet and staggered to the front of the bouncing, lurching vehicle. I tapped the driver on the shoulder. He turned and smiled. Would he mind stopping? He turned and smiled again. I asked if he would stop. He smiled once more. I suddenly realized I was the only one on the bus who spoke English. Desperate by now, I reverted to the familiar tactic of most tourists. I shouted.

Not only did the driver turn, but the rest of the passengers on the bus looked up, fearing that the only Englishman on board had been out in the midday sun too long and had become a raving lunatic. I didn't care what they thought. The main thing was that the bus had come to a screaming halt. I banged on the door, which was immediately thrown open. I looked around at what was quite possibly the flattest area on earth. There was not one tree in sight. I headed for the only cover available – the bus – and dropped my trousers. Here was a show the likes of which few on board had ever seen. Faces, including the driver's, were pressed to the back window. Their huge grins told the story. Rarely had these passengers been so royally entertained.

17

THE ORGANIZATION STARTED by Doreen had now grown out of its original space and moved to a fourteen-thousand-foot warehouse. Beds and medical supplies that had been donated from across Canada sat in boxes and crates marked for areas in need around the world. She now had a staff of three full-time workers and several volunteers who each week wrapped and pack the various materials before shipping them.

Her biggest challenge had been met and achieved such success that the phone rarely stopped ringing. One thing I had learned in Ethiopia was that the temperatures fell rapidly once the sun went down. There was a desperate need for blankets, not just food and medicine. Doreen went into action. First she secured the help of various agencies in the field to ensure that if blankets were sent, they would get to the people who needed them most. The campaign was put into place and resulted in donations of forty thousand blankets from across Canada. Workers at Cadet Cleaners laboured throughout one weekend, for no pay, to ensure that each blanket was cleaned, wrapped in plastic and bundled for shipment to Ethiopia. The fact that each blanket arrived at the various points where the need was greatest was entirely due to the persuasive talents of a certain Doreen Wicks.

One funny aspect of the exercise was the fact that fourteen thousand of the blankets were new electric blankets. These were from generous Canadians who had, no doubt with the best of intentions, gone to their local store and asked for the best blankets they had, unaware that the areas they would be sent to were thousands of miles from the nearest electrical outlet.

Happy with the two-part series I had written for them on Ethiopia and the Sudan, the *Toronto Star* asked me if I would be interested in writing a weekly column. I certainly was. By now "The World of Wicks" had been cancelled, and the column would allow me to interview the kind of people I had enjoyed filming for the program.

John and I had met hundreds of interesting people in the six years the show had aired and were happy with our success. After it was all over, we wondered what it was that had attracted us to our subjects and decided that the one thing they all had in common was their gentleness. Their eccentricity had caused no harm, but rather had helped to brighten an otherwise serious, unkind world.

Some months earlier, the *Globe and Mail* had redesigned its front page and, in doing so, cancelled my cartoon. Fortunately the *Star* picked it up almost immediately and placed it in a regular spot on the front page. Now, in addition to the cartoon, I would have my own column on the inside in which I was free to say whatever I liked, provided that the six hundred words were fun and arrived at the office on time.

Since Vincent had always taken an interest in politics and world affairs, it seemed that the ideal job for him would be to assist me. He had recently married a nice young woman, Lori Pearson, and they were settling down to life together in Toronto. Ours was a perfect arrangement. He quickly got a grasp of what was required to be a cartoonist, and within months had replaced me in drawing "The Outcasts" strip, leaving me time to concentrate on the daily single-panel cartoon.

Interesting job offers continued to come my way, such as when the executive producer of "Arts National," a CBC-FM program, called me to do a three-part series on Vera Lynn.

"Three hours on Vera Lynn? Is this a joke?"

"We think it would be a popular program for our listeners."

"But isn't 'Arts National' a little, er, you know, artsy, to be featuring someone like Vera Lynn?"

"We don't think so." He sounded annoyed. "We've just finished a series on Paul Robeson. Is that artsy?"

"Okay, count me in."

"Good. Now, how well do you know her?"

It's a strange fact that the moment North Americans find out you were raised in Britain, they are sure of two things: one, that you have seen the Queen and two, that you have seen Vera Lynn. I had to think fast. I was certainly a fan and wanted to meet her.

"Well, I don't know her well and, to be honest, it's been a long time since we've seen each other . . ."

I managed to get her home phone number from Ray Sonin of CFRB. When I phoned the number in England, a man's voice answered.

"May I speak to Vera Lynn, please?" It sounded stupid, like asking someone if you may speak to the Queen.

"This is her husband speaking. May I help you?"

"Er, my name is Ben Wicks and I . . ."

"Oh, Ben, we were expecting your call. Ray just phoned to tell us you'd be calling. You're lucky to catch us in. We've just got back from shopping."

Was this a joke? Vera Lynn shopping?

"Vera is in the kitchen unpacking the groceries. Anything I can do?"

We arranged a time and place for an interview. I was tremen-
dously excited at the prospect of meeting Vera Lynn. I booked
my ticket for London and friends at Air Canada upgraded me to
the front of the plane, in the posh section.

On the day of my flight I had a great deal to do around the
office before my cab arrived, so I was a little irritated to hear the
phone ring. My friendly Air Canada contact had news. A VIP
would be travelling first class on the same flight as me. "He's
travelling under the name of Aulde," Air Canada's Deep Throat
whispered.

"Who the hell is Aulde?" I asked, "and why all the secrecy?"

"Because, my dear Ben, Mr. Aulde is really Prince Andrew,
who has been on a canoe trip here. He doesn't want anyone to
know how he's travelling, and you must promise not to bother
him for an interview." I promised and immediately phoned the
Toronto Star.

I deliberately left for the airport early to get a seat, if not next
to the prince, as close as possible. Deep Throat handed me my
ticket.

"Did you get me a seat next to him?" I whispered back.

"What are you, some sort of joker? It's worth more than my
job is worth to do that."

After a heated discussion about the favours he owed me, he
selected a seat for me beside the security man and Prince
Andrew.

As it was mid-week the first-class lounge was almost empty. I
was reading when the young prince walked in, his security man
close by. They ordered coffee. The beard the prince had grown
during his canoe trip was a perfect disguise. No one else recognized him as they quietly sat chatting. I lifted my magazine in spy
fashion and glanced over the top. The prince was getting restless
and left the room to board the plane early with his escort.

"Excuse me, sir."

I looked up at the tall man standing in front of me.

"My name is Johnson. I'm with airport security, and I was wondering if we might have a little chat."

Damn, I thought. I knew I should have declared the bottle of rum I had taken through customs three years before.

"Er, I know who you are, Mr. Wicks, and I'd just like to ask you a few questions. Er, I understand that you're flying to London tonight, and I know you're flying first class."

"That's right. I am."

"Are you aware of who is also travelling first class?"

"Well, I, er, yes!"

"I want to put this as diplomatically as I can, Mr. Wicks. Great pains have been taken to make sure that the prince's return to England is a relaxing one. As such we decided that it would be best that the prince travel by a commercial airline with a false name, in order to protect him from the media. Everything has gone extremely well."

"Wonderful. Congratulations."

"The point is, Mr. Wicks, we had cleared first class, or thought we had. Now we're in a sticky position."

"Yes, I can see that. Well, I'd love to help, but I have a ticket and, frankly, I like to be comfortable when I travel."

"Do you plan to interview the prince?"

I confessed that I did.

"Would you mind waiting here and I'll be right back."

Fifteen minutes later he returned. "I think we have a solution, Mr. Wicks. We've all agreed that if you don't do an interview on the plane, you can write what you like when you get off."

"Now look here. I haven't agreed to do . . ."

"Or we can have you transferred to another class."

"Being a loyal subject and a great fan of the Royal Family, naturally I shall do whatever you want me to do," I replied.

I left the lounge to board the aircraft. It was pouring rain outside.

"Good evening, Mr. Wicks," the purser smiled as he saw the

first-class ticket and steered me towards the front of the aircraft.
Andrew was sitting with his security guard in the empty cabin.

"I have a lovely seat over here," said the purser, and showed
me through the cabin to a seat in the corner.

"That's fine," I smiled. "I'll take the seat on my ticket."

I turned and sat beside the security man, as an astounded
purser, prince and escort stared at the empty seats around us.

"Are you sure you wouldn't like to . . ." The purser's red face
was almost touching mine.

"No, this is great, thanks."

I turned to the security escort. "My name's Wicks."

He mumbled something in return.

I leaned across him. "Wicks," I said.

The prince was about to offer his hand when he looked up at
a steady stream of drips.

"Has anyone got an umbrella? There's a leak in the roof," said
the prince. "Maybe I should take another seat."

He squeezed around my legs and made his way to a seat
beside the one the purser had suggested I take earlier and went
to sleep.

We never did get the chance to chat.

When we landed I contacted my CBC soundman. Like me, he
had never met Vera Lynn and, also a fan, was just as anxious as
me to get to her home. Our train pulled to a stop in the pretty
village of Ditchly, just an hour's ride out of London. We took a
taxi from the station. The driver turned in his seat and glanced
at our recording equipment.

"Going to visit our Dame Vera, are you?"

"Do you know her?"

"Know her? Of course I know her. See her shopping all the
time."

"Do you like her?"

He smiled. "You know, there's only one word that describes
Dame Vera."

"And what word is that?"

"She's charming."

The taxi driver dropped us at a large comfortable house that I later learned had been designed by the star herself. A short man in his sixties opened the door. Harry had married Vera forty-four years before.

"Come on in." Harry led the way into the living room, where a large fire was blazing in the hearth. Vera came into the room with her hand held out. I was surprised. Far from being the epitome of glamour, the British superstar was, well, she was an ordinary person – the kind of woman you would ask to take care of the kids while you dashed up to the launderette to do the week's wash.

She was far more attractive than any photograph I had ever seen. She certainly didn't look her age, sixty-nine. Maybe the answer was that her inner self had not changed. She seemed to me to be the same young woman who had sung about blue-birds flying over the white cliffs of Dover. I sat back and chatted with Harry as I listened to her bustling in the kitchen. How had they met?

"It was at an audition. Not for Vera, she was already a star. But a new band was starting up, and I went along and there she was." Harry leaned towards the fire and poked it as Vera returned carrying a tray.

She was born in London in 1917 to a father who worked on the docks and a mother who was a dressmaker. It was a time when the poor of Britain were waiting in their sooty slums for sons and fathers to return to the miserable lives they were fighting to preserve. Music was the link that held them together. From the trenches of France to the back streets of London great songs were being sung. For Vera Lynn this world was the perfect campus. Here she developed an early understanding of those who craved a better yet simple way of life.

Like most stars, Vera had changed her name. "I was born Vera

Welch. I borrowed Lynn from my grandmother. One lump or two?" She poured the tea.

"By the time I was three, my Uncle George was already teaching me the songs of the day and having me perform for the family. I hated it. I still do. I'd run a mile rather than stand up and sing at a private party. I was seven when I started performing in the working clubs of East London. Got seven shillings and six-pence for three songs."

So the afternoon went. I left her house thrilled that I had finally met one of the two voices that had played such an impor-tant part in sustaining Britain's courage during the Second World War. I never did meet the other one – Winston Churchill. Now when people ask if I've ever met Vera Lynn, I lean back on the counter with my pint and answer, "Met her? 'Course I've met her. 'Ad bleedin' afternoon tea wiv 'er."

Over the last few years our family had moved around Toronto quite a bit. But now that both Susan and Vincent were married and out of the house, and Kim was in her final year at Havergal College, Doreen and I decided to move to a downtown condo-minium. We bought one on the top floor of the building, with a glorious view across the Don Valley.

I found that in order to write a regular column, it was vital to keep in touch with the type of people that I had interviewed for television. It was also a good excuse to take Doreen and Kim and, once again, visit family in England. With them safely settled in Bristol, I headed for London to follow through with a couple of interviews I set up.

The little chain of shops wound its way along a depressing part of London made all the more miserable by the light rain falling from an overcast sky. The headquarters of the Aetherius Society was easy to find. Hanging outside was a model of a flying saucer. Dr. Richard Lawrence led me to a back room and introduced me to his assistant, a young woman named Chris, who quickly set the table for afternoon tea.

"Let's start by talking about your leader, Sir George King. Is the title for real?"

"It's not from the Queen, if that's what you mean. But not all titles come from Her Majesty," said Dr. Lawrence.

"But does he have a title?"

"Absolutely. It's from the Order of St. John, and was given for his work in the field of healing."

I leaned forward.

"I've been told that you are in communication with outside worlds."

"Sir George is in contact with the other worlds. Yes."

"Since when?"

"Since 1954. You may smile, he has yet to be proven wrong."

"I'm sorry. I don't mean to doubt you, but it is a little unusual."

"Of course it is. One lump or two?"

"I'm sorry?"

"In your tea? Sugar?" We all laughed and Chris passed me the cup and saucer. It was hard to believe that we were involved in a serious conversation about contacting beings from outer space.

"Let's start at the beginning, Dr. Lawrence. How did Sir George first make contact?"

"It was back in 1954. Sir George was practising advanced techniques in yoga. Incidentally he is what is known as a master of yoga. One day he was contacted by a master on Venus."

"The planet?"

"Of course, the planet. Anyway, the master on Venus introduced himself as Aetherius."

"Hence the name of the organization."

"Right again. And that's when the organization was formed."

"How was he contacted?"

"By voice."

"Someone spoke to him from Venus?"

"He was contacted audibly, yes."

"What did it say?"

"You are about to become the voice of the interplanetary parliament."

"Blimey, that sounds like a pretty big job."

He ignored my statement. "Naturally he investigated the voice thoroughly and has since been contacted regularly."

"Why was Sir George chosen by the other planets?"

"Because of his unique ability as a yogi, but he certainly wasn't chosen haphazardly. There isn't another yogi, even in India, as advanced."

"I see. So when this master from Venus contacted Sir George, why did he call? Just for something to do?"

"Certainly not. He was not just calling for the sake of calling. The planets are organized. They were using the master on Venus as their spokesman."

"You mean that the other planets have a form of interplanetary parliament?"

"Right. Something like our parliament."

"I hope not." I answered.

We all laughed as Chris poured more tea.

"So who heads up this parliament?"

"There's a hierarchy that's based on Saturn, since that planet contains the most advanced masters."

"Is Sir George still in communication?"

"Naturally."

"Incidentally, where is Sir George now?"

"In California."

"What's he doing there?"

"He was sent there."

"You mean there's something on the minds of those masters of the other worlds?"

"I do."

"What?"

"Nuclear war."

"Wow, that's the same thing that's on our minds. Anything else bothering them?"

"Communism."

"They don't like it?"

"It's anti-Christian."

"They're religious?"

"Of course. Jesus came from Venus."

I was beginning to get a headache.

Chris leaned over. "More tea?"

"No thanks. But I wouldn't say no to something a little stronger." I turned back to Dr. Lawrence. "Your organization claims that the star of Bethlehem was, in fact, a flying saucer bringing Jesus from Venus?"

"That's correct."

"So the other worlds hold Jesus in high regard?"

"Absolutely. God is over all." He lifted the cup of tea and took a sip.

It was hard to imagine that here in the back of a small shop in a scruffy part of London, I was having this kind of conversation with an obviously bright person.

"Let's go over the details once more so that I can get them right. Your leader, Sir George King, is in communication with other worlds."

"Correct."

"An interplanetary governing body meets and sends various messages to Sir George, who in turn passes them on to his followers."

"Right again."

"Look, I don't have to tell you that a lot of people hearing you talk like this would think you were completely off your rocker."

"Do you mean those people who believe that a star hung suspended over a manger two thousand years ago?"

"Can I take a photo of Sir George with me?"

"Why do you want it?"

"I'd like my editor to see it."

"Will he publish it in the newspaper? It will help us gather members and convince those who doubt what Sir George is saying."

"I'm sure we'll publish the photo."

"Is that a promise?"

"Would I lie to you?"

I joined Doreen and Kim back in Bristol for the remainder of the week. Although I was tempted to discuss the interview I'd had in London with Doreen's family, I hesitated. The last thing I needed was for them to associate me with the kind of people I had met in London. It was bad enough that they felt that all I did as a cartoonist was sit around all day scribbling on pieces of paper for a living.

Back home once more we were anxious to know how GEMS was doing. Although Doreen had a first-class paid staff of three, she was always uneasy to be away from her office. The media coverage that we had generated by the series on Eritrea and Operation Blanket had increased our visibility. Requests for help were forcing her to now spread her basic operation to other areas of the world besides Haiti. Supplies were coming in and going out of the warehouse on a daily basis, and the number of volunteers had increased to twenty.

As a nonprofit organization, we were soon in touch with others working on behalf of those in desperate need. One friend was involved with the African Medical and Research Foundation's flying doctor services. The idea had begun in Australia and, through the leadership of an exceptional man, Sir Michael Wood, it had now spread to Africa. Like us, AMREF was constantly in need of funds. In order to raise them it was necessary to get the media interested enough to publish stories on their work. Would I be interested in travelling to Africa to write a story for them? I thought it was a good idea and immediately contacted what I was sure was the perfect match: *En Route* magazine. The editor agreed. Where better to place a story about flying doctors than in Air Canada's in-flight publication?

I had a wonderful welcome at AMREF headquarters in Nairobi, and after a tour of the city I went to bed. We had to make an early-morning start, and I wanted to be fresh. From what I had heard, the pilot doctor I was about to travel with was quite a character.

As the plane began to pick up speed and race up the tarmac, I gripped the seat and turned to the plump, grey-haired female pilot at the controls.

"We're running out of runway."

"Rubbish! Of course we're not running out of runway." She pulled slowly on the stick and lifted the aircraft. "We're carrying a heavy load. Do you want me to pull up the nose too soon and stall?"

It was the last thing I wanted. As beautiful as Kenya was, I had no intention of finishing my days six feet below its surface.

"Where are we heading?"

"Masai country." Dr. Anne Spoerry, a native of France who had been working in Africa for thirty-five years, turned to the radio and began to give her position. A member of AMREF, she had obviously fallen in love with Kenya and its people. For the next hour we travelled in silence, as I marvelled at the beauty of the expansive plains below us.

"Masai!" Her voice came through the cackling radio.

"Where?"

"There!"

Dr. Spoerry lowered a wing. I glanced down as we circled. A thick bramble bush formed a protective barrier around a half-dozen mud huts.

"The first hut on the right after the entrance is for the man's first wife. The first hut on the left is for the second wife. The second hut on the right is for the third wife, and so on."

The doctor grinned as she tugged at her peaked hat and turned the plane back on course.

"They're a remarkable people. I remember once being called to fly in to collect a young Masai boy who had been guarding his goats when a leopard suddenly appeared. He was just ten years old, yet he attacked that leopard with the only weapon he had – a small stick. The animal clawed him from the centre of his forehead to the middle of his stomach. It was touch and go, yet we managed to save him."

"Boy, that kid must have had tremendous courage."

"He did, but when I asked him about it later, he explained that he was more afraid of what his father would have done if the leopard had got one of the goats."

She suddenly banked the plane. "Well, here we are."

I looked down at a vast nothing. "Here we are where?"

"Where we're delivering medical supplies."

"In the middle of nowhere?"

"Of course not. We'll land on the strip."

"What strip?"

"That one."

We levelled off and headed for a piece of dirt the size of three tennis courts laid end to end. Once again I gripped the seat. This was not easy since all my fingers were crossed. Suddenly we were down, shaking and bouncing our way along an obstacle course disguised as a landing strip.

"Open the door." The doctor gave my arm a shove.

"I'm trying."

"Here, let me do it." She glared, leaned across and gave the door a whack. It opened and I jumped down. A deserted African plain lay between me and the distant Mount Kilimanjaro. Nearby, five Masai boys stood staring at our plane. Dr. Spoerry followed my gaze.

"They're young Masai boys who are preparing to be circumcised and become Masai warriors."

"How long will it take them?"

"As long as it takes them to make a crown of dead birds." We strolled to the nearest boy. "There, you see, he already has one." Dr. Spoerry turned the boy's head. Hanging down from his headband was a brown, pheasant-like bird.

"How did he catch it?"

The doctor spoke to the boy and pointed to the bird. She translated for him. "He chased it and hit it with his stick."

We watched as the young boys drifted off to continue their search. Our supplies safely delivered, the small plane banked away from the country of the Masai, where this rare breed of human lives happy and content.

Back in Nairobi there was disturbing news. There had been a coup in the neighbouring country of Uganda. This hapless country had suffered under the leadership of Idi Amin, who had been ousted by an equally brutal leader, Milton Obote. The most beautiful country in Africa had been run into the ground by two evil madmen and was now, in 1986, in the throes of a civil war.

The rebel army was led by a patriotic Ugandan, Yoweri Museveni, who had a sincere love of his country. He was making dramatic advances, and the country was in turmoil. Drunken government troops, who had not been paid in months, had closed the borders and no one was getting in or out. Once again I found myself being drawn into a potentially dangerous situation. It is difficult to explain why this is often the case. Maybe I am living in a Walter Mitty world, one where I act the part of the experienced foreign correspondent carrying news to an anxiously awaiting pubic. Certainly being on radio and television back in Canada expounding on world events has its appeal, and maybe is the simple answer. Whatever the reason, the news of what was happening in Uganda drew me like a magnet.

Although it was a stupid idea, my one thought was to get inside Uganda and be the only journalist to report from inside the country. I explained to Sir Michael Wood what I had in mind. He asked the obvious question, "How do you expect to cross the border?"

I had thought it out and, although the idea seemed ridiculous, I was sure it would work. I would go in as a doctor. Surely they'd let a doctor in? All I needed was an identity card stating that I was. I could see no other problem. Excited at the thought of being involved in a scheme outside their normal medical missions, the flying doctors readily agreed. Within hours I was holding a photo ID card. In bold print at the bottom it said I was Dr. Wicks and worked for AMREF. "I'll fly you," said one of the doctors. "But only as far as the border, then you're on your own."

Once again I took off in a small plane and headed across the plains of Kenya. As the Ugandan border came into view, the pilot began his approach. Although the grass field seemed small, he was convinced we could land on it. On our final approach, he suddenly became uneasy.

"Would you mind getting out as soon as you can?" he asked. "I don't like the look of those trucks in the corner of the field."

"What about the trucks?"

"They may be troops."

I left the plane before its propeller stopped, wearing a backpack over one shoulder, and made it to a small group of white men standing on the edge of the field. I turned to wave to the doctor who had flown me in, but he was already climbing into the sky.

"Where the bleedin' 'ell 'is 'e going?" said a short, scruffy individual leading two others.

"Er, he's going back to where he came from. Who are you?"

"Us? We're with ITN. British television. What about this bleedin' film 'e's supposed to take wiv 'im?"

"I think there must be some mistake. He was just giving me a lift."

"But what about this film?" He held up a can. They had been filming at the border all morning and were waiting for a small aircraft that could speed the film, via Nairobi, to London. I apologized for giving him the wrong impression and explained that I was also in the media and hoped to get across the border into Uganda.

"Nofink is getting across that border, and I mean nofink, mate."

"How far is it?"

"About two miles." He saw the look of disappointment on my face. "But I tell you what. Since we've got nofink better to do 'til our plane arrives, we might as well drive you to the border as wait 'ere in this bleedin' field."

Once away from the field, a long line of delivery trucks, which had been stopped by the closed border, clogged much of the road to Uganda. I left the car a hundred yards from the border, thanked my new friends for the lift and strolled towards the first crossing. Since this was the Kenyan side and I appeared to be a doctor, there was no problem. The guard pointed to the Ugandan checkpoint, a small shed twenty yards farther on. There I faced an incredibly untidy individual and showed him my card.

"Why do you want to enter Uganda?"

"I'm anxious to help those wounded in the struggle."

"What's in your bag?"

"Various things for me to record conditions, so I can tell my medical friends what's needed."

He left the shed and asked me to lower the backpack to the floor. I did as he asked and for the first time saw that he was missing one arm. I held the bag for him as he searched inside. He lifted out the tape recorder I had packed at the bottom of the bag along with my camera.

"I need to record what problems I see." I explained

Satisfied that I was who I said I was, he pointed with his stump at a road.

"Follow this road for a mile until you see a group of huts. One of these is the local chief of police. Report in there and he will stamp a card that will allow you into Uganda."

I set off down the road. It was hot and dusty and already busy as the Saturday morning crowds began to make their way to the market. Birds were singing in the trees, and it was hard to imagine that these atrocities were being committed, perhaps somewhere nearby.

I was anxious to begin work and, needing to be away from prying eyes, I decided to scramble down into a ditch and begin recording my impressions. I discovered that I had left a tape in the recorder. At a small dinner with the AMREF pilots, I had been introduced to an Ugandan who fled the country after being imprisoned and tortured by Obote's men. I quickly checked to see that his interview was not in danger of being erased and began to record what the other side of the border looked like. Suddenly there was a voice from above the ditch.

"Hey, you. What are you doing down there?" He was young, about twenty-five years old, and pushing a bike. His coloured shirt hung over ragged trousers. He was not happy.

"Me?" I asked.

"Yes, you! Come up here!"

I did as I was told. I had been warned that the area was infested with government special-service death squads, who were happy to pull a gun on anyone they suspected of being on the other side of the conflict. As I scrabbled out of the ditch I noticed that, sure enough, this cyclist was not out for a jolly jaunt, but was carrying a gun.

I smiled the biggest smile of welcome I had ever given anyone.

"What were you doing down there?" His face frowned.

"I'm a doctor, and I was recording details of potential medical problems in the area."

"You're a journalist!"

I grinned. "You've got to be joking. I'm a doctor." I reached for my ID card. It was no longer in my pocket. I reached into each of my pockets and could find nothing.

"Let me hear what you were recording."

"It's all medical stuff. You wouldn't be interested."

"Play it!"

"Okay, okay." I began to fiddle with the machine in the pack, trying to turn the tape away from the previous interview. My greatest fear was that the section I played for him would include the tortured Ugandan saying that his country was run by a gang of thugs.

"What are you doing?"

"I'm trying to get the machine. It's caught on my laundry."

He glared. "Then empty everything."

"There's no need," I said as I lifted the recorder clear of my pack.

"Put it on the seat of the bike."

I did as he ordered and began to reverse the tape. I pressed the play button. My voice describing the border came out. I breathed a sigh of relief.

"Let me work the tape. Reverse it, and when I bang my fist on the seat of the bike, stop the tape."

This guy was no idiot.

"Stop! Now play."

It could not have been at a worse spot. "I never want to see anything like that again. It was horrible . . ."

I immediately stopped the tape.

"What was he saying was horrible?"

"An operation that he was witnessing. It was the worse wound he had ever seen."

We stood staring at each other for what seemed like an

eternity. Finally he turned, climbed on his bike and pedalled away. My knees were wobbling, and for the first time I noticed that sweat was pouring down my neck. I had been stupid. "Trust no one. The secret police are everywhere." Ugandans living outside the country had warned me of this many times, yet I had ignored them.

I walked on until I saw the mud hut attached to a low building and waited for the chief of police. A pleasant young chap entered and, upon hearing that I was a doctor, mentioned how sorry he was that I had not been in the area the week before.

"My brother had the worst gunshot wound in his arm that you've ever seen. You could have helped him."

I agreed, but did not mention that my solution would have been to remove his brother's arm. He liked doctors, he said and, pleased at this news, I asked if he could help me get to the capital city, Kampala.

"Since the coup many people need my help there," I explained.

He scribbled a note on a piece of paper, explaining that I should hand it to those at the checkpoint a few hundred yards up the road. When I reached a barrier across the road, with a small sentry box at one end, I showed the guards the letter. A car approached, and an extremely nervous white driver rolled down the window. Sitting beside him was a young black lad.

"Where are you going?" demanded the guard.

"Er, Kampala," said the nervous driver.

The guard moved his machine gun to his other shoulder, opened the rear door and turned to me. "Get in!"

I got in and closed the door as the guard waved us on. The driver was a German engineer and his companion worked for Ugandan customs. Both were extremely nervous, convinced I was with the Ugandan secret police. I explained that I was a doctor and needed to get to Kampala to help. He took this explanation to mean that his vehicle had now become an ambulance. We leapt down the road passing anything in our way. At the dozens of army checkpoints, we stopped at he explained that I was a doctor on an emergency call. As we approached the first town, getting past the checkpoints became more difficult. Most were occupied by drunken soldiers who had decided that the best way to stop vehicles was by stringing empty beer bottles across the road. Although anxious to get to Kampala, we were just as anxious to do as we were told.

Near the town of Iganga, an intoxicated soldier swaggered towards our car leaving another soldier sleeping by the roadside. He leaned on the door and swung one of the world's most devastating weapons, the Russian-built AK-47, in front of him. I showed him the scribbled note and, although I was sure he was too drunk to read it, he waved us on.

The streets of Iganga were almost empty. We stopped at a hotel and wandered through the corridors looking for something to drink, but it was deserted. Hours earlier the army had gone through the town and destroyed everything in its path. One witness on the road told me that he had watched two soldiers arguing over a radio as they stood in a store window. The disagreement was finally settled when one turned to the other and shot him dead. He then calmly stepped across the body and strolled down the street, the radio under his arm.

We finally entered the city of Kampala. Drunken soldiers wandered through town looking for some form of action to occupy their beer-sodden minds. The sounds of gunfire echoed between the buildings. Those civilians who could be seen were either hurrying through the streets of broken glass and rubbish to the depot to catch the last bus out of town that day or scurrying to get to the shelter of their homes before a 7 P.M. curfew. I said goodbye to my companions and wandered towards the centre of town.

The best place for me to be, I decided, was the university. One of AMREF's doctors had given me the name of a Canadian doctor

who was living there. If I could find him, I might be able to persuade him to give me shelter. It could not have been a better
piece of advice. It was after dark when I knocked on his door. It
opened immediately and I was invited into a room filled with the
music of Beethoven. Dr. John Ross from Newfoundland was not
only my landlord for the night, but became a friend for life. We
spent the night listening to music and drinking, as the world
outside slowly went crackers. Fortunately, John's wife had
managed to escape before the trouble and, although many others
had also left, this remarkable Canadian doctor was still there
caring for the sick.

The next morning John took me on a tour of a children's
hospital. Of the twenty youngsters, only four had mothers
beside them. "The other parents just ran and left their children
behind," John explained.

It was beginning to dawn on me that I had made a mistake in
coming. Although it was true that I was one of the few journalists in the country, I had no transportation and, worse, had no
means of getting a story out. There was no point in staying. This
assignment was going nowhere. John offered to drive me to the
only airport still operating in the country. Entebbe Airport was
a just an hour away. The closer we got to the airport, the more
frequent the checkpoints became.

Entebbe was an important military location, and the damage
here was extensive. The local commander had already fled, and
soon afterward his home was blown up. Now, just months after,
he was back and once again in charge. Such was the politics of
this mixed-up country.

The first plane since the coup began had tried to land at the
airport the day before. A voice informed the tower that on board
were representatives of the London *Times* who wished to land.
The troops in charge of the airport and the surrounding countryside were delighted and explained that this would give them
the opportunity for much-needed practice on their anti-aircraft

guns. The days of British rule had long gone, and with them any respect for Britain's oldest, most influential newspaper.

Despite this unwelcome attitude towards *The Times*, things were changing. The Ugandans decided to open the airport the next morning to allow one international flight to leave. John and I were there at 9 A.M. The airport was deserted and the shops were ransacked. Goods were scattered everywhere, and broken glass littered the floor.

One young Ugandan woman in uniform asked me for ten dollars. It was an airport tax, she explained.

"I only have three dollars," I answered.

"That will do," she answered and promptly snatched it out of my hand.

An hour after the customs' inspector had stamped my passport, he appeared in the empty lounge and grabbed me by the shoulder. He apologized for having stamped the wrong date. I was happy to hand him back my passport. He stamped it again and handed it back. No one seemed to know what they were doing. The sooner I was on the plane, the better.

Once on board I looked around at the ninety empty seats and answered the request to fasten my seatbelt. It was broken. As we lifted off, I looked down at this beautiful country and puzzled over how such a people could be so badly treated by their leaders. Maybe the rebel army would be able to achieve what others had not and bring peace to a devastated, lawless land where killing and brutality had become a way of life.

Today I am pleased to report that President Museveni has done just that.

18

BACK AT HOME, THE WICKS family continued to grow. We received an excited phone call from Vincent telling us Lori was about to give birth to our very first grandchild. We raced to the hospital and watched as Vincent, dressed in a green gown, sprinted between the labour room and the waiting area.

"She's going into labour." He vanished, only to reappear. "Things are going fine, I think." Vincent finally gave us the news that a little girl, Brittany, had arrived. It was August 18, 1986, and Doreen and I were grandparents. A new Wicks had come into the world to expand our family tree. Within months, Susan gave birth to a beautiful baby daughter, Caleigh. In the next five years, Lori had two more children: Rhia, a girl, and two years later, Toran, a boy. Doreen and I were now the proud grandparents of four children.

The latter half of 1986 was proving to be quite satisfying indeed. This day, in particular, started like most days. What was in the news? How many cartoons did I need to complete that week's output? Was there anything important in the mail? Apparently there was. The outside of the letter gave the return address as Her Excellency the Right Honourable Jeanne Sauvé,

Governor General of Canada, Government House. I was surprised. Why would Madame Sauvé be writing to me?

I quickly read the short note, and although the letter asked me not to mention its contents, I immediately handed it to Doreen. I had been recommended to receive Canada's highest civilian award, membership in the Order of Canada. The award was yet to be made official, and for this reason I was requested to say nothing. This was not easy. My first reaction was to throw open the window and tell the world that the country I loved more than any other had just told me it felt pretty good about me.

My second thought was, Why me? The letter had neglected to tell me why I was to receive such an honour. Although I was sure most Canadians about to be inducted into the Order of Canada have no doubt why they are being recognized, I was genuinely puzzled.

When the all-important date – November 12, 1986 – arrived, Doreen and I left for Ottawa. I was still puzzled as to why I was being so honoured; however, not puzzled enough to tell the Governor General she had made a mistake. When the time came to leave for Government House, we assembled in the lobby of the Radisson Hotel. Pierre Berton was about to be made a Companion of the Order, and standing close by was Peter Gzowski, a man who each morning links this great country of ours together by radio.

We were shown into a beautiful room in Government House. Those receiving awards were seated at the front, friends and relatives at the back. A wonderful fanfare preceded the entrance of a smiling Madame Sauvé. As each name was called, the reasons why that person was being honoured were given.

"Claude I. Taylor. He has turned Air Canada into a world leader in air transportation . . . Lister Sinclair. This author, actor, critic . . . George Manuel, founder of the World Council of Indigenous Peoples . . . Joanne E. McLeod, the first paraplegic to graduate from the University of New Brunswick . . ."

As my name was read out, I stepped into the centre of the room and walked to the front to face the Governor General. She turned and lifted the medal from a cushion and smiled as she waited for the announcement to be read: "Ben Wicks. An extremely popular author and cartoonist, he gives greatly of his time and talents to help community organizations, local hospitals and, most recently, a project to raise money and obtain hospital equipment for Third World countries."

I felt extremely uneasy. Although Madame Sauvé did lean forward and whisper in my ear, "and for all the many years of laughter you have given us," I returned to my seat too embarrassed to look at Doreen. When I finally had the courage to look up, she was smiling. But it was difficult. She had looked on as her husband received the highest honour his country could bestow for *her* achievements. She had given herself to help those in the developing world, only to hear her husband receive the credit. As we walked towards the magnificent meal that had been prepared under a canopy, I took her arm. It would be three more years before she was rightly recognized, and although I was proud to be a member of the Order, I was not comfortable until Doreen was also honoured.

I had been back in Toronto for just a few weeks when I received a phone call from the Prime Minister's Office. Would Doreen and I like to have dinner at 24 Sussex Drive with Brian and Mila Mulroney and a few of their few friends? We would.

The first surprise was that the prime minister personally opened the door and asked us in. He was charming, and made small talk as he led us into the living room to meet the other guests. Michael Wilson, the minister of finance, an obvious regular, quickly put us at ease. It was a beautiful house and the room was cosy, yet try as we may, the conversation was strained. Then a breath of life came into the room.

Mila had the newest member of the family in her arms, and in an instant the whole group became animated. How many

Canadians really got to know this fabulous woman, I wonder. She and her husband were deeply devoted to each other and their children. Although I said some terrible things about Mulroney through my cartoons, he was a man who could be proud of two things: he had succeeded in capturing the heart of an incredibly beautiful, caring woman and had tried his best to hold together the country he dearly loved.

A few months after this visit we were again asked to Ottawa, but this time by the prime minister's wife. President Reagan and his wife were paying a visit to Canada and, since the president and prime minister were holding meetings during the day, Mila had invited friends to a luncheon to meet Nancy.

Mila had decided to seat me between her and Nancy, who proved to be engaging and easy to talk to. One American guest leaned across me to suggest that we in Canada should constantly guard against communism. Nancy asked if I agreed. I told her I did not. She smiled and changed the subject. We began to discuss the ridiculous prices being paid for some of the world's most famous paintings. I mentioned that I felt the same value should be placed on cartoons, particularly those of a guy called Wicks. She and Mila laughed. I took the opportunity to steer the conversation to Doreen's work, but Nancy was not interested.

I had now found another outlet for my work: cartoon books. These were simple to put together since the work had already been done. Just grab a year's supply of cartoons, throw them between a couple of covers and there you have it: a book. It was a hit with Christmas shoppers and so I vowed to do a book a year for as long as people bought them.

My working days were full of variety: cartooning, writing, speaking engagements and occasional interviews, which I enjoyed since they invariably dealt with my favourite subject, me! The interview with Mike McManus of TVOntario began simply enough. He was obviously very good at what he did and asked me about growing up in South London. I began to relax

and was quite enjoying the attention when suddenly I was hit
with a broadside.

"Tell me about 1939?"

"In 1939 I was living at home with my two sisters. It had
been a wonderful summer and . . ." I suddenly found myself
relating, for the first time, the story of my days as an evacuee
when, as a small boy wearing a large label, I gripped a pillowcase and said goodbye to my mom. Suddenly tears began to
roll down my cheeks and a large lump in my throat made it
impossible to continue. There was silence in the room as each
crew member looked at his shuffling feet. The producer suggested that we stop for a break before continuing. I could not
believe what had happened. This childhood experience had
obviously been buried deep in my mind and had been suddenly dragged to the surface. Later I was able to finish the
interview.

The next morning I related my experience to my friend and
agent of fifteen years, Matie Molinaro. When I told her that
three and a half million British children had been whisked away
from their homes in 1939 to avoid being bombed, I heard a loud
gasp on the phone. She was intrigued. I picked up a pencil and
began to scribble as I talked. What did she think about the idea
of my writing a book on the subject? Although I had done the
cartoon books, I had never tackled nonfiction. Matie thought it
was a wonderful idea and asked if I had a title. I looked down at
the pad and read her the line I had scribbled.

"How does *No Time to Wave Goodbye* sound?" I asked.

"Terrific," she replied and then advised me to write an
outline. I wrote twenty pages explaining that it was my intention
to contact as many of the original evacuees as I could and gather
their stories. Matie sent the outline to various publishers, and
soon I had contracts with a British and a Canadian publisher.

I needed help to do the book, and was delighted when my
friend Robin Fawcett and her daughter, Linnet, offered to help

me contact former evacuees in Britain. This dynamic duo turned the country upside down in their efforts to find information relating to the period. They contacted the British newspapers and asked for former evacuees to write to us. Within two weeks, five thousand letters arrived at our office in London. It was a seven-day-a-week job just to open the envelopes, sort the letters and answer the phone calls.

Like me, these people had buried their experiences during the war deep in their minds. Most were telling their stories for the first time. Some had been married for more than thirty years and had never told their wives or husbands. Many were so upset recalling their experiences that they found it difficult to talk. A few laughed so hard that it was impossible for them to speak. Some sent photographs of then and now, and many included letters written by them to their parents at the time of their evacuation.

I knew that the actor Michael Caine had been an evacuee and I knew that a foreword from him would help sales of the book. I contacted Jerry Pam, his agent in Los Angeles. As Jerry was a former Londoner, I was sure he'd help. I was surprised to learn that he had also been an evacuee. I asked him if Michael would be interested in writing a foreword.

"I don't think so," he answered. "He's so busy and, frankly, I'm not so sure it's a good idea for him to endorse any book. But I'm sure he'd agree to an interview."

A few days later, I was sitting in a hotel suite in Montreal with Michael. I had always thought that he had had a wonderful time as an evacuee; that the evacuation from our miserable area had given him his love of the countryside and gardening. I was quickly disabused of this idea.

He was six and his brother was three when they left home. At first they were billeted to a kind lady, but then the authorities decided her home was too far from school, so he and his brother were moved. Worse, they were sent to different homes. For the first time, Michael spoke of the horrors of the house in which he found himself.

"What we later found out was that this woman hated kids. Clarence, the evacuee sharing the house with me, had a terrible time and eventually was taken to the doctor with a broken arm." The woman had hit him with a tennis racket. Word reached Michael's mother in London, and she raced to where he was staying.

"My mother arrived through that front door and nearly killed the woman," he grinned. "I'd heard there was a war on, but I didn't know what they meant until I saw my mother on top of that woman in the living room."

At the end of the interview, I thanked Michael and casually asked if he would write the foreword for the book.

"Sure. Just let me know when it's time to send it to you."

After long months of winnowing through the thousands of accounts, making hard decisions over which to include and which to leave out, the book was finally finished. While the publishers readied it for printing, we started to think about how to grab the attention of the daily press. Robin and Linnett supplied the solution. Why not take over one of the London train stations the evacuees had left from and recreate the scene for the media? It took months of planning, with most of the time taken up trying to convince a major London station to close one of their platforms for five hours during a weekday. Once the railway authorities agreed to this extraordinary request, however, they came through with flying colours.

On September 1, 1988, forty-nine years to the day since they had gathered at this station, six hundred former evacuees from across Britain walked onto the platform at Marylebone Station, reliving a period of their lives they had left behind so long ago. A train more than fifty years old was shunted into the station to help recreate the scene. Members of the Women's Royal Volunteer Service, dressed in their wartime uniforms, handed a small bag of sandwiches to the former evacuees as they stepped onto the platform, just as they had done in 1939. On a small stage a band played melodies from the war, and Lee Leslie, dressed in the army uniform of the day, sang the songs made famous by Vera Lynn. Many people, unable to control their emotions, were crying openly and hugging each other. I was one of them.

I have never seen so much media. CNN, CBS, the BBC and CBC were all there jostling with newspaper reporters from around the world. One CBS producer asked if I could help him choose a story. I waved my arm around. "Take your pick, mate. There are six hundred here."

An elderly woman asked if I could get her on camera. I said it would be no problem and asked her if there was a reason for her request. I was shocked by her reply. "Well, you see, I was evacuated with my sister and when we got to being picked out I was separated from her. I never saw her again." I grabbed the nearest television crew and introduced her to them.

As expected, I spent the publicity tour that came after our day at Marylebone Station dashing from one studio to the next. The most popular TV show I was invited to was Terry Wogan's talk show. After an eight-minute interview with me, Terry brought on an elderly woman in a wheelchair.

Gwen was grinning broadly. She explained that she had been living in a small cottage in the country during the war. She had heard a knock on the door late one night and opened it to find the local billeting officer. There had been a problem. Evacuees had been arriving all day and they had run out of homes for them. He had a family with him, a mother and her children. Would Gwen take them in just for that night? Gwen explained that there were only three rooms in the cottage and that she had two children of her own. But since her husband was away in the army, yes, she would do her bit for the war effort. The billeting officer was delighted and stepped to one side to allow the mother and her *nine* children into the house. Gwen did more than keep them overnight. She shared her home with them for three years.

"Do you remember their names?" Wogan asked. "It was forty-nine years ago."

"'Course I do. There was Willy, Joyce, Adam . . ." She went on until she had named all nine children and their mother.

"Did you ever hear from them after they left?" he asked.

"No, never did," replied Gwen.

"Don't you ever wonder what happened to the children?"

"Aye. Many times." She smiled thoughtfully.

"Well, then, why don't we find out?" said Terry and, as the orchestra struck up a march, all nine children walked onto the stage. It was a very moving moment. But Gwen stopped everyone's sniffles when she almost leapt from her chair and in a loud voice declared, "Blimey, it's like 'This Is Your Life'!"

No Time to Wave Goodbye received very positive reviews, which shot it onto the London *Times* best-seller list for sixteen weeks. In Canada it did even better, hitting the number-one spot in both the *Toronto Star* and the *Globe and Mail* lists.

Its success gave my publishers the idea of producing a similar book to commemorate the fiftieth anniversary of the evacuation. *The Day They Took the Children* was a picture book and included many stories that had not made it into the first one. It also hit the best-seller lists. The only strange twist involved the cover. The photograph of a little boy and girl looking at each other's name tags resulted in a call to my British publishers, Bloomsbury. A man phoned to say that it was his picture on the cover. He was wondering if he could get a copy. He was asked if he knew who the young girl with him might be. "Sure," he answered, "that's my sister."

Excited at the prospect of a reunion picture that might boost publicity for the book, the publishers contacted his sister. She had yet to see the book but, upon hearing she was on the cover, was so furious that she threatened to sue them. It seemed that she felt that publishing her photograph without her permission was against the law. I tried my best to reason with her, but to no avail. I had no doubt that the hurt of a war long gone remained with her, as it did with many of us.

The publicity tour in Canada consisted of one hundred and ten interviews in three weeks. It was exhausting, and by the end of the first week, most of my generosity towards the interviewers had vanished. Two interviews in particular I will never forget.

With a black mass of hair set on a fine body, he swept into the makeup room and stared into a mirror as he held out a hand for me to shake. "Hi, Ben, I'm . . ." As he stated his name, he carefully took a strand of hair and gently pushed it back into place. "Great book, Ben. Haven't had time to read it, I'm afraid . . . can't read 'em all," he laughed. "Did take a quick look at the back cover, though, so no prob."

When he was finally finished fixing his hair, we made our way to the studio and sat facing each other. He leaned forward and slapped my knee.

"Tell you what, Ben. Why don't you take it? Like, you've read it, right?" He laughed again. "I'll kick it off and away you go." He was as good as his word. His opening remark was "Welcome to Montreal, Ben . . . and what brings you to town?" For the next six minutes he did nothing but nod his head as I described the book.

I went to Winnipeg next. The interviewer was young and nervous. This would be her very first interview. Most interviewers started with one of three questions: How did you get into cartooning? What made you want to be a cartoonist? and the ever-popular, How do you get your ideas? As I followed her into the studio, I wondered which of the three she would use. The floor director began his countdown. Suddenly a look of horror appeared on her face. She grabbed my arm. "Quick," she whispered, "what is it you do again?"

No Time To Wave Goodbye showed me that not only could I put a good book together, but one that could make money. This was the very ingredient Doreen and I needed for GEMS. Forty thousand people living in a slum on twenty-one acres at the edge of Monrovia, the capital city of Liberia, were in desperate need of Doreen's help. We decided a book would be the ideal vehicle for raising funds to build a clinic there. Using the same format as *No Time to Wave Goodbye*, we would ask Canada's schoolchildren to write their answers to the simple question: What would you do to put the world right? Their replies would go into a book titled *Dear World*.

Twenty-two thousand youngsters wrote, drew and painted their replies, a remarkable outpouring. From these we chose four hundred essays, poems and drawings. Every part of Canada was represented, and every ethnic group was involved.

Dozens of volunteers from more than fifty Canadian publishers sorted the entries and passed on their choices to our judges: Mila Mulroney, Knowlton Nash, Margaret Atwood, Margaret Laurence, Pierre Berton, Roger Caron, Pierre Tisseyre, Laszlo Gal, Doreen and me. It was great fun working with all these people, especially Mila, who tackled the job with her customary enthusiasm.

"I was sitting up in bed going through some of the letters last night," she said, "and I would constantly stop reading and shake Brian. 'You must listen to this one,' I'd say. Eventually Brian said, 'Mila, I know they are all marvellous, but I've got a country to help run tomorrow.'"

One seven-year-old wrote that he would put all the soldiers in the world on farms so they could help feed the people, and he would use their guns for fence posts. A six-year-old wrote that to put the world right he would stop his mum and dad from shouting at each other.

Smithbooks and Coles, Canada's biggest retail book chains, donated the profits they made from the book to our clinic.

Once again I found myself saying, "This is one hell of a country we live in." *Dear World* did more than help the people of Liberia. It opened the eyes of Canadians to the needs of children everywhere. Despite the civil war in Liberia, the clinic remains open to this day.

Proud of the efforts of Canada's children, Canada House in London decided to hold an exhibition of the art in *Dear World*. Princess Anne had been sent a copy of the book. She not only asked for more copies, she agreed to open the show.

Doreen, Kim and I flew over to London for the event. I was asked to make a four-minute speech. In it I said that I was not all that happy to see Her Royal Highness. There was a shocked silence.

"You see," I turned to Princess Anne, "although thrilled at the thoughts of an exhibition, my wife told me four weeks ago that she was much too busy to go to London, and that I would have to go alone. When I gave her the news that you, Your Highness, were going to attend, wild horses couldn't have kept her and Kim off the plane. Thanks to your being here, my single fare expanded into three, plus two new outfits." Anne smiled and the crowd relaxed.

We arrived home to fantastic news. At long last Canada had recognized the contribution Doreen was making to her country. She was to be awarded membership to the Order of Canada. A few months later we returned to Government House for the presentation of the awards. I watched proudly as the most remarkable woman I have ever known stepped forward to be recognized for the unselfish devotion she has shown to those in desperate need around the world. We had become a rare couple, one of the few honoured with Canada's highest civilian award.

19

BY 1990 THE GEMS WORKLOAD for Doreen had increased so much that, although she hated to disappoint people, she could no longer help everyone who contacted her. One new area of the world that did interest her was northeastern Brazil, where an old friend she had been assisting in Africa, Sister Mona Kelly, had been transferred. Within weeks of her arrival Sister Kelly wrote to Doreen about her plan to help mothers and children living in a particularly bad slum in the city of Fortaleza. Would Doreen visit and work on the plan with her? Unfortunately there was a problem. Doreen had promised to visit a group in Haiti that had asked for her help. There was only one solution. I would have to go to Haiti in Doreen's place. I agreed and left for the troubled island a few weeks later.

He was dead. His young, rag-clad body was still lying beside the car that had hit him. Drivers eased their way around him, irritated that one more obstacle had appeared to slow the dense Port-au-Prince traffic. After all, he was just one poor child among thousands in Haiti.

It had been some years since I had been in the country. I had thought things were bad enough on my first visit, but they were nothing to what I saw on my return. The country had gone mad.

"There were fourteen killed yesterday when a tap-tap [a Haitian taxi] collided with a truck," said Jim Heslip, the Canadian aid worker who was my guide.

Thousands of children were struggling to survive in this impoverished country, begging or scrambling for scraps in the gutters of the markets. The lucky ones found refuge in one of the thirteen shelters run by the order of the Little Sisters of St. Theresa of the Baby Jesus. Started forty years ago by the late Father Louis Charles, the homes gathered in as many orphans as they could feed and house. Although all of the shelters were struggling to survive, one orphanage in particular had been forced to seek GEMS' help. The water they took from a nearby mountain stream was down to a trickle and they were desperate.

I hitched a ride to the orphanage with Susan Grace of GEMS, who had hurried from our Toronto headquarters in response to their plea. The four-wheel-drive vehicle banged and jostled its way along the back roads, which threaded between the cardboard shacks so many Haitians called home. We crossed a shallow river filled with women beating clothes against the rocks, then climbed into the mountains. An hour later we nosed our way through the large gates of the orphanage and came to a stop in the courtyard.

Sister Solange, a short, jolly woman, hurried over and, after kisses all round, insisted that we rest after the journey. She had been with the order for twenty-two years. Born in the north of Haiti, she had four brothers and a sister. When she came to the orphanage six years earlier, the building had been nothing more than a shell. She had saved it and built it into a home for ninety girls and a day school for five hundred local children. Now she was fighting for its survival.

The view from the balcony was magnificent. Bottles of pop were passed around. "This is to celebrate," explained Sister

Solange. "We have so few visitors to our home, and you're all the way from Canada." She laughed and clinked glasses with us before telling us that some of the girls in her care were without parents and others were there because their mothers or fathers were too poor to care for them.

A pretty little girl stood shyly swaying back and forth with her arms behind her back. Sister Solange smiled. "This is Nadia, the youngest member of our family." She took Nadia's hand and together they led us on a tour of the home. "Nadia has been with us just ten months. She is five and has two brothers and three sisters."

"And what of her parents?" I asked.

"Her mother died and her father was unable to take care of the children." She smiled reassuringly at Nadia and quickly changed the subject. "Nadia sings and dances beautifully, you know." Nadia grinned and looked at her feet.

Their needs were mind-boggling, from food and clothes to the most vital need of all – water. An engineer had inspected the problem, and had said that a well was the only answer. An underground lake could be reached by drilling down three hundred and fifty feet. The Mennonite Central Committee in Winnipeg had offered to do the drilling for free, and I was happy to tell Sister Solange that GEMS would provide the money for the pipe.

I had completed one assignment for Doreen and had a few days to spare before starting on the next. I decided to do some research for a story on a subject that has always intrigued me – voodoo, a popular religion in Haiti, which is based on ancestor worship and seems to involve a great deal of magic.

"He makes you not afraid of nothin'." Marcel, the Haitian cabdriver, half-turned in his seat, slipped his car between two gaily coloured buses and gave them both a loud blast on his horn. The hot sun bounced off the dirt road as we drove away from Port-au-Prince and headed for the village of Merne Mian.

"Is the guy we're going to see the best?"

"Absolutely, boss."

"Would you go to him if you had a problem?"

"I has no problems, boss."

"How come?"

"I'm a Macon Lodge."

"You're a Mason?"

"No, boss. I'm a Macon Lodge – a person who is protected from the spirits."

"You believe in voodoo?"

"You don't believe?" He turned and looked like he was ready to leap from the car. I suddenly remembered that 90 per cent of Haitians strongly believe in voodoo.

"I always figured you needed darkness and that the sounds of voodoo drums from far off hills were needed to experience the strange world of the witch doctor."

He shrugged, obviously puzzled by my notions of voodoo.

"You want to stay at the village when we get there?"

"That depends. How long will the ceremony take?"

"What spirit do you need?"

"I don't understand."

"Some spirits take as long as ten days."

"Can we get one to visit for ten minutes?"

"You ask the voodoo priest when we get there."

Eventually we came to a small group of huts that hugged a clearing in the forest. A band of children laughed, kicking at the dust with their bare feet.

"You wait here, boss. I go find the priest," said Marcel.

"Before you go, who are they?" I pointed to a family sitting under a tree.

Marcel turned. "They wait for evil spirits to leave them before going home."

"Patients?"

He ignored the remark and hurried towards the centre hut.

A bearded man of medium height, wearing plaid trousers, appeared in the doorway. As Marcel talked, the two of them became very excited and turned towards me.

"This is Lucien Nelson, boss." I shook his hand and we entered the hut. It was just light enough inside to see the hut's furnishings – three battered chairs and a machete leaning against a small drum. We sat down and Marcel opened the conversation. The priest stared at the floor.

"The priest wants to know what we can do for you, boss."

"First, I'd like some information."

Marcel translated.

"He say forget this information stuff. What's your problem?"

"Tell him I have no problem."

"He wants to know why you come to see him if you have no problem."

"I am a newspaperman, and I would like to do a story about him."

The priest suddenly stood, glared and headed for the door.

"What's wrong with him?"

"He say he only interested if you have a problem."

"Okay, tell him that I have a problem."

"What problem?"

"I don't know. Give me a problem."

"Want no fear is a good problem."

"Great, tell him I'll have a no-fear spell."

Marcel explained. The priest twirled around, grabbed the machete and spun it around his head before beginning to draw small circles in the hut's dirt floor. Terrified by this sudden spurt of activity, I held up a hand.

"Hold it! How much is this spell going to cost?"

"A thousand dollars U.S."

"What! Is he joking?"

The mood in the hut changed rapidly. The priest slowly turned and began to hiss at poor Marcel. A look of horror appeared on the cabdriver's face. "The priest is very angry," he explained needlessly.

I took up a position just behind Marcel's right shoulder.

"Tell him a thousand dollars is a lot of money."

"But this is a no-fear-for-life spell." Marcel had begun to sound as though his own no-fear spell was fading fast.

"Ask him how much for a no-fear spell for about an hour?"

The priest let out a scream. Marcel dropped into a chair and held his hands above his head. "The priest says you make fun of him."

"He doesn't understand. Tell him that if my editor finds out I've spent a thousand dollars on a spell, he'll stick pins in me."

Marcel translated. To my great relief, the priest didn't reach for his machete again. In fact, he wasn't at all insulted by my rather flippant remark. Instead he began to grin and Marcel laughed.

My other assignment for Doreen was to see if funds donated by the Canadian Editorial Cartoonists Association would be well spent helping three Catholic sisters from Quebec – Sister Simone St. Pierre, Sister Marguerite La Rouche and Sister Janine Carrière – care for the sick at a mountain clinic in Haiti. I wanted to see for myself what the sisters needed in the way of medical supplies.

I flew from Port-au-Prince in a missionary plane with a Sister Superior, and, after landing in a small field, we drove to the village of Jeremy situated at the base of a mountain where we spent the night at a seminary. The next day before dawn, we began our climb up the mountain to the clinic in a Jeep that bumped, banged and clunked its way over rocks, stones and holes disguised as road. We were lucky. The rainy season that turned this route – the only way up the mountain – into a raging river had been delayed, making it possible for us to cover the seven miles up in *only* two hours. As we were rocked and thrown about the inside of the Jeep, I had ample time to ruminate on what a sister invited to join us on the trip had meant when she answered, "I'd rather scrub three floors." If I'd known what I was in for, I'd have offered to scrub the inside of Buckingham Palace to avoid the trip.

As we climbed higher and higher, farmers in their fields grinned and waved at the rare sight of a vehicle attempting a trip normally made by mules. At one point, we passed a family making its way slowly up the steep slope. A young woman, with what looked like malaria, sat slumped over in a chair, which was being carried high on the shoulders of four men.

I had long given up arriving anywhere when the nose of the Jeep finally lowered to a sensible angle. We were at the top, on a small plateau that held a clump of crumbling structures. We chugged our way towards the clinic and were met by grins as wide as the valley that stretched below.

Two hours before the clinic opened, more than fifty patients had already started to wait outside its door. Now all eyes were on a tiny house thirty yards from the clinic where Sisters Simone, Marguerite and Janine, who had risen at 5 A.M. for mass, appeared to treat the sick among the crowd outside the clinic. After quickly greeting us they turned to their patients, many of whom were lying on the ground.

Sister Marguerite saw the anxiety in my eyes and reassured me. "They're not all sick. Many of them are just tired from carrying their sick friends and relatives for hours to get here." She laughed. "Some of them are probably sleeping off the effects of Klaren, a form of alcohol. The relatives of the sick person give them a tiny bottle as payment for carrying the patient. Not all of the carriers wait to drink it on the way down."

I glanced around. It seemed such a long way from Sister Marguerite's home in Jonquière, Quebec. Surely she must miss it, I asked.

She smiled. "Being one of twelve, I do think of my brothers and sisters at times, but I joined the order when I was eighteen, so it's a long time ago." She turned to feel the head of a baby girl sitting on her mother's lap. "Actually, I started out to be a teacher, then later switched to nursing."

"What diseases were most common?"

"Well, like this little one here," she smiled at the baby. "Diarrhoea, worms and, of course, malnutrition. At first, we did try a feeding program, but gangs roaming the mountains heard about it and raided us, stealing all the food."

Sister Janine joined us. Born on a farm in Les Boules, Quebec, she had taught for many years before coming to Haiti in 1985.

I pointed to one of the small, crumbling buildings and asked what it was.

"Oh, that's Sister Simone's pride and joy – the school."

Sister Simone, the eldest of the sisters, had left her home in Quebec at the age of thirty-four, and, after serving in Africa for fourteen years, began teaching in Haiti in 1977. This was her sixth year on top of the mountain. She was justly proud of her school, which, she told me, accommodated four hundred students. If she had more room, she said, she could teach twice that number.

"The parents are so anxious for them to learn, and they are wonderful children. They get up very early because, before they come to school, they must do their chores. Some come from as far as four hours away, so we have to let them out of school at two o'clock or they'd never get home."

Sister Marguerite hurried over to a child coughing nearby. After a few reassuring words to the mother, she said, "I was afraid it might be tuberculosis, but we get very little of it up here, praise the Lord. We're too far removed from the city slums."

"We're not always sure what the illness is," Sister Janine told me. "One time I saw a man of about thirty who I thought had syphilis. I gave him penicillin. He died soon after. It turned out that he had AIDS."

"Do any doctors ever visit?"

Sister Simone smiled. "I'm afraid not, though we do get dentists once in a while."

Despite the sounds of sickness surrounding me, I felt strangely peaceful as I watched the three sisters touch each patient, smiling, listening and reassuring them. In the crumbling clinic, Sister Janine showed their meagre medical supplies – mostly Aspirin and chloroquine.

"We always make them pay something for their treatment," she said. "They have their pride, the same as you and me."

"How do they pay?"

She placed a hand to her mouth and grinned. "Sixty cents to a dollar."

"And if they don't have the money?"

She laughed. "Eggs and pineapples are the most popular."

Not for the first time since Doreen had started GEMS did I find myself wondering what motivated people like these sisters. Why would someone choose to live on a mountain top in one of the poorest countries of the world? I could only marvel at their spirit in the face of such desperate poverty. One in four children in Haiti die before they reach the age of five, and the average life expectancy for a man is fifty-three and for a woman, fifty-seven. A hundred and twenty-five people a day arrive at the clinic for treatment.

By afternoon many of the patients had left, and it was time for us to do the same. As our Jeep made its way down the mountain I noticed that the young girl with malaria had been treated and was now back in her chair, hoisted onto the shoulders of her friends and relatives. They were moving off when one of the sisters hurried after them, opened a large umbrella and handed it to one of them to use to shelter the girl from the blazing sun.

On my way to the airport for my return flight to Canada, the car radio spluttered out a report of a new killing. That morning the head of the human-rights movement had been found murdered, his body tossed beside the airport road, like a piece of garbage.

Haiti was not just poor; it was being devastated by violence. Yet in the midst of its misery were people who, in spite of the danger, worked for the poor with selfless compassion.

A few months later, the Association of American Editorial Cartoonists held its annual meeting in Washington. Doreen was too busy with GEMS to come with me, so I took Vincent along instead. Since he was working as my assistant, I thought this would be a good opportunity for him to meet President Reagan, one of the characters he was learning to draw. I had never been a fan of his and, although he was gracious at a reception for the association in the Rose Garden, I was not impressed by him.

The highlight of the Washington visit was quite unexpected. One visiting cartoonist told me that he had become deeply involved in the plight of the missing American prisoners of war in Southeast Asia, or MIAs (missing-in-action) as they were called. He was convinced that some of them remained alive. I had heard this story but, in truth, had paid little attention to it. He was so convincing and so anxious for me to hear the facts for myself that he suggested I join him for a meeting with a friend who would, as he put it, "blow me away" with her story.

Elizabeth Stewart was a lawyer who looked to be in her early thirties. She had had a successful law practice in Florida but had given it up to work in Washington, lobbying the government to take action on the MIAs.

"It was not an easy move, but I had to come," she said as we sat down in the hotel bar for a coffee. "It's a long story, if you don't mind listening . . ."

I nodded my head. The temperature was in the nineties outside, so listening to her story sure beat stomping the hot Washington streets sightseeing.

She explained that her father had been a pilot during the Vietnam War and was reported missing in 1966. She had been eleven and remembered the two uniformed men delivering the news. When the first POWs arrived home, she sat glued to the TV set watching as each of them came off the plane, hoping that the next man to appear would be her father. But he never reappeared.

"We carried on like any good air force family. Mom never talked about it, and we tried to get on with our lives. Eventually we stopped waiting for the telephone to ring. Watergate came and the story of the POWs was pushed from the papers, and I carried on with my schooling and eventually started a law practice.

"Four years ago I decided to meet with other families of POWs and joined a group called the League of Families at a convention here. I started to talk to them and was astonished to hear them tell me that my dad was probably alive."

"You had never been told that he might be?"

"The closest we ever got was when Mom was invited by the air force to look at pictures of captured flyers and she picked out Dad."

Elizabeth said that the photo showed her father in a prison camp, with a Vietnamese guard standing behind him. Her mother had asked where the picture had been taken, but the military refused to tell her. Later they phoned to say they had made a mistake.

"They said the picture was of a Colonel Stockman. We thanked them and forgot about it. But I began to feel uneasy. So last year I moved to Washington to dig a little deeper. I phoned Colonel Stockman and found he was in Washington on business for two days just two blocks from my office. I raced over and showed him the picture."

"And he said?"

"He said it wasn't him."

"Did you talk to other former POWs?"

"They told me about leaving buddies back there, but many

had been told to shut up. The fact is that six hundred men were shot down over Laos and not one has come out."

"Do you really feel deep down that your dad is one of them?"

"Maybe my dad did not survive the crash, but Mom and I have the right to know what happened to him."

As she lifted her coffee cup, a red bracelet slid into view. It was a bracelet like those worn by the loved ones of MIAs. "Col. Stewart" was engraved on hers.

Back in Toronto again, I thought about the meeting I had had with Elizabeth. I decided to phone her.

"It's strange you should call," she said. "I was about to phone you. A small group of relatives and friends of MIAs are leaving for Thailand in a week, and I was going to suggest that I send you material on what we found when I get back."

I broached the subject with Doreen. Would she like a trip to Thailand? She would not. She had enough to do with GEMS. How about taking Vincent? Since he was now working with me, why not involve him more deeply in my activities? He loved the idea. I phoned Elizabeth back and asked how she felt about adding two more to her list of travellers.

It was a rush to get prepared, but eventually Vincent and I made it to the airport in New York. After pushing our way through the Sunday evening crowds we found our small group waiting near the ticket counter. Our leader was not too difficult to spot: An ex-congressman standing six foot four and wearing glasses, Billy was every cartoonist's idea of what an American tourist looked like.

Billy immediately took control. His booming voice and waving arms soon had us scurrying to check our luggage. Once on board we were given the first of a dozen military-type briefings. Vincent and I leaned in close. Since we had a sixteen-hour flight ahead of us and not the faintest idea what was planned for the other end, we were anxious to learn as much as we could.

What we were told was incredible. Vincent and I looked at each other to see if we had heard right. Billy maintained that he and a group of congressmen had raised $2.4 million to be used as a reward to the first Laotian, Thai or Vietnamese to deliver a live American prisoner to the U.S. authorities. As proof of the existence of such a vast sum of money, Billy and the congressmen were photographed beside a table bearing the $2.4 million. He handed me the photo.

"Okay," said Billy, taking the photo from our hands. "Now the next thing is to get this here news into the hands of the little suckers who may be in a position to grab one of our boys and get him to us."

The biggest problem facing Vincent and me was how to stop ourselves from laughing, then I glanced across at Elizabeth and, from the expression on her face, knew that for her this was no joke. She was searching for the truth and was determined to find it.

Billy's voice barked out again. He had spread out a map of Thailand and was pointing to an area in the north.

"I figure we get to Bangkok and, after a couple of days' rest, we hire a small plane to take us here." He slapped a finger close to the Laotian–Thai border. "We then get a small bus, somethin' like one of them German babies, and follow along the banks of the Mekong River."

The very names began to conjure up images of the past war in Vietnam and the terrible wounds left in its wake; wounds, like those suffered by Elizabeth, that would take a lifetime to heal, if they ever did.

"I still don't understand how we're going to get word of the reward to people living in the areas that may hold missing prisoners," said Vincent.

Billy smiled. "I'm pleased you asked that, son. Here's what

we do." He took the large photo he had shown us from his brief-case. "I've had copies of this photograph reproduced in hun-dreds of leaflets." He once again delved into his briefcase and pulled out a small pamphlet. "As you can see, the leaflet is in three languages – Vietnamese, Thai and Laotian. It tells whoever reads it that this picture is living proof that we'll be giving a reward of two point four million dollars to whoever hands us one of our missing boys. Now turn it over." On the back were four cartoons showing a peasant leading an American POW to safety and receiving a gold brick as a reward.

"Er, I have a question," I piped up. His loud voice was making me uneasy. Not only was he big, but his accent reminded me of a plantation owner I had seen whipping slaves in the television series "Roots."

"What's yer question, son?"

"Since the drawing shows an American prisoner being brought from Laos into Thailand, does this mean we may go into Laos?"

"Well, no . . . The last time we were there, we had a little problem, and they won't let me back in."

"What kind of problem?"

Billy described how they had taken hundreds of leaflets to northern Thailand where they had tied them to balloons, intending to let them drift them across the Mekong River into Laos. Unfortunately for Billy, the Thai police chief had been forewarned and decided that Billy's efforts would provide ideal target practice for his troops. As fast as Billy and his group launched a balloon, the police shot it down. Despite Billy's attempts to explain to the Laotian authorities that his intentions were honourable, the Laotians were not amused at the sugges-tion that they were holding American POWs. They warned Billy that the less they saw of him, the better.

The cab from the Bangkok airport weaved its way through the hectic traffic, which spewed out a million tons of pollution into the crazy city. Once we had settled into the Windsor Hotel, I took another member of our group to the coffee shop to find out more about him. It was easy to like Leo. His darkly suntanned skin was stretched in a permanent smile. I had never lost my love of flying and when he told me he was a crop duster, our friendship was sealed.

"My mother got two cables: one to say that my brother hadn't returned from a mission in Vietnam, and the other one confirmed that he'd been shot down. One of the crew of the other aircraft looked back and saw him rolling up his parachute. While I was serving in the Philippines, I walked past a newsstand and, I don't even know why, I stopped to look at one of the Chinese newspapers. There on the front page was a picture of my brother David. Behind him was a Vietnamese soldier with a machine gun. I later found that the picture had appeared in *Pravda*."

The rest of his story was like the others'. His folks had written to the Pentagon and, dissatisfied with the military's response, decided that they were being lied to. Now Leo was here, convinced that David was out there somewhere.

Billy had hired a small plane to fly us to northern Thailand. After a bumpy landing on a deserted airfield, we made our way to a nearby hotel. I must say this for Billy: he knew how to organize things. A little bus complete with driver-cum-interpreter was waiting for us.

The Thai driver introduced himself. At least, I think that's what he did.

"What the hell did he say?" barked Billy.

"He said he's pleased to meet us," I lied.

Billy threw his hands in the air. "I arrange to have an interpreter and I can't understand a damn word he's saying."

It was not a good start.

The plan was to follow the Mekong River and stop at each small town along its banks on market day to deliver our pamphlets. And so we set off, with me gazing out of the window at this lush, beautiful country and its hardworking people. This area, which so few North American civilians have ever seen, was crowded with families just like ours, all intent on one thing, being left alone to live in peace and watch their children grow.

At each stop Billy would instruct our "English-speaking" translator to spread the word.

"Tell everyone you see that an American is in town, ready to pay big bucks for a live American POW."

His announcement made Vincent and I extremely uneasy. This was hardly the area to declare that not only were you American, but that you had enormous amounts of dollars to throw around. Vincent did little to ease my concerns when he said, "Dad, have you any idea where we are? This is the centre of the Golden Triangle. The largest heroin crop in the world is grown here."

It was wonderful to have him with me. Although he was as intrigued by the mission as everyone else in our group, he alone took the time to film and to study the culture of the places we passed through. Whenever we walked through a village, small children followed us everywhere, obviously puzzled by these strange-looking people and, in particular, by the giant with the loud voice who carried a map wherever he went.

One night, after we had booked into a small, cheap hotel by the river, I decided to go to bed early. At midnight Vincent woke me.

"Dad, wake up. I've got something to tell you."

I rubbed my eyes and sat up.

"A guy just came up to me in the bar and said he knows where we can find an American prisoner."

I was instantly wide awake.

"He wants me to go with him back to his house, and he'll tell me where."

I told Vincent that he shouldn't leave the hotel, but instead make arrangements with the contact to meet us in the lobby the next morning.

After breakfast Vincent explained to Billy what had happened, and together our little band of explorers set off for the lobby, where we met a thin Thai man. His English, for reasons I never did find out, was better than our paid translator's. We agreed to follow him to his house and, after walking down a narrow street, we climbed up rickety stairs to an apartment that sat precariously atop a wooden structure. Our contact went in and waved us to follow.

The low door forced Billy almost to double over. A young woman was sitting on a bed. To the side of the room was a tattered curtain that didn't quite hide a dirty sink. Tied to a chain under the sink was an animal. It was, without doubt, the ugliest creature I have ever seen. It looked like the result of an uncomfortable union between a baboon and an anteater. To make matters worse, it stank.

Our friend immediately got down to business. He spoke with the woman and translated for us. It seemed she knew a guard at one of the river crossings who knew someone who had seen an American prisoner working in Laos. If this information resulted in our getting our prisoner, would they get anything? Billy assured them they would. He took the map from his pocket, laid it on the bed and watched as the man pointed to where we might find the guard.

We quickly set out in our van for Nakhon Phanom to hunt out the guard. It was late-morning when we came to a stop at a busy market. A few of the Laotian traders, who had paddled across the Mekong River with their wares, were already making their way back home in their flat-bottom boats. Billy leapt from the van shouting instructions.

"Liz, you, Vincent and Leo give out the leaflets. I'll hold up the big picture of me with the money, and you" – he turned to our interpreter – "tell them what we're all doing here, giving away easy money."

"What do want me to do, Billy?" I called out as I ran beside him.

"Take pictures of me."

We settled on a spot on the muddy beach. Most of the traders were by now climbing into their boats.

"Don't let them get away," shouted Billy as Liz and Leo tossed leaflets at the them. Billy turned to the interpreter.

"Tell them I want to talk to them," he shouted. The interpreter called out, and soon a crowd of giggling families was surrounding the biggest man they had probably ever seen. Billy felt sure that an instant translation could be achieved by shouting in a slow Carolina drawl. Nevertheless, the translator repeated everything, or said he did. The Loatians nodded and whispered and got back into their boats. If they knew anything, they weren't saying. As we watched them slowly paddle their way back across the Mekong, Billy lifted his arms like MacArthur about to invade, declaring in a loud voice, "Shit, look how close it is. You could piss across it and still miss the beach."

Billy finally gave up his search for the guard. This sad man, who was convinced that across a narrow stretch of river lay the answer to all his political dreams back home, lowered his head and slowly made his way back to the van.

By now, word of our mission had reached the newspapers, and although this was an excellent way to get our news out, it also meant that the Thai government knew what we were up to. They were not happy with us. They felt, and rightly so, that promises of quick riches would undermine their efforts to convince the peasant farmers that their way of life was the best on earth. Furthermore, they were still suffering the headache caused by Billy's last visit to the area.

Nevertheless, they didn't stop us, and so we carried on along the river from market to market, spreading the word. We met many people who, once they heard Billy's offer, claimed they knew where prisoners were, but we got no closer to our goal of finding one.

Our last stop was in the area from which Elizabeth's father had taken off for the last time. All of us agreed that we should hunt out the base. A short drive through the jungle took us to a clearing, and there it was. The deserted huts were now decaying in the humid air. We stopped the van beside the runway. Any gate or fence that may have guarded the base had long since disappeared, and nature was already weaving a cloak across the concrete landing strip.

As we stretched and looked around, Elizabeth strolled slowly towards the nearest hut. A few moments later I heard sobbing. Elizabeth was standing still, unable to enter the building. The memories of her father were now sharp in her mind as she stared into the shelter that had been his temporary home. I was about to move towards her when I felt a hand on my arm.

"Leave her, son," said Billy. "It's better that way."

Bloody war!

20

I WAS ITCHING TO WRITE ANOTHER story and was considering
what subject to tackle. Although I wasn't sure I was up to the
task of writing a book on it, one subject that had always interested me was the problems in Northern Ireland. I decided to go
to Belfast and see the problems for myself, then I would make
up my mind about whether to write a book on some aspect of
the troubles. A close friend from Belfast, Ted McConnel, said
that if I did decide to go, his family would be there to help.
Another friend, Joe Kennedy, the head of the Irish Tourist
Board, also offered to contact his family and friends.

Joe's brother was there to meet me at the Dublin airport and,
after settling into the comfortable boarding house he had found
for me, I phoned a Catholic contact given to me by a CBS journalist. The next morning I made my way by train to Belfast
where the contact, a cabdriver, was there to meet me. He
offered to tour me around the city.

The black cab crawled slowly between crumbling buildings
in the Catholic ghetto of West Belfast before coming to a stop
beside a heap of debris. We watched as a few people parked their
buggies at a tiny store that clung to the corner. Up and down

the street, destruction co-existed with survival. The year was 1993 and talk of peace was once again in the air.

After a couple of hours I was fed up with my host. I could have taken a tour bus for all the information I was gathering. I took the advantage of a lunch break to lay my cards on the table. I was here as a journalist and had seen nothing and, what was worse, he had introduced me to no one who could give me any insight into the problems in Northern Ireland. What I really needed, I told him, was to talk with some members of the IRA. He stared at me for a few minutes and, without answering, left the café. I paid the bill and followed him back to the cab. We drove off in silence. A few minutes later we turned down one of the district's many narrow streets.

Paddy leaned from the cab window and called to two young mothers leaning in a doorway. "Is the club open?"

"A couple of hours ago."

We left the cab a few blocks from the club and walked to a two-storey building with a metal cage around the outside. "That's to stop unwelcome objects from being thrown through the window," Paddy explained.

I waited as he rattled a rusty door beside a bricked-up window. A head appeared through a hole above the door.

"What d'yer want? Oh, it's you, Paddy. Come on up."

We left the sunny morning outside and entered a dark, dismal space with a cramped stairway leading up to a scruffy bar room. A solitary pool table stood in one corner and a small bar in the other. A circle of ten men of various ages pushed their pints of beer to one side and, after greeting Paddy, introduced themselves.

"So what brings you to Belfast, Ben," said a small man with chalky skin pulled tightly across a bony face.

Aware that my Cockney accent could present a problem, Paddy quickly answered. "Ben's from Canada, and he's going to do a story on us. He's going to make us famous."

"So what are you looking for, Ben?" asked Chalk Face.

Once again Paddy did the talking. "He's looking for all types of people to talk to."

"Like those that have bullets put through their knees as punishment and those who do the kneecapping?" Chalk Face suddenly leaned forward and took my knee between his thumb and first finger. "About a size five and a half, I'd say." Everyone began laughing.

"Hey, take your hand off my knee!" I made a sorry attempt at a laugh.

"Don't be shy, Ben. One pull of the old trigger and you won't feel a thing."

After more laughter, he explained that punishment came in various degrees. For severe crimes a .45 shot from the back of the leg would take off the kneecap entirely. Lesser crimes were punished with a shot to the knee from the side. For the least serious, the shot was through the muscle below the knee.

"And for the worst offenders?"

"You mean informers?" He put his forefinger to his head.

The door opened and a large man in a plaid shirt entered the room.

"So, how did it go?" asked Chalk Face.

"The judge let him off wid a warnin'."

I introduced myself to the new arrival and asked him to explain. An eighty-six-year-old man named Mickey had appeared in court that morning, and everyone in the club was anxious to know the result of the trial.

"When was he arrested?" I asked.

"Yesterday," said the newcomer.

"I saw him get picked up." Chalk Face said. "They had to back him into the police car since his arthritis wouldn't allow him to step into the back of the car front ways." Everyone chuckled.

"So, what happened in court this morning?" I asked.

The newcomer stood and began to describe the scene. "The judge looked down and said, 'Were you in possession of an AK-47?' Mickey put one hand up ta his ear and said, 'I was never in any organization in '47.' The judge den shouted, 'Did you have an AK-47 rifle hidden under your stairs?' Mickey looked at the judge and shouted, 'Under the stairs? What stairs? I live in a bungalow!'"

As Paddy and I left the club, a helicopter hovered overhead and a six-wheeled Saracen armoured personnel vehicle whined slowly by. We climbed back into our cab and made our way through a warren of nineteenth-century houses where children were playing on the usual rubble found in poor districts every- where. Then suddenly we were in the area of Queen's Univer- sity, where shoppers bustled through delightful narrow streets bordering green lawns.

I contacted the relatives of my friends, and within the hour I was sitting around a supper table with a family of Catholics. My story of the visit to the IRA club was met with polite laughter. The humour I had tried to inject into the story was quickly squelched.

"It happened late one night," said the husband. "My brother had arrived home and was putting away the car. His wife opened the front door to greet him, and before my brother reached the front step, Protestant gunmen stepped from the bushes and shot him dead."

Each person sitting around the table had a similar, grim story.

"Do you know that in the ten years we've lived in the area, we've had ten cars stolen? And do you know how they was stolen? A knock on the door at night. You open the door and standing there is a guy with a gun. He asks for your car keys and, if you're lucky, the car is back in the morning. If not . . ."

His wife interrupted, "Tell him about the last time, dear."

Her husband nodded. "I opened the door and a guy was

standing there wearing a woollen mask over his head. He was carrying a machine gun and had his hand out for the car keys. Next day the police were in the house telling me that one of their men had been murdered and that my car had been found at the spot. Four hours I spent at the police station while they asked me why I hadn't phoned to tell them about the guy who asked for the car keys – someone who knew where I lived and had a machine gun."

The phone rang. A Protestant friend was quickly told about the visitor from Canada. Two hours later I found myself in Frank's bar in the Protestant area of Belfast. I was anxious to hear from the Protestant side and listened carefully as Frank explained that the problem had nothing to do with religious beliefs.

"You see, Ben, it's like when you wear a rosette in your coat at a football game. That just identifies what team you support. Well, that's the same with the Catholic and Protestant factions. The religion just identifies what people want. It's really territorial. Two sets of minds about the kind of border they want dividing Ireland."

I liked this man and watched as various customers slapped him on the back in friendly greeting. I wondered if I was ever going to meet someone from Belfast I did not like.

Frank laughed. He obviously enjoyed the compliment. "Except for the ones that don't want ta work – con men and the like – eighty per cent are very good."

"So how come they can't get along?"

"The biggest part of the problem as I see it is with us Protestants. We had two-thirds of the majority and what we should have been doing is leaning over backwards to help the one-third, and we didn't."

"And the Catholics?"

"Sure, they also made mistakes, but when the Protestants

asked the British to come in to protect us, they just made it worse."

"How do the Protestants feel about the British soldiers? Do they feel as bad as the Catholics do about them?"

He laughed. "Now that's quite funny. Look, if you brought the Queen into this bar tonight, this crowd of Protestants would all stand up."

At the end of my visit, Paddy drove me to my plane. The radio was tuned into a phone-in show. One of the leaders of the Sinn Fein was attempting to explain why the IRA was justified in fighting for its cause. In the sixty minutes it took us to get to the airport, not one caller phoned to sympathize with him. Without exception everyone said that they were fed up with the killing and cruelty on both sides of the conflict, and all they wanted was peace.

I leaned back in the plane. It had been only forty-eight hours since I arrived in Belfast, but already I knew that the book idea I had had wasn't going to work. Still, I had met some wonderful people – all of whom deserved better from their lives. They had suffered over two decades of war. The words of my Protestant publican friend came back to me. I had asked him whether he thought it was getting any better.

"It will never get better," he answered.

I hope he is wrong. Certainly the chances for a lasting peace look better now, in 1995, than they have for a long time.

Our children had spread their wings. In 1991 Vincent took his family to live close to Laurie's parents on the West Coast. Susan, too, headed in a new direction. In addition to working at her daycare centre, she had written a series of children's books called *Katie and Orbie*. I illustrated them, and although the books themselves were not as successful as we hoped, the world of television saw their charm. In 1992 Ottawa's Lacewood Studios decided to make twenty-six half-hour animations based on the book for PBS. We were especially thrilled when we heard the news that the voice-over narration would be done by the Canadian actor and Hollywood star Leslie Neilsen.

In July 1992 there was wonderful news from Kim, who was studying for her science degree in England. She had been selected to further her summer studies in South Africa and planned to go there with Shane Barker, a young man she had met at university. A few weeks after they left I received a phone call in the middle of the night. Kim was at a phone booth in the middle of nowhere having just climbed down from a mountain. She wanted us to be the first to know that, as she and Shane stood on the summit, he had proposed and she had accepted. And I thought proposing in the middle of Trafalgar Square had been a big deal. They returned to Toronto to get married in July of 1993. Meanwhile Kim learned she had been accepted into McMaster University Medical School.

Nothing, it seemed, could happen to change our good fortune. We were wrong. The bad news arrived via the telephone. It was my sister Nan. Doll was terminally ill with cancer. I caught the next flight back and raced to her side. Although Doll was almost eighty years of age, I had never thought of her as an elderly person. I knew her as a brave protector who was never far from my side.

When I arrived I found Doll's husband, Howard, was so eaten up with grief he had drawn all the curtains against the sun. They had always been a most loving couple, and I dreaded the thought of his being left alone. Doll was lying in bed and only slowly opened her eyes when I went into her room. As she recognized me, a huge grin crossed her face.

"Hello, Alf, what are you doing here?" she asked.

"More to the point," I replied, "what the hell are you doing in bed this time of day?"

We both laughed. I was not happy sitting in the dark and, although Howard was against moving Doll, I persuaded him to let her get up and join me in the living room. I pulled back all the curtains to let in the sun and, with her hand in mine, we went through her photo album. As I stroked her thin wrist and hand, we relived the remarkable life we had seen together.

Time and time again we are told that you can't go back. Well, you can and we did, my sister and I. We journeyed back to Southwark to revisit London Bridge on Guy Fawkes Day, when Doll and Nan would dress me up and parade me around. In our minds we watched the many ships from all over the world being loaded and unloaded, and threw pebbles into the water below.

We travelled throughout the borough and, as I held a picture of our mother, we could hear the sound of her voice calling after a son who had once again let go of her hand and dashed off.

"You were always doing that," said Doll in a weak voice. "You loved to wander off on your own and would return with your eyes staring into the pavement saying, 'All right, Mum. Don't tell the world I'm lost.'" We both laughed and for a moment Doll forgot her pain.

St. Georges' Building, where we had spent such a happy childhood, was long gone, but not to us sitting in the quiet of Doll's home. The sound of Johnnie Bastin's windup record player seemed to come through the walls, and from afar we could hear Bing Crosby singing "In the Blue of the Night."

In one photo a tiny sparrow perched on a windowsill.

"Maybe that's Joey," said Doll. He could have been Joey, but he was the wrong colour. The bird that Dad had taken me to Petticoat Market to buy from a barrow loaded down with wooden cages had been a blue budgie. Dolly remembered him well.

We talked of George and his pawnbroker's shop with the three brass balls hanging outside and remembered the day Mum stood in the rubble after a particularly heavy bombing raid had demolished poor George's shop. "I've got the ticket and I want my old man's only suit," Mum had yelled at the poor man as he stood with arms held out shouting back. "You'd think I'd dropped the bleedin' bomb meself!" he said.

Doll smiled at the memory, and as she did she slowly pulled together the covers of the album in her lap. She was tired. I took her by the elbow and helped Howard ease her into bed. She lay back, closed her eyes and squeezed my hand.

We had gone back. Back through time to tour a life that she had loved but that was about to come to an end. I kissed her cheek and left. Two weeks later she died.

But with death comes new life.

My twin died as a newborn. But, two generations later, life seems to have come full circle. In 1994 Kim gave birth to the first of her children. They're wonderful, healthy twins. Twin boys.